OurSpace

OurSpace

Resisting the Corporate Control of Culture

Christine Harold

Christine Harold

University of Minnesota Press

MINNEAPOLIS • LONDON

Portions of chapters 2 and 3 were originally published as "Pranking Rhetoric: 'Culture Jamming' as Media Activism," *Critical Studies in Media Communication* 21, no. 3 (September 2004): 189–211; reprinted with permission of the Taylor & Francis Group.

Published by the University of Minnesota Press
111 Third Avenue South, Suite 290
Minneapolis, MN 55401-2520
http://www.upress.umn.edu

Library of Congress Cataloging-in-Publication Data

Harold, Christine.
   OurSpace : resisting the corporate control of culture / Christine Harold.
     p.   cm.
   Includes bibliographical references and index.
   ISBN: 978-0-8166-4954-9 (hc : alk. paper) / ISBN-10: 0-8166-4954-5
   ISBN: 978-0-8166-4955-6 (pb : alk. paper) / ISBN-10: 0-8166-4955-3
   1. Rhetoric—Political aspects.   2. Mass media and culture.   I. Title.
   P301.5.P67H37   2007
   808—dc22   2006037863

Printed in the United States of America on acid-free paper

The University of Minnesota is an equal-opportunity educator and employer.

12 11 10 09 08 07   10 9 8 7 6 5 4 3 2 1

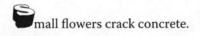She knows too much about the processes responsible for the way product is positioned in the world, and sometimes she finds herself doubting that there is much else going on.

IIII III II I IIII IIIIIIIIII IIIIIII III I IIII

—WILLIAM GIBSON, *Pattern Recognition*

Small flowers crack concrete.

IIII I II IIIIII IIIIIIII III I II III III

—SONIC YOUTH, *NYC Ghosts & Flowers*

Contents

Acknowledgments

This project is the result of an ongoing jam session with a variety of talented friends and scholars. Despite my interest in collaborative invention, however, I take sole responsibility for this project's shortcomings. My most heartfelt thanks go out to the following people, many of whom contributed rich and textured "riffs" to the ideas expressed in the pages that follow.

My friends and colleagues at Penn State were a great inspiration to me throughout this project. Marco Abel provided immeasurable encouragement and feedback, and my work has benefited greatly from his insights. Thank you, Marco. Rich Doyle and Jeff Nealon inspired, in individual ways, a unique intellectual culture in and around the Department of English at Penn State that I am fortunate to have experienced. Rich, among many other contributions, helped me discover early on the governing theme of this project simply by asking, "What's the difference between sabotage and appropriation? And what else is there?" I'm not sure I have sufficiently answered that question, but I have learned much in the attempt. Jeff will likely see many of his insights about markets and contemporary capitalism expressed (however clumsily) in these pages. Stephen Browne was an ideal mentor over the course of this project. He is the kind of writer I aspire to be — artful, specific, and generous. His love of words and texts has always ennobled for me our work as critics.

I have had the opportunity to learn from many outstanding scholars over the years and I indulge myself by thanking a few of them here. My sincerest thanks to Tom Benson, Nancy Love, Mike Hogan, Evan Watkins, Jim Aune, Henry Giroux, Catherine Collins, Bob Trapp, and David Douglass.

My conversations and readings with friends over the long course of this project have been invaluable. For sharing their time, friendship, intellects, and talents, I am grateful to Pat Gehrke, Gina Ercolini, John Muckelbauer, Dan Smith, Ryan Netzley, Debra Hawhee, Megan Brown, Jeff Karnicky, Roger Stahl, and Jim Roberts.

My friends and colleagues at the University of Georgia made what could have been a difficult transition a surprisingly smooth and even pleasurable one. For this, I am especially thankful to Bonnie Dow, who continuously goes out of her way to be a supportive colleague and friend; John Murphy, whose kindness and enthusiasm for the art of rhetoric inspire me; and Celeste Condit, who is a role model of academic rigor and professional generosity. Amy Ross and Victoria Davion provided perspective and encouragement when I needed it most. Justin Killian provided research assistance. Kevin DeLuca has been a steadfast mentor through every step of my academic career, from Pennsylvania to Georgia. I hope he knows he has earned himself a lifelong friend and fan. I am also thankful to the many students who served as my captive audience as I thought through some of the ideas expressed here.

Thank you to Mike and Lynn Harold for their love and unwavering support, especially in the year I began this project — a year when getting words onto pages was supposed to be the greatest challenge I faced. My love, Ken, is my greatest resource, from whom I unabashedly draw. He is a rigorous editor, a provocative interlocutor, and a tireless cheerleader. His belief in this project and me makes everything feel possible. Thank you, Ken. This project is dedicated to him and our beautiful daughter, Helena; and also to the memory of my mom, Diane, whose lessons for me continue and grow more meaningful every day.

I am extremely grateful for the financial support given to me by the University of Georgia: for the travel support provided in the form of a Sarah Moss Fellowship by the University of Georgia Center for Teaching and Learning, and for the gift of time provided by a faculty research grant from the University of Georgia Willson Center for Humanities and Arts. For permission to use artwork or imagery for which they are often undercompensated, I thank Ron English, Andrew Baio, Kieron Dwyer,

The Yes Men, Artists Rights Society (ARS), the Breast Cancer Fund, the Media Foundation, and the American Legacy Foundation. Finally, I want to thank the staff at the University of Minnesota Press, especially the generous and insightful Jason Weidemann, who has made the publishing process a genuine pleasure.

Introduction

The Brand Politics of Consuming Publics

> Marketing is now the instrument of social control and
> produces the arrogant breed who are our masters.
>
>
> —Gilles Deleuze, *Negotiations*

> America is no longer a country. It's a
> multitrillion-dollar brand . . . America™.
>
>
> —Kalle Lasn, *Culture Jam*

upert Murdoch knows a good thing when he sees it. In July 2005, the media mogul purchased MySpace.com for $580 million, a move that many suspected would sound the death knell for the hipster social-networking site. MySpace had risen, in just two short years, to the upper echelon of the Internet—despite the fact that many people (especially those over thirty) had never heard of it. MySpace was founded in 2003 by Web entrepreneurs Tom Anderson and Chris DeWolfe. At the time Murdoch's News Corporation (News Corp) bought MySpace's parent company, Intermix Media, MySpace was the third-most-visited site on the Web.[1] It had more members than America Online (AOL) and more overall hits than Google and eBay combined. MySpace boasts over 50 million members, with new members joining at a rate of 150,000 per day. MySpace's innovative mix incorporates "elements from other sites popular with the young: the instant-messenger capabilities of America Online, the classifieds of Craigslist.com, the invitation service of Evite.com and the come-hither dating profiles of match.com."[2] What seems to have been crucial to MySpace's success is that all of its elements are woven together by the thread of indie rock, meaning its public is composed of the holy grail of marketing demographics — sixteen- to thirty-four-year-olds.[3] Rupert Murdoch knows a good thing when he sees it.

For the half-million bands with profiles on the site, MySpace has provided the tools for a kind of open source marketing, allowing up-and-coming acts to gain far more exposure than they ever could under the traditional big-label/big-radio approach to distribution. "It's become the new paradigm," says one musician. "At first I thought, 'Why would people randomly go to our site?' But that's the way it works. People are actively searching out new bands on MySpace. It's an experimental marketing tool right now. I don't know if it translates to record sales or getting heads to a show, but it's exceeded my expectations as far as getting us exposure."[4] One successful club promoter in Los Angeles is also enjoying the benefits of MySpace membership: "I conduct my entire business through MySpace," he says. "I haven't made a flyer in years" but he is nonetheless seeing fans line up around the block to see the shows he promotes.[5] MySpace allows bands, solo acts, and promoters to post song and video clips, tour schedules, pictures, and blogs on the site, all free of charge. As a result, many acts have enjoyed huge success, just through MySpace; in fact, the site has produced its own kind of star system. And it's not only small up-starts capitalizing on the MySpace phenomenon. Indie-rock veterans such as Depeche Mode, Nine Inch Nails, Foo Fighters, Billy Corgan (of Smashing Pumpkins fame), and Weezer have all used MySpace as a venue for promoting albums before they landed in stores, on Amazon, or on iTunes. REM even launched its 2004 album *Around the Sun* exclusively on MySpace.

As a venue for rock bands in search of a following, MySpace provides a grassroots alternative to MTV, which has largely given itself over to reality programming and hip-hop.[6] Virgil Dickerson, who owns the independent label Suburban Home Records, told the *New York Times,* "I'd say, as a cultural phenomenon, MySpace is as important, if not more important, than MTV."[7] Tom Anderson, the younger and more visible of the two MySpace founders (every new member is immediately granted the privilege of automatically becoming one of "Tom's friends"), has launched MySpace Records in order to tap into the huge population of unsigned acts. As he meets with bands, he says that many ask, "How are you going to get me onto MTV?" "They don't quite get it, and I'm only starting to get it myself," says Anderson. "We've got our 26 million, with a lot more people logging in each day. . . . It's kind of like, who cares about MTV anymore?"[8] Unlike MTV, which long ago lost any sense that it is anything other than a twenty-four-hour shill for pop-culture conglomerates, MySpace promoted itself as a *people's* space, a space where members could express themselves and interact with others (in the form of sometimes hundreds of online contacts — a process known as "friending") under the radar of the corporatization that has taken over public life. The success of MySpace stems from its chaotic and democratic presentation of *user-generated content.* It should not be surprising, then, that Murdoch's purchase of MySpace was met with some ire.

The greatest fear among MySpace members seemed to have been that Murdoch, much like a grandpa showing up and killing a good party, would start softening the edges that made MySpace so popular among the cool crowd in the first place. After all, as many MySpace bloggers complained, Murdoch is the money behind a number of conservative media outlets — the most prevalent being GOP-friendly Fox News. Sites began popping up all over MySpace deriding Murdoch and claiming, for example, "Rupert Murdoch owns your soul!" As the *San Francisco Chronicle* explained, "Some of the hipsters in the online hangout fear their freewheeling ways, celebrated in naughty notes, brash blogs and provocative photos, won't mesh" with Murdoch's values. "I'm opposed to what Rupert Murdoch has done to the media, and I don't want him involved in MySpace," one user told the paper. "Democracy depends on media capable of performing without having people like Murdoch interjecting his personal political views."[9]

MySpace's supposed censorship of references to video-sharing site YouTube.com, a MySpace competitor, seemed to realize fears that News Corp would end MySpace's nonmonopolizing past. Although YouTube insisted that the deletions were "a simple misunderstanding, and MySpace has re-enabled all YouTube embeds" on MySpace pages,[10] the issue served briefly as a lightning rod for critics concerned that "Big Brother" News Corp was meddling with the democratic MySpace. One user wrote of the matter: "This is soooo like Fox and News Corp to try and secretly seal our mouths with duct tape."[11] Another user wrote: "My friends and I are trying to make the blogging community aware of a stealth censorship campaign that is being conducted by MySpace. . . . They are not admitting to it, and are trying to do this in secret."[12] Misunderstanding or not, the links to YouTube were apparently restored only after "600 MySpace customers complained and a campaign began to boycott the site and relocated to rival sites such as Friendster, Linkedin, Revver.com, and Facebook.com."[13]

Although members' concerns over Murdoch's conservative politics may be understandable, what members seem to forget is that this is also the man who brought us *The Simpsons, Married with Children, 24,* and the *X-Files* — hardly what one would call red-state fare. Indeed, Murdoch seems just as happy to cash in on the tastes of tattooed indie rockers as the tastes of the family-values crowd. Perhaps more so. What seems more significant for the future of the News Corp–MySpace alliance is not the political predilections of Murdoch the individual, but the effects of a seemingly organic, unfettered public being shaped by the dictates of *brand management.* A writer for the University of Houston's *Daily Cougar* sums up nicely the stakes for many MySpace members: despite the grassroots feel of MySpace, its members are essentially "content providers" for those who own the online community:

> Once you've logged on and automatically become one of Tom's friends, you "hereby grant to MySpace.com the nonexclusive, fully paid, worldwide license to use, publicly perform and display such content on the Web site." This means all photos, art, blog entries and music clips from your band are now property of News Corp. They've just acquired the biggest gold mine of target market research since *The Real World.*[14]

This explains why the burgeoning protest surrounding the MySpace–YouTube issue may have worked; News Corp knew that in the fickle world of the teen and twenty-something marketplace, getting labeled "the Man" could easily spell an end to your product's popularity. MySpace president Tom Anderson undoubtedly understood this when he quickly began "teenspeak damage control," assuring members, "I'm not going to let things suck," in the wake of the News Corp acquisition: "We are not deleting any content or censoring people in any new way. We are not exploiting anyone's data or violating anyone's privacy. MySpace has been my life for almost two years now. . . . I won't let it get jacked up."[15]

It remains to be seen whether or not the brand equity of MySpace will hold, but at this early stage in the development of social-networking sites, one thing seems clear: old media brand strategies just won't work. MySpace will have to continue to distinguish itself without jealously guarding its turf from competitive interlopers, because the boundaries between MySpace and everyone else's space are too porous. MySpace cannot ensure that the brand images it promotes remain wholly consistent, as the old branding model would have it (the Pillsbury Doughboy, the Trix rabbit, and Mr. Peanut, for example, all have strict guidelines hundreds of pages long that specify in great detail what each character can and cannot say and do),[16] because to compete in new media environments a brand must allow users to interact with it in ways that can't easily be controlled. Ryan Hupfer, who is making a documentary about MySpace, agrees that the site may change the future of marketing: "This totally blows all that out of the water.... They can't just put their TV commercials on their MySpace page and sit there and expect people to buy things."[17] *Adweek* tells advertisers who want to appeal to MySpace members that they must (however artificially) become part of the community itself, "rather than just look for eyeballs": "'They definitely have to think outside the box when it comes to the MySpace audience,' CEO Chris DeWolfe said, noting its under-30 users are typically skeptical. For advertising dressed as in-demand content, however, MySpace members eagerly interact."[18] A number of corporations such as Proctor & Gamble, McDonald's, and Sony Pictures are offering free music downloads, film trailers, and contests tied into their products. All this interactivity — corporations allowing members to "friend" with their products by linking to their branded content — makes protectionist branding strategies seem old school. This is likely precisely why Rupert Murdoch wanted in.

"The lesson here," writes *New York Times* reporter Saul Hansel, "is that on MySpace there is no distinction between personal and mass media. A teenager can post a photo from last night's party, a poem for a lost boyfriend, buttons that play her favorite song and a clip from her favorite TV show."[19] If the goal of marketing is to gain evermore a public's "mindshare," then MySpace seems like the perfect place to do it, by letting young people do what they have done for decades: decorate their "space" with the imagery and sounds of popular culture. That a savvy businessman like Rupert Murdoch wants to get in on the action should come as no surprise. As Hansel reminds us: "You do not have to have a pierced tongue to know that anywhere that teenagers congregate, soda vendors and sneakermongers will pay to follow."[20] However, as has been shown, by the time the "suits" come to a scene, young people are usually compelled to move on to something else.

But MySpace, it must be said, was *never* some pure, unbranded space, untarnished by the dictates of marketers. Like MTV, it serves in part as a portal through which pop-culture giants weave messages into the lives of young people by providing free and entertaining content, by becoming, as best they can, one of them. Unlike MTV viewers, MySpace members have the capacity to talk back (MTV's pseudo-democratic *Total Request Live* notwithstanding), reorganize, and influence the tastes of their peers at a rate impossible to achieve through the media of television and radio. Advertisers flock to MySpace because they say it's "sticky," meaning it's an environment in which a well-embedded ad can resonate with members on a personal level by infiltrating everyday interactions. It "sticks" by not appearing to be an ad, in effect slipping under consumers' well-tuned ad radar. Corporations even hire "influencers" — members of the online in-crowd who, for money, talk up brands in MySpace. Malcolm Gladwell — who has become something of a guru for a new generation of brand managers, thanks to his bestselling book *The Tipping Point* — convincingly illustrates that ideas spread through cultures more like epidemics (like a flu being passed in a schoolyard) than by way of top-down corporate campaigns. By embedding brands in the peer-to-peer world of MySpace through content tie-ins and buzz-generating influencers, marketers hope to facilitate the epidemic spread of their messages.

News Corp may even adopt the interactive, user-generated model for its "old media" outlets. "If we can enable the MySpace model across properties, that's terrific," says Ross Levinsohn, president of News Corp's Fox Interactive Media division, "but [consumers] are not going to listen to me, they are going to tell me. We have 30 million trend and style opinion-makers."[21] In any case, it looks like the MySpace brand won't be going anywhere soon. As I write, plans are in the works for a MySpace record label, a MySpace satellite radio channel, MySpace mobile phones, and even a MySpace film company. "There hasn't [yet] been a Web site that has established itself as a lifestyle brand," Chris DeWolfe told *Advertising Age*.[22] If the company has its way, that will soon change, and MySpace members will have plenty of MySpace brand content to buzz about. Jamie Kantrowitz, vice president of marketing and communications for MySpace, says the company's "marketing mission is that we are driving our brand, keeping it authentic."[23] But the trick will be to drive the brand without seeming to drive product down users' throats.

News Corp's purchase of the MySpace community is but one high-profile instantiation of an all-too-familiar story: a countercultural haven is turned into an advertising vehicle by corporations hoping that a little authentic "cool" will rub off on their brands. As a result, the story goes, the life gets sucked out of an otherwise thriving public, forcing that public to move on to purer pastures.

Naomi Klein, whose best seller *No Logo* (2000) was a runaway hit with anticorporate activists, offers a compelling analysis of public life under corporate branding. Klein helped popularize the sentiments that have inspired the rash of protests against global trade organizations throughout the early part of the new millennium, beginning with the so-called "Battle in Seattle" in late 1999. Klein argues that the voraciousness of corporate brand campaigns — their mission to infiltrate every part of our daily lives — has left us with "no space" to call our own, "no choice" but that determined by the bottom-line thinking of the multinationals, and, for many North Americans, "no jobs" but those in the increasingly undependable and disloyal service industry. Through a multitude of timely examples, Klein argues that we can blame these losses, at least in part, on a recent shift in the mission of late capitalism. Her book begins: "The astronomical growth in the wealth and cultural influence of multinational corporations over the last fifteen years can arguably be traced back to a single, seemingly innocuous idea developed by management theorists in the mid-1980s: that successful corporations must primarily produce brands, as opposed to products."[24]

Klein explains that producing things simply became too expensive, with cumbersome factories full of employees required to make them. Thanks to the success of neoliberal economic efforts to revise trade laws and undermine labor reform, factories could be moved elsewhere and could be run by contractors less encumbered by fair wages and organized workforces. "What these companies [brand giants like Nike, Microsoft, and Tommy Hilfiger] made were not things, they said, but *images* of their brands. Their real work lay not in manufacturing but in marketing." The success of this formula, Klein continues, has been extremely profitable and has "companies competing in a race toward weightlessness: whoever owns the least, has the fewest employees on the payroll and produces the most powerful images, as opposed to products, wins the race."[25] Given this formula for success, Murdoch's purchase of MySpace was an incredibly smart one: it earned him instant access to the evanescent world of youth culture, a virtual hotbed through which contagious brands spread. However, the selling out of MySpace also seems to illustrate Klein's point that there is *no space* left where people can create their own communities independent of the logic of the big brands.

In their book *Nation of Rebels,* philosophers Joseph Heath and Andrew Potter go to great lengths to dispel as myth the notion of an unbranded, utopian space populated by countercultural outliers that Klein's analysis seems to mourn. In this often-scathing analysis of the anticorporate movement (that includes Klein), Heath and Potter argue that rather than offering an *alternative* to rampant consumerism, countercultural "rebellion" is actually the engine that drives the competitive consumption on which neoliberal capitalism thrives. Contemporary culture, according to Heath and Potter, does not *lack* choice, or simply offer a mass-produced conformity masquerading as choice, as Klein suggests. Instead, our love of all things "alternative," "indie," and "authentic" produces "cool" assets (like MySpace), which capitalists such as Murdoch want desperately to add to their holdings. Hence, for Heath and Potter, "Countercultural rebellion is not just unhelpful, it is positively counterproductive."[26]

Following Heath and Potter's analysis, the selling out of MySpace was not a sellout at all, because the individualism it celebrates is the governing trope of marketing. Murdoch didn't "co-opt" MySpace; MySpace was already teeming with competitive cool kids all on the prowl for the "next-big-thing," which is what makes it the ideal marketing venue. Ultimately, Heath and Potter's position is not that different from Klein's, despite their handy dismissal of her work. They charge that the countercultural or anticorporate position that *No Logo* inspires is wrongheaded because its all-or-nothing revolutionist posture "encourages wholesale contempt" for the benefits that good old-fashioned incremental policy change can provide to the real lives of citizens. Although Heath and Potter are onto something here (an argument I will elaborate on in chapter 2), they unfortunately trade one hegemonic villain for another. If the counterculture rebel sees "the Man" in mainstream commercial culture, Heath and Potter see him in the stubborn revolutionary posture of the rebel. However, the countercultural myth they so malign does not persist over decades because people are suckers. I suggest that, given the market's appetite for edginess, the countercultural rebel is indeed something of a myth, which in no way voids its importance as a story that inspires people. Countercultural rhetoric, mythological or not, continues to win converts generation after generation because it affords powerful creative possibilities. It provides rich political fodder.

This story—one in which robust countercultural spaces are consistently reduced to mere markets—raises a series of questions that will animate this book. Whether this story is proof of a brand-saturated dystopia to be rallied against, as Klein might have it, or of a harmful myth that preoccupies a generation of activists whose energies would be better spent doing the work of "real" politics, as Heath and Potter contend, I find myself asking, "Is this the only story we have?" For Klein and Heath and Potter alike, this is a story in which the counterculture, the Left, or the "people" are always in danger of losing out to the corporate hegemon. Be it through deception or complicity, the public is stripped of the tools (what rhetorical scholars would describe as the inventional resources) with which to produce meaningful political discourse.

For both analyses, the way out is to appeal to institutions and movements outside the marketplace: the courts, the antiglobalization movement, fair-trade treaties (Klein), or an ambiguous call for the return to traditional political action (Heath and Potter). I certainly do not want to suggest that these extra-market avenues (if such a thing even exists) are not worth pursuing. They are. But recent history has shown that these avenues, in and of themselves, are not sufficient for inspiring progressive and innovative political change. The rhetoric and imagery of the market has proven incredibly compelling to people, and not, I will argue, because people are merely duped into behaving against their own self-interest. So, in response to the "problem of the market," should we, with Heath and Potter, content ourselves with a return to the state? Should we simply dismiss the counterculture as nothing more than a myth, with which the masses must be readily disabused? Or, might we instead consider modes of "resistance" that are not predicated on *independence* from markets? Toward this end, one goal of this book is to try to imagine the public and public space in ways other than what the traditional "independence versus co-optation" binary might afford. What might such public spaces look like? What other stories might we tell about the relationship between markets and publics?

Brand Politics

Branding functions almost exclusively through repetition and emotion. A successful brand must have simple but striking imagery and emotional resonance with the public. Since markets are often saturated with mass-produced products that are more or less indistinguishable from one another, brands — by attaching to consumer goods a carefully crafted lifestyle, image, and attitude — provide the mechanisms for the individualization necessary in a competitive marketplace. As one *New York Times* writer argues, "Over the last fifty years the economic base has shifted from production to consumption. It has gravitated from the sphere of rationality to the realm of desire: from the objective to the subjective."[27] As most marketers and biz-lit gurus contend, the North American economy is no longer primarily driven by industry, but by marketing.

Increasingly, the referential link between brands and their products is becoming dislodged. In a very real way, products are the *vehicles* that deliver their brands to consumers, rather than vice versa. For example, Tommy Hilfiger, one of the great branding success stories of the 1990s, is a company that exists almost exclusively via licensing agreements. That is, as Klein tells us, Hilfiger manufactures no products. He purchases products — jeans, sneakers, sweatshirts, etc. — from other companies, brands them with the well-marketed "Tommy" logo, and sells them at high prices. Hilfiger is above all in the business of *marketing*. David Ogilvy, the famed American ad man, popularized a marketing perspective that was later perfected by Nike's Philip Knight. As advertising executive Abe Novick describes it: "Corporate advertising conveys a vision. Its message is aimed not so much at tactically selling the company's products as it is in having a defined purpose. A *raison d'être*."[28]

This book engages in a critical examination of the public discourse surrounding the increasing political influence of multinational corporations and of the discourse of marketing and branding that aid multinationals' expansion. Commercial rhetoric is a central and crucial element of the global economy, an economy driven less by the industrial production of tangible goods than by the *marketing* of goods produced in the factories of developing nations. In American culture, for example, economic value is increasingly created at the level of corporate brand identities and the suasory production of consumer desire to affiliate with these brands.[29] As an article in the *Wall Street Journal* titled "So Long, Supply and Demand" concludes: "The bottom line: Creativity is overtaking capital as the principal elixir of growth. And creativity, although precious, shares few of the constraints that limit the range and availability of capital and physical goods."[30] In the current economy, *rhetoric* emerges as a key site of economic and cultural production. Ideas and the ability to communicate them are valuable currency in an economy for which one good brand campaign can change an entire industry.

Ideas are also valuable currency for those marketers known as "politicians." As a commentator in the *San Francisco Chronicle* noted: "Branding is the new federal mega-project, as serious as the guns-and-ammo war on terrorism or the quest to inflate a new bull market."[31] Like corporate marketers, government marketers are finding that controlling the way one's brand is received is a challenging task indeed. Just two weeks after the atrocities of 9/11, for example, U.S. Secretary of State Colin Powell hastened to remedy America's brutally evident public-relations problem by appointing a new undersecretary of public diplomacy and public affairs, handpicking Charlotte Beers to revamp the United States' image abroad. While Powell's move to bolster the State Department's leadership may have seemed like an obvious response to a diplomatic crisis, his choice of Beers was a novel one, because Beers had no experience in diplomacy or international politics. The so-called "Queen of Madison Avenue" was an advertising executive who headed three of the country's top ad agencies and who served as the brains behind some of the best-known U.S. advertising campaigns, including American Express's "Don't leave home without it" and Uncle Ben's "perfect every time." At the State Department, Beers faced her greatest marketing challenge — selling America to the international community.

As Powell's appointment of Beers illustrates, even those speaking on behalf of the nation-state are increasingly employing the tropes of the market. Indeed, Beers described the world's only superpower as simply "the most elegant brand I've ever had to work with." And, while she claimed to be confident that "poster people" George W. Bush and Colin Powell were "pretty inspiring symbols of the brand,"[32] she told members of Congress that she and her team hoped to undermine the salability of future Osama bin Ladens by "brand[ing] this kind of fanatic as a false prophet."[33]

Although nations and leaders may pose greater challenges to advertisers than other less complicated products, Beers's model of political rhetoric—one governed by the logic of branding—has little to do with rational arguments and with people of character moving audiences with eloquent speech. One wonders what it is that the State Department and others hoped to gain by deploying the language of marketing when describing its agenda. Does wrapping diplomacy and propaganda in the vocabulary of branding make it more palatable to domestic audiences? Perhaps. In 2002, when reporters asked about a possible attack on Iraq, Andrew Card, then chief of staff for the George W. Bush White House, responded as any good adman would. The administration planned to wait until after Labor Day: "From a marketing point of view . . . you don't introduce new products in August." [34]

Consuming Publics

As people try to negotiate the world of brands, many express concern that the insatiable appetites of corporations are destroying what we most cherish about public life: that there is increasingly less room for *public* values in which sharing and openness trump property and profit. Indeed, our notion of "public" may be changing in this age of the brand. What kinds of public spaces and public discourses are available to us in an environment that increasingly encourages us to see ourselves as consumers or as members of niche markets? Are we simply becoming a *mass* that is duped into thinking we are participating in something more profound? That is, *has TheirSpace finally devoured OurSpace*? Certainly, branding invites us to identify ourselves with others who consume as we do, or to differentiate ourselves from those whose tastes are seemingly inferior to our own. Even politicians, our public servants, presumably see us in relation to what we consume: we are NASCAR dads, or the *Sex and the City* set, or the iPod generation. And many of us seem to embrace these visions of ourselves. For example, take the current abundance of those black and white "W the President" stickers on cars across the United

States. Although the "W" brand has outlived its explicit usefulness (as a logo promoting the reelection of President Bush), its cultural stock has actually gone *up* since November 2004. It now serves as a quick and easy way for drivers to announce to others passing them on the freeway: "I'm with the winning team."[35] So pronounced has this brand logic become that people continue to identify with it even though its function as an advertisement has passed. As good advertisers understand, maintaining brand loyalty is key; successful brands must keep promoting themselves, if only to remind consumers they made the right choice. Indeed, "W," as the more recent bumper stickers declare, is "*still* the president."

This is an example of one way we might understand "consuming publics." That is, we might ask: What are we if not people defined by the things we consume — be those things presidents or iPods? This trend toward relegating citizens as consumers is at the heart of a growing critique of commercial culture. Further, many fear that in seeking to create consuming publics, corporate marketers also *consume publics*, absorbing and perverting the very entity on which democracy and citizenship depend. This second, related concern sees consumer culture as an environment in which the public is obliterated, turned into nothing more than a marketing ploy. By increasingly seeing others as those who consume as we do or those who consume differently, any notion of civic connectedness is extinguished, consumed by the fickle flames of greed and competitiveness.

A diverse, international alliance of activists is responding to what they see as this consumption or disintegration of publics. The central task of this book is to examine a set of strategies currently being tested and deployed in response to the proliferation of commercialization in civic life — the insurgent political movement known loosely as "culture jamming." As explained by Mark Dery, who first theorized the concept in his pamphlet *Culture Jamming*, culture jamming takes its name from the CB slang from which it is derived — "the illegal practice of interrupting radio broadcasts or conversations between fellow hams."[36] It usually implies an interruption, a sabotage, a hoax, a prank, a banditry, or a blockage of what are seen as monolithic power structures governing media and culture. Like Umberto Eco's "communications guerrillas," culture jammers seek to "introduce noise into the signal" that might otherwise obliterate alternatives to it.[37] In this sense, culture jamming is a kind of "glutting" of the system; it is an amping up of contradictory rhetorical messages in an effort to force a qualitative change. Dery notes that the phrase "culture jamming" was first introduced by the sound-collage band Negativland. One band member explained the strategy "as awareness of how the media environment we occupy affects and directs our inner life grows, some resist. . . . The skillfully reworked billboard . . . directs the public viewer to a consideration of the original corporate strategy. The studio for the cultural jammer is the world at large."[38] As I will argue throughout this book, "jamming" as a metaphor does not have to be interpreted only as a damming or stopping of corporate media. More interestingly, it can be a strategy that artfully proliferates other media and messages that challenge the ability of corporate messages to make meaning in predictable ways — to jam *with* rather than *against*.

Although culture jammers define themselves in various ways, common themes emerge from their discourse. Gareth Branwyn, in his culture-jamming handbook *Jamming the Media,* prefers the term "media hackers," whom he describes as "those who enjoy tinkering with various forms of media and who believe in a similar hacker ethic. Media hackers are to big media what independent computer hackers are to big computer corporations. They share the hacker's mistrust of imposed limitations, the challenge of doing more with less, and the joy of finding creative solutions to systemic problems."[39] Like computer hackers, media hackers also depend on commercially funded resources to do their work. Branwyn's book offers inspirational case studies showcasing successful do-it-yourself media makers, including 'zine publishers, pirate radio broadcasters, pranksters and art hacks, and billboard "liberationists."

Like Branwyn, Kalle Lasn, founder of *Adbusters* magazine, the Media Foundation, and Powershift Advocacy Advertising Agency, sees the culture-jamming movement as following in the tradition of the French situationists, surrealists, and Dadaists, who sought to challenge hegemonic cultural codes by appropriating and reconfiguring them in novel ways. Lasn enthusiastically describes culture jammers as "a loose global network of media activists who see [themselves] as the advance shock troops of the most significant social movement of the next twenty years."[40] Lasn may overstate the case, but his magazine's style of ad parody and cultural spoofing seems to be gaining momentum. Overall, this brand of culture jamming may be less the cause of significant social change than the "revolutionary poetry" that attends it.

As I will argue throughout the book, this poetry emerges from *within* commercial culture. As self-described "hacktivist" Jamie Batsy explains, "Advertisers and other opinion makers are now in a position where they are up against a generation of activists that were watching television before they could walk. This generation wants their brains back and mass media is their home turf."[41] By engaging a variety of responses to consumer culture, I will examine how this movement seeks to undermine the marketing rhetoric of multinational corporations, specifically through such practices as "media pranking," "adbusting," corporate sabotage, "billboard liberation," "brand-jacking" and copyright infringement. In a way, these strategies of resistance can all be seen as attempts to rescue publics from being consumed by consumption.

The reader may note that there is a collusion between the two senses of "consuming publics" thus far elaborated. In both senses, if publics are defined exclusively by their consumption, then publicness itself has no function outside consumer culture. For those resisting this collusion, through what I will describe as sabotage or appropriation, the strategic response is dialectical — to re-craft or save the public from its sublimation to consumption. However, these strategies of resistance are insufficient, if not counterproductive to the goals of culture jamming. Among the questions raised in this book, I ask: Has "resistance" reached its limit as a diagnostic category for critics and activists waging struggles over cultural messages in the new brand economy?

Fortunately, there is a third way we might understand this age of "consuming publics," one that affords the public much more agency. Rather than conceiving of publics as inherently passive or vulnerable to the dictates of markets, I consider publics as *all-consuming*. Rather than ceding to a dialectical model of understanding the relationship between publics and markets, I start from the assumption that publics *are everywhere*. And rather than joining those who bemoan the duping or eradication of publics, I encourage readers to explore what kinds of publics are currently emerging (and receding) in contemporary culture. What possibilities for political action are afforded *within* the logics of postindustrial capitalism?

In this book, I frame the practice of culture jamming through a specific description of contemporary capitalism. Taking my cue from the work of Michel Foucault and Gilles Deleuze, I take seriously a shift in political culture they describe as a shift from *disciplinarity* to *control*. In a 1990 interview with Toni Negri, Deleuze distinguishes between three modes of power: sovereign power, disciplinary power, and the control over communication. Sovereign societies were organized to meet the needs of feudalism, in which a lord took a cut of what was produced but had no real hand in organizing production. Under disciplinary societies, explored in great detail by Foucault, the modes of production were brought together, organized, and confined in order to maximize efficiency and profit. Disciplinary societies operate primarily through the confinement and atomization of individuals (e.g., through the familiar models of the prison, the classroom, or the factory). This mode of power was most appropriate in a Fordist world, where assembly-line-style production was the most efficient way for capital to expand. To function, Fordism required a certain level of *standardization*. Workers were more or less interchangeable and labor practices were repeated with as little variation as possible.

Deleuze further pursued an observation Foucault made late in his career that we were undergoing a transformation from the disciplinarity necessary for an industrial economy, to a service economy organized in part through the *control* of consumer desires. Control societies do not operate through the confinement and silencing of individuals, but instead "through continuous control and communication."[42] In a control society, people are not denied access to information and knowledge, but are instead granted ever greater access to them through the opening up of technologies and the hybridization of institutions. However, what might appear as new freedoms enable business to increasingly modulate every aspect of life. I suggest that the proliferation of branding strategies, in part, marks this shift from discipline to control. Because of this emerging shift from disciplinarity (which spotlights the political rhetoric of the nation-state) to control (which increasingly relies on the visual rhetoric of the market), the possibilities for political resistance have changed as well.

At this stage, I see at least three modes of intervention that emerge out of and in response to the logics of disciplinarity and control: *sabotage, appropriation,* and *intensification* or augmentation. In the chapters that follow, I loosely affiliate sabotage and appropriation with disciplinarity, and intensification with control. I try throughout to complicate any neat distinction between the two. Although appropriation may be increasing in the face of greater control, both strategies continue to function in response to similar problems by deploying different tools. As Deleuze has suggested, disciplinarity does not operate dialectically; it does not disappear with the emergence of control. Control is itself an intensification rather than a replacement of discipline.

This book is organized according to these three sets of strategies. The first strategy, explored in chapters 1 and 2, is composed of two types of culture jammers who engage in symbolic *sabotage*, an explicitly dialectic engagement with the rhetoric of consumer culture. Sabotage is a direct attempt to thwart the repressive disciplinarity of the Spectacle. The rhetoric of sabotage is best exemplified by *Adbusters'* approach to commercialization as a monolithic *machine* or "image factory" that must be stopped or slowed down.

The second strategy, explored in chapters 3 and 4, is composed of two culture-jamming strategies that attempt to *appropriate*, rather than sabotage, commercial rhetoric. Through the practices of pranking (what I describe as a rhetorical folding) and pirating, these appropriation artists attempt to take seriously consumer culture on its own terms, and engage it accordingly. I suggest that appropriation art, in its celebration of the "criminal" artist, tends to perpetuate (although less so than with saboteurs) a dialectical relationship with commercial culture. By positioning themselves as outlaws, appropriation artists run the risk of solidifying the codes they challenge.

Finally, chapter 5 addresses a third set of responses to commercial culture — responses that, as I suggested earlier, take advantage of the ubiquity of publics, of their all-consuming nature. The activists discussed in this chapter do not so much thwart the brand giants, nor do they liberate small pieces of culture from their clutches. Rather, by actively promoting the concept of "the commons," these activists *augment* and *intensify* certain aspects of markets. Importantly, this strategy is unavailable to those who see markets and publics as mutually exclusive. Rather than saying "no" to consumer culture as the antithesis of healthy, thriving publics, an intensification strategy says "yes, *and*" to the tools markets afford.

Chapter 1, "Detours and Drifts: Situationist International and the Art of Resistance," investigates the rhetorical strategies of Situationist

International (SI). From 1957 to 1972, SI, a group of artistic and political subversives, sought to overthrow the conservatism that dominated Western Europe. Most crucially, SI slogans and tactics were at the forefront of the Paris student-worker revolts in May 1968. Situationist rhetorical theories and strategies—primarily those outlined by SI leader Guy Debord in his *The Society of the Spectacle*—are enjoying a renaissance through contemporary culture-jamming discourse. According to Debord, the Spectacle articulated a novel mode of social domination in which the industrial age's coercive manual labor was replaced by capitalism's deceitful promise of fulfillment through consumption.

Chapter 1 focuses less explicitly on situationist critiques of media-dominated capitalist society than on the strategies situationists employed in an effort to propel capitalist society *elsewhere*. They did so largely by manipulating existing rhetorical forms toward their own ends. And although they described their project as one opposing the Spectacle at every turn, situationists often found themselves forced to negotiate the tension between their desire to overturn the Spectacle and their inevitable contribution to it. In an effort to explore this tension, I investigate the rhetorical force of three of the group's more predominant political strategies: *détournement, dérive,* and psychogeography. SI theories and practices have very much influenced a particular version of dialectical culture-jamming, one that is best exemplified by the work of *Adbusters.*

Chapter 2, "Anti-Logos: Sabotaging the Brand through Parody," focuses on the most prevalent and defining organization in the culture-jamming movement: the Media Foundation (Vancouver, British Columbia), best known for its bimonthly *Adbusters* magazine. *Adbusters* strives to undermine the brand identity of multinational corporations, largely through parody. Adbusters founder Kalle Lasn and his comrades articulate their position clearly in their "Culture Jammer's Manifesto": "We will jam the pop-culture marketers and bring their image factory to a sudden, shuddering halt."[43] Chapter 2 details one version of the practice of jamming—jamming as dialectical opposition. For the activists at *Adbusters*, jamming is akin to creating a logjam in order to stop the flow of water or, like turn-of-the-century industrial saboteurs, to throwing one's clogs into the machinery in order to stop the flow of production. This chapter addresses the shortcomings of a rhetorical strategy that engages primarily in negative critique. Culture jamming as negative critique responds by saying "no" to disciplinary power—a mode of power most prevalent in industrialization.

In the remaining chapters, I investigate practices that illustrate the transition from this mode of response to those that, in contrast, engage *and deploy* the logic of markets. Chapter 3, "Pranks, Rumors, Hoaxes: 'Dressing Up' and Folding as Rhetorical Action," explores the rhetorical strategies employed by commercial media pranksters, who appropriate rather than negate current lines of power. Pranksters consist of media hoaxers and performance artists (e.g., Guerrilla Media, Joey Skaggs, and 1960s "yippies") who use tools of the mass media and marketing to call attention to the constructedness of the Spectacle. Through the concept of "pranking," I suggest that pranksters resist less by negation and opposition than by playfully appropriating commercial rhetoric, both by "folding" it over on itself and by exaggerating its tropes.

Chapters 2 and 3 are attended by brief, anecdotal intermezzos that explore the preceding ideas. My use of this venue plays on the enthusiastic embrace of Michael Hardt and Antonio Negri's *Empire* as the "next big thing" in academic circles. Indeed, *Empire* has become something of a scholarly *brand*. Hence, in a somewhat tongue-in-cheek attempt to keep with academic fashion, I borrow Hardt and Negri's stylistic strategy of offering dramatic intermezzos to speculate more subjectively about the discussion at hand.

Chapter 4, "Pirates and Hijackers: Creative Publics and the Politics of 'Owned Culture,'" looks at culture-jamming practices that "hijack" the so-called tools of control to produce different rhetorical effects, rather than try to stop production of the mass media. If we are indeed moving into a political terrain that superficially permits rather than denies access to information, then rhetorical responses seeking to liberate speech from the hands of the market may be less effective than many have hoped. I also explore the ways in which "pirating" and "hijacking" as practices might force a reconfiguration of how we conceive authorship and invention. Unlike the situationist and *Adbuster* perspectives, the pranksters and pirates discussed in chapters 3 and 4 recognize that they never have the final revolutionary word, because appropriation is not only a tactic of resistance, it is also the rule that governs corporate marketing.

Chapter 5, "Inventing Publics: Kairos and Intellectual Property Law," is a discussion of the open-content movement, which adopts the "copyleft" principles of open-source communal software development for cultural production. As I have suggested, this *intensification* of marketing logic and rhetoric may be the most compelling version of culture jamming to date. Open content does not engage consumer culture dialectically, as do sabotage and appropriation (to greater and lesser degrees). Rather, it serves as a *provocation* to commercialism by taking market values more seriously than many free marketers themselves. That is, open content *frees* markets from the modernist categories of property and authorship in such a way that disallows the hoarding of resources that makes contemporary capitalism, for most culture jammers, so unjust. Open content takes the notion of free market seriously, in that it shuns the rhetoric of protectionism that dictates contemporary intellectual property law. Open content, like a free market, promotes innovation and creativity, but by design it displaces the vastly unequal distribution of resources we see in the current economy.

An underlying assumption of this project is that corporate and anticorporate rhetorics do not *oppose* one another so much as feed off and respond to one another. Increasingly, the market is able to mutate in response to adversity. As Hardt and Negri illustrate in their *Empire* thesis, crises provide the conditions for novelty and difference on which global markets thrive.[44] Indeed, corporate marketers have already added culture-jamming tactics to their rhetorical palette. It is increasingly common for corporations to "jam" themselves. Companies such as Dodge, Diesel Jeans, Tanqueray, and Sony have recently launched campaigns that mimic the subversive strategies of culture jammers.[45] As I write, a popular cell-phone company is running a commercial in which a grey-haired executive tells his young employee that his new, more flexible wireless service allows him to "stick it to the Man." His employee replies, "But, sir, you *are* the Man." "I know," the executive replies. "So, you're sticking it to yourself?" the employee asks. "Maybe," the executive concedes, smiling.

In a sense, neosituationists are faced with a Spectacle far more protean than even Debord described. In effect, detouring, hijacking, and pirating are no longer exceptions to capitalism, *they are the rules.* This book advances the position that this appropriation of the rhetoric of culture jammers does not inevitably lead to their impotence, as many culture-jamming activists fear. Rather, I suggest that in the brand economy, successful resistant rhetorics are not those that avoid being co-opted but those that deploy tactics for getting co-opted in productive ways.

As I have suggested, one of the primary questions I asked as I began this project was whether the binary between independence and co-optation holds under careful scrutiny. One of my goals has been to avoid approaching corporate rhetoric as a monolith asserting its will on a bewitched public (readily containing any resistance to it). On the other hand, I avoid assigning an overly romantic role to evasive readings of polysemic texts as the Davidian deathblow to a hegemonic giant. Rather, as I have tried to make evident throughout the analysis, it is my observation that corporate and consumer rhetorics are engaged in a dynamic, fluctuating relationship and they continuously inflect and infect one another.

At present, the full story of MySpace has yet to be written. Given the capricious nature of markets, by the time you read this it may be an Internet has-been, gone the way of Kibo or CompuServe. Or, it may be, like MTV, little more than one big commercial, stripped of its authentic spirit. Either way, the larger story of OurSpace, of which MySpace is but one example, will undoubtedly persist, as will attendant debates about its meaning. So far, debates about the corporate control of culture seem to have broken down in this way: the commercialization of countercultural publics is either a phenomenon to be mourned and evaded or a predictable outgrowth of wrongheaded rebels unwittingly feeding the system they claim to resist. I suggest that it is neither. To more fully make sense of the relationship between markets and publics (between TheirSpace and OurSpace), we need to interpret this story in a way that doesn't so readily offer answers before one even begins. We need, in effect, to be sensitive to the play of rhetorical *invention* and the subsequent unpredictable formation of public life.

Detours and Drifts

Situationist International and the Art of Resistance

In those mystical days of May [1968] the poets of Paris were
the International Situationists, who have attained a similar
state of frenzied anti-doctrinal comic anarchism to the
yippies, though suckled on Dada, not L.S.D.

— Richard Neville, *Play Power*

Are you consumers or real participants?

— Situationist-inspired graffiti on the Sorbonne, Paris, May 1968

n October 29, 1952, Charlie Chaplin was giving a press conference in Paris to promote his latest film, *Limelight.* Chaplin, long considered the patron scamp of the workingman, had always enjoyed the enthusiastic support of the political Left. Indeed, "the little tramp" had defiantly shuffled, flat-footed, through the first half of twentieth-century America, poking his cane in the ribs of the establishment. At the height of American anticommunist paranoia, Chaplin was even "officially cited by the [U.S.] attorney general as a subversive"[1]—a label that should have contributed much to his "red cred" in the United States and abroad. Therefore, Chaplin seems an odd target for a small but boisterous group of Marxists who organized an angry protest outside the Ritz Hotel where Chaplin was promoting his film. The protestors shouted derisive epithets and distributed a scathing leaflet titled "NO MORE FLAT FEET," which chastised Chaplin for selling out to the Hollywood culture industry:

Because you've identified yourself with the weak and the oppressed,
to attack you has been to attack the weak and the oppressed — but in
the shadow of your rattan cane some could already see the nightstick
of a cop.

You are "he-who-turns-the-other-cheek" — the other cheek
of the buttock — but for us, the young and the beautiful, the only
answer to suffering is revolution. . . . Go to sleep, you fascist insect.
Rake in the dough. Make it with high society. . . . Have a quick death:
we promise you a first-class funeral. . . . Go home, Mr. Chaplin.[2]

The leaflet was signed by four members[3] of the Lettrist International (LI), a group of avant-garde poets, artists, and activists that had
emerged out of the heady, irreverent spirit of Dada. The Chaplin protest
ultimately inaugurated a splinter group of LI that became known as Situationist International. When, after the protest at the hotel, LI founder
Isodore Isou distanced himself from his four disciples and aligned himself instead with "the homage everyone has rendered to Chaplin,"[4] his
four followers responded in the publication *Combat:* "We believe that the
most urgent expression of freedom is the destruction of idols, especially
when they claim to represent freedom. The provocative tone of our leaflet was a reaction against a unanimous and servile enthusiasm."[5] For the
new founders of Situationist International, idols ripe for destruction now
included not only Chaplin, but the "servile" Isou as well.

From 1957 to 1972, Situationist International (SI) sought to overthrow the political conservatism and American-style consumerism that
dominated postwar Western Europe, as well as to confront the hypocrisy
of an ineffectual Left that had failed adequately to combat it. Although
the situationists, whom one contemporary media activist describes as "a
group of grumpy French anarchists,"[6] faded into relative obscurity in the
years following their disbandment, their ideas are currently enjoying a
significant renaissance in academic and political circles. The main reason
situationist thought remains so relevant is that the "Society of the Spectacle" — the phrase coined by SI leader Guy Debord in his 1967 book of
the same name — articulates for many people the increasingly invasive
presence of mediated consumer culture. According to Debord, the "Spectacle" named a novel mode of social domination in which the industrial
age's coercive manual labor was replaced by capitalism's deceitful promise
of fulfillment through consumption. Human experience under the Spec-

tacular hype of consumerism became mediated rather than immediate, passive rather than active, and inauthentic rather than authentic. The situationists encouraged people to choose authentic and spontaneous action in order to live life as "a moral, poetic, erotic, and almost spiritual refusal to cooperate with the demands of consumer culture."[7] The idea was to create *situations* that could not easily be represented (and hence, contained) by the machinery of the Spectacle.

The concept of the Spectacle updated for the media age Marx's conception of an exploitative society in which workers are pacified into compliance by an economically driven false consciousness. The Spectacle marked a transition in Western capitalist societies, where human beings began to identify less as workers and more as *consumers.* Debord, following Marx, detailed the ways in which consumer capitalism reduces humans to commodities that are readily exchanged for a profit. This reduction of communal life to a system of exchanges was accomplished, Debord argued, through a constant deluge of mesmerizing images (produced by advertising, Hollywood, television), which replaced everyday human relations. Steven Best and Douglas Kellner point to the novelty of the situationists' focal shift to a new locus of cultural value:

> Whereas traditional Marxism focused on production, the Situationists highlighted the importance of social reproduction and the rise of a consumer and media society. . . . While Marx spotlighted the factory, the Situationists concentrated on the city and concrete social relations, supplementing the Marxian emphasis on class struggle by undertaking cultural revolution and the transformation of everyday life.[8]

For Debord, if commodities were the basic unit of the economy, then images served as such for a Spectacular society. However, neither commodities nor images could replace real human emotion and involvement. Indeed, he argued, the new image economy alienates humans from authentic life, reducing them to nothing more than passive spectators experiencing only the artificial dreamland of the market. He wrote that human experience, under Spectacle, could be characterized by the "degradation of *being* into *having*" and, ultimately, by a "generalized sliding of *having* into *appearing.*"[9] In response, Debord and the situationists promoted spontaneity, play, and fascination. They encouraged fellow citizens to "free the passions," "live without dead time," and "don't change employers, change the employment of life." The return to authentic, unmediated *being* was the central goal.

Ironically, although they described their project as one *opposing* the Spectacle at every turn, situationists often found themselves forced to negotiate the tension between their desire to overturn the Spectacle and their inevitable contribution to it. And, although the situationists (who have been aptly labeled "Groucho Marxists"[10]) were theoretically committed to playfulness and ambiguity, they ultimately had quite clear categories defining what was truly revolutionary and what was merely reform in service of the establishment. For the situationists, the work and art of many of their potential comrades on the Left fell into the latter. Their disdain for Charlie Chaplin is but one example.

To a significant degree, SI concepts and strategies continue to set the general tone and specific goals for many of today's anticorporate activists. Several new studies of the situationists as well as anthologies of their writings have been published in recent years, and Web sites and discussion boards devoted to SI and Debord actively debate how to best implement their ideas.[11] This contemporary surge of interest in a movement that formally dissipated thirty years ago marks an increasing appetite for ways to combat the commodification and mediation of everyday life. To better understand the rhetorical tropes and strategies the situationists provide contemporary activists, I will attend in some detail to the concepts and practices of Situationist International. In this chapter, after a brief discussion of Situationist International's social milieu, I explore the rhetorical nature of three of the group's more prominent political strategies: détournement, dérive, and psychogeography.

Situationist International and the "Spirit of '68"

"That which presently characterizes our public life is boredom. The French are bored. . . . Youth is bored. . . . General de Gaulle is bored." So wrote a French journalist for *Le Monde*, contrasting the general public and their ennui with those people who did not have the luxury of being so bored, the "unemployed, marginal peasants, pensioners."[12] Historian Bernard E. Brown writes that this volatile formula—middle-class malaise coupled with working-class dissatisfaction—"was striking and captured the spirit of the times."[13] Just two months later, in early May, a police crackdown on students occupying the university at Nanterre provoked student occupations across the country and a swell of public support for the cause of the revolutionaries. By some reports, public opinion favored the students by a ratio of four to one. That spring, the superficial docility of France was shattered as the country underwent a major political upheaval that resulted in the most massive staging of barricades since the French Revolution, thousands of arrests, countless worker strikes, and the near upheaval of the national government.

Historians Andrew Feenberg and Jim Freedman observe that the most surprising aspect of the movement was its "rapidity and short duration." As they describe it: "It started at the University of Nanterre, where a small kernel of twenty-five grew into over a thousand in a month's time." After the closing of Nanterre, "the group of radicals swelled to fifty thousand and, in another ten days, ten million."[14] Yet, in only a month, except for a few concessions to workers, some minor changes in de Gaulle's government, and "specks of unwashed graffiti on the walls of the Sorbonne, there was hardly a visible trace of its passing."[15] Debates still rage as to the significance of the New Left movements of the 1960s.

The mood of 1960s Paris, made most manifest in the events of May 1968, was one characterized by a multifaceted denunciation of state- and market-sanctioned norms in favor of finding new ways of living. Certainly, North Americans were undergoing their own version of leftist revolution, but in a somewhat less organized and less centralized way. Parisian students, laborers, and artists articulated their suspicion of the hierarchical bureaucracy of the state, but also of the tranquilizing effects of consumer culture. The late 1960s revolts in Paris, like most people's uprisings, can be seen as an experiment in nay-saying, a collective repudiation of the status quo.

Brown points out that underlying much of the rhetoric of the revolts, the playfully antagonistic rhetoric that endures in our collective memory of the so-called "Spring of '68" was already theorized in detail by Debord and the situationists. Brown writes: "In the confusion and tumult of the May Revolt the slogans and shouts of the students were considered expressions of mass spontaneity and individual ingenuity. Only afterward was it evident that these slogans were fragments of a coherent and seductive ideology and had virtually all previously appeared in situationist tracts and publications."[16] Although the avant-garde SI was among the least noticeable of the many revolutionary groups at the time, the group's *rhetoric,* in the form of short, pithy slogans that inverted conventional values, was literally scrawled across Paris in the form of graffiti and wheat-paste posters. Greil Marcus describes the situationist rhetorical style thus: "A blindside paradox of dead rhetoric and ordinary language floated just this side of non sequitur, the declarative statement turning into a question as you heard it: what does this mean?"[17] Situationist slogans, which invoked bemusement as much as vitriol, were perfect for a generation standing at the precipice of the mass-mediated consumer culture we know today. Brown notes, "In retrospect ... the 'spirit of '68' was perhaps best captured, one might even say incarnated by the situationists."[18] Indeed, he adds, "most of the slogans chalked on the walls of French universities in May 1968 came straight out of" Debord's *The Society of the Spectacle* and fellow situationist Raoul Vaneigem's equally influential *Revolution of Everyday Life.*[19]

The situationists contributed to the growing vocabulary that expressed people's dissatisfaction with life under the related ideologies of Gaullism and consumerism. SI did not instigate people's dissatisfaction so much as provide the rhetorical tropes with which they could make themselves heard. If growing numbers of people wanted to say "no," then situationist rhetoric offered them the perfect lexicon for doing so. Although the situationists were heavily influenced by Marx, they had no use for the communist bureaucracies his work inspired. SI was interested in negating not only deGaulle's conservatism and the market's greed, but communism's rigidity as well. Brown writes that "the situationist critique of modern communism is total: anti-Lenin, anti-Stalin, anti-Trotsky, anti-Mao, anti-Ho, and anti-Castro. The debt to anarchism is obvious, except that the situationists repudiate the anarchists as well."[20] If it was nay-saying the people wanted, it was nay-saying they would find, as the situationists' increasingly popular writings were laden with it.

Since their emergence in the early 1950s, the situationists anticipated a growing frustration that manifested in one of the most significant uprisings of the twentieth century. Importantly, situationist rhetoric did not stop at negating the validity of one's present conditions, as this was only one step in a dialectical process. In order to transcend the shackles of modern life, situationists offered specific and detailed strategies for engaging in what they hoped would be a *post*modern world. Heavily influenced by the precepts of Dada, "a laboratory for the rehabilitation of daily life," they hoped to provoke people into a "rediscovery of joy and a reversal of perspective."[21] The situationists were, at their base, surrealists in the most general sense — they celebrated the imagination, the passions, and the fantastic in response to the rational constraints of modernity.

Détournement

Internationale Situationniste (IS),[22] the group's main journal, defines détournement as a detouring of preexisting Spectacular messages and images in an effort to subvert and reclaim them. Détournement was an effort to "devalue the currency of the Spectacle,"[23] which the situationists claimed had "kidnapped" authentic life. Examples include rewording conversations between popular comic-strip characters, reworking the sign on a storefront, making subversive collages out of familiar advertising images, and "hijacking" a public sermon, where a situationist dressed as a priest declares that "God is dead." Détournement can be translated as "detour" or "diversion," but other, more subtle meanings in the French include "hijacking," "embezzlement," "corruption," and "misappropriation."[24]

SI often used common images of the state and the market and paired them in ways that rendered them absurd. For example, Debord and Asger Jorn's early piece *Fin de Copenhague* (1957) is a collage book that lampoons the Spectacle's hollow promise by piecing together disparate images and text from periodicals purportedly collected during one stop at a Danish newsstand. The collage expressed the situationists' concern that the Spectacle was killing authentic urban life; it also conveyed their confidence that the falsity of its world would inevitably lead to its demise. One scholar of situationism notes that "In *Fin de Copenhague* Jorn and Debord gave the spectacle just enough rope to hang itself by, presupposing that a critique of 'spectacular' society was already present within the language of that society."[25] The situationists made it their mission to exacerbate what they saw as the inevitable implosion of the Spectacle — what they saw as a rhetorical house of cards, built only on illusory images and false promises. However, utilizing the rhetoric of the Spectacle while still maintaining the contrarian posture that SI so valued demanded tricky rhetorical footwork.

According to *IS*, two "fundamental laws" govern the successful practice of détournement: first, "the loss of importance of each detourned autonomous element—which may go so far as to lose its original sense completely—and at the same time the organization of another meaningful ensemble that confers on each element its new scope and effect."[26] The first move of détournement, then, is always a negation, or a decrease in value of a particular organization of a message. This "devaluing" was often attempted by making opaque the Spectacle's rhetorical manipulation. As Best and Kellner put it, détournement can be seen as "a means of deconstructing the images of bourgeois society by exposing the hidden manipulation or repressive logic (e.g., by changing the wording of a billboard)."[27] As I suggest in chapter 2, détournement continues to characterize much of contemporary culture jamming.

Debord once detourned a familiar image of Stalin by "placing a barebreasted woman on his forehead with the caption 'The Universe Turns on the Tips of Breasts.'"[28] Such alteration is an effort to undermine the authoritative political portrait—in this case, Stalin's. Further, the alteration reorganizes the image in a way that not only interrupts the original meaning but creates a new meaning, or opens up potentials for new meanings. The nonsensical phrasing is not incidental—the situationists did not necessarily want to offer a clear prescription for how to read their messages. Rather, they sought to force viewers to grapple with detourned artifacts and, hopefully, to derive from those artifacts meanings or responses of their own.[29]

Elsewhere in SI writings, Debord and his comrades establish a more explicit set of guidelines for détournement than the mere "tweaking" they discouraged. In a hesitant effort to theorize the concept, Debord and Gil Wolman outline the following four-part détournement "methodology." They write that, first, "It is the most distant detourned element which contributes most sharply to the overall impression, and not the elements that directly determine the nature of this impression."[30] For rhetorical scholars, this point should resonate with Kenneth Burke's notion of "perspective by incongruity," in which the force of a rhetorical artifact is an effect of the degree of dissonance it produces.[31] For situationists, this meant that the most directly oppositional components of a détourne-ment were often not the most productive.

Debord and Wolman offer the example of a leftist poem-collage from the Spanish civil war in which the most compelling image is also the least assuming: a fragment of a lipstick advertisement that declares, "pretty lips are red."[32] Given the situationists' commitment to altering the consciousness of those they confronted, it seems that the lipstick ad is less sensical, and thus requires a more significant engagement from viewers than the more explicitly political components of the piece. In the ad's orig-inal form, pretty red lips are the advertiser's promise to female consumers. Put in another context, however, the phrase associates beauty with com-munism, albeit in a relatively ambiguous way. A similar example during the situationists' heyday is the popular poster of a woman standing in front of barricades, throwing a brick accompanied by the familiar situationist slogan "La Beauté est dans la rue" (Figure 1). In keeping with Burke, both the collage and the poster link seemingly incongruous concepts — beauty and war — making these texts potentially more powerful as a result.

Debord and Wolman also suggest that "the distortions intro-duced in the detourned elements must be as simplified as possible, since the main force of a *détournement* is directly related to the conscious or vague recollection of the original contexts of the elements."[33] Détour-nement relies not only on an existing form for its critique, but also on people's familiarity with it. For example, Debord's mockery of Stalin's portrait garners its rhetorical effectivity from the French public's mem-ory of the original image, or at least of the formal conventions of politi-cal portraiture in general. Given this dependence on a viewer's previous knowledge, it was necessary to keep the alterations simple, so as not to render the original image completely indiscernible.

A third "law" of détournement, according to Debord and Wol-man, is that "*détournement* is less effective the more it approaches a rational reply."[34] Although situationists clearly sought to create oppor-tunities in which the people could talk back to the unilateral monologue spewed by the Spectacle, they were careful not to resort to mere reac-tionary engagements that would only reinforce their subordinate role. This is evident in Debord and Wolman's warning to leftist comrades who wanted to detourn an anti-Soviet poster by the fascist organization Peace and Liberty, "which proclaimed, amid images of overlapping flags of the

Figure 1. Beauty is in the street.

Western powers, 'Union makes strength,' — by adding onto it a smaller
sheet with the phrase 'and coalitions make war.'"[35] Although Debord and
Wolman were likely sympathetic to the ideology behind such a detourn,
they ultimately disapproved of the tactic, which served merely to bolster
the enemy's message by contrasting it with what amounted to little more
than an enfeebled "no."

An extension of this position is the fourth and final rule that "*détournement* by simple reversal is always the most direct and the least effective."[36] The characteristic implied throughout all the rules — the necessity for a certain level of irrationality — establishes the tension that situationists had to negotiate, maintaining some familiar elements of a detourned artifact while at the same time refusing to engage in logical argument. Importantly, the negation that situationists argued was so integral to détournement was not to be waged as the flip side of a binary pair, but as a radical rerouting that troubled the authority of rational logic itself. Similar to their dissatisfaction with the plan to detourn the Peace and Liberty posters, Debord and Wolman questioned the rhetorical force of the Black Mass, a group that sought to undermine the metaphysics of Catholicism by inverting its convocational framework. The inevitable, if unintended result, SI warned, was a simultaneous *conservation* of those very metaphysics. Again, although negation is an important function of détournement, the situationists insisted it must not remain mired there, ardently opposing dominant discourse while failing to say anything new.

It is important to look more closely at the sociopolitical forces within which the strategy of détournement emerged. Practitioners saw détournement as the ultimate tactic to mobilize a revolutionary consciousness, a tactic that would clash head-on with juridicopolitical conventions. Indeed, Debord and Wolman write that "[détournement] cannot fail to be a powerful cultural weapon in the service of a real class struggle. The cheapness of its products is the heavy artillery that breaks through all the Chinese walls of understanding. It is a real means of proletarian-artistic education, the first step toward a *literary communism*."[37] "Literary communism" was intended as a response not only to the reigning conservative rhetoric of Gaullism, but also to the leftist discourse of other predominant French intellectuals and artists of the 1960s, discourse the situationists described as "passionless polemics between the celebrities of Unintellingence" serving only to "mask real problems by expatiating over false ones."[38] Included on this list of intellectual phonies were none other than Roland Barthes, Claude Levi-Strauss, Jean-Paul Sartre, and Henri Lefebvre, among others.

Foremost among those earning SI's scorn, however, was the administration of Charles de Gaulle. In addition to the more obvious political maladies that de Gaulle's Fifth Republic came to represent for many avant-garde activists — such as its isolationist foreign policies, eager development of atomic power, and enthusiasm for American-style capitalism — the situationists actively opposed the Gaullist urban *aesthetic,* a kind of modernist functionalism that Debord and his comrades suspected was by design confining and oppressive. Although I focus here primarily on the more conventionally understood *rhetorical* strategies of SI, it must be noted that a crucial component of their thought and practice centered on innovating an architectural style that would revolutionize the modern city.[39]

The situationists abhorred the conservative approach to urban planning that ruled much of postwar Europe. According to SI, de Gaulle's France, of which Paris was the undisputed cultural and political nexus, was a deliberate experiment in spatial control of the masses. Situationist A.-F. Conord suggested sarcastically that "one can only admire the ingenuity of our ministers and our urbanist architects. . . . So as to avoid a complete rupture of consensus, they have put in place some model slums, the plans of which serve the four corners of France. . . . It is the 'barrack' style.'"[40] Situationists further charged that de Gaulle's administration designed "premeditated ghettos" to house Paris's Algerian immigrant population. Importantly, for SI this militaristic governing of community space related directly to the Fifth Republic's attempts to control public discourse in the tumultuous 1960s.

SI activists carefully negotiated a tension between the detour's dependence on the public's familiarity with discursive and graphic formal conventions, and the need to radically differentiate those conventions toward different, revolutionary ends. This negotiation was a response to another deeply held belief about the Spectacle in the age of Gaullism. Like their Frankfurt School predecessors, who articulated similar themes under the "Culture Industry" rubric, the situationists "believed that the Spectacle had become so sophisticated that it could successfully recuperate rebellion, strip it of its threatening content, and re-sell it as pure image."[41]

This understandable belief in the Spectacle's ability to appropriate the rhetoric of those who dared resist it haunted the situationists and girded their contempt for many of their artistic contemporaries who celebrated the Spectacle's artificiality. Pop artists of the 1960s are a telling example of those whom SI saw as enemies of the revolution; in one SI publication, the group describes pop art as "materially and 'ideologically' characterized by *indifference* and dull complacency."[42] Another such culprit was New Wave filmmaker Jean-Luc Godard, who "presently represents formal pseudofreedom and the pseudocritique of manners and values — the two inseparable manifestations of all ersatz, recuperated modern art," according to SI in an essay berating Godard.[43] Although SI shared with pop artists an opposition to the conservative Fifth Republic and to market capitalism, SI had little patience for those who found any creative or political potential in experimenting positively with establishment images.

In addition to the situationists' concern with the failure of pop artists to make their critiques sufficiently explicit, SI felt that the pop artists merely perpetuated the class divide over what counted as "literature" or as "art," in part by maintaining the primacy of the auteur-genius. Indeed, it was SI's disdain for the bourgeois "auteur" that fueled their attack on Chaplin, who, despite his respectable proletariat résumé, was one of Hollywood's first true movie stars. The situationists were keenly aware that formerly insurgent art movements had failed to live up to their revolutionary potential and had allowed themselves to be ingested by the insatiable Spectacle. Debord and Wolman write in an *IS* essay: "Since the negation of the bourgeois conception of art and artistic genius has become pretty much old hat, [Marcel Duchamp's] drawing of a mustache on the *Mona Lisa* is no more interesting than the original version of that painting. We must now push this process to the point of negating the negation."[44]

I suggest that this argument highlights a potential weakness in the situationist conception of détournement — if one must always "negate the negation," one can never "detourn" sufficiently and is destined for eternal disappointment. Such a politics seems, in many ways, mired in a Hegelian logic that resentfully longs for a future that will never be. SI's struggle to capitalize on Spectacular conventions without being infected by them brings to mind Foucault's affectionate discussion of Hegel, in which he suggests that those of us who wish to escape his influence must recognize how much we confirm his presence by doing so: "It implies a knowledge, in that which permits us to think against Hegel, of that which remains Hegelian. We have to determine the extent to which our anti-Hegelianism is possibly one of his tricks directed against us, at the end of which he stands, motionless, waiting for us."[45] As I suggest in the chapters that follow, perhaps it is the logic of negation itself that must be reconsidered — especially as a strategy of resistance in the contemporary cultural milieu.

It is unlikely that Debord and his comrades would be particularly surprised at how adeptly *today's* Spectacle recuperates rebellion. As late as 1988, Debord returned to the concept. In his *Comments on the Society of the Spectacle,* he argues that Spectacular power had now become wholly integrated. As Debord biographer Anselm Jappe describes: "Unlike its predecessors, the integrated spectacle lets no part of the real society escape its control: instead of hovering above reality, it has 'integrated itself into reality.' Reality thus no longer 'confronts [it] as something alien,' for the integrated spectacle has been able to reconstruct reality to suit itself."[46]

Under this "integrated spectacle," the avant-garde critic is left with little employ, as her strategies cannot be said to deliver something like "the real" to her audience. Indeed, advertisers are as clever as any activist when it comes to spoofing advertising. "Political resistance" is readily branded and sold back to consumers through edgy lifestyle campaigns for "Xtreme" products. One especially stark example is the game "State of Emergency," produced in 2000 for Sony PlayStation (Figure 2). In this game, players become antiglobalization activists fighting the so-called "American Trade Organization"—modeled after the protests at the World Trade Organization's 1999 Millennium Round in Seattle. The game's images of young antiestablishment warriors taking to the streets look eerily similar to the well-known images of the Paris protests of May 1968, in which the situationists played an integral role (Figure 3).

Dérive: The Drift

The situationists define dérive as "a mode of experimental behavior linked to the conditions of urban society: a technique of transient passage through varied ambiances."[47] Elsewhere, they describe it thus: "In a *dérive* one or more persons during a certain period drop their usual motives for movement and action, their relations, their work and leisure activities, and let themselves be drawn by the attractions of the terrain and the encounters they find there."[48] In his description of dérive, *Adbusters* founder Kalle Lasn focuses on the everydayness of the practice. By being open to one's immediate surroundings, he explains, one discovers what one truly loves and hates. He adds: "The Situationists believed the *dérive* could largely replace the old twin occupations of work and entertainment, and become a model for the 'playful creation' of a new way of life. The *dériviste* is a drifter in the best possible sense, not someone down and out

Figure 2. Activists take to the streets against a fictional international
trade organization in Rockstar Games' "State of Emergency" for
Sony PlayStation.

but up and beyond, living outside the stifling roles society prescribes for
us."[49] Drifting, then, was at once a material and a rhetorical practice—an
attempt to redefine oneself by inhabiting space in new ways. It was akin
to surrealist novelist André Breton's notion of a "perpetual promenade in
the middle of a forbidden area."[50]

Although drifting was largely a physical exercise, its goals may
resonate with students of rhetoric. Like more conventional rhetorics of
resistance, dérive was an attempt to drop one's "usual motives" and allow
oneself to be "drawn by the attractions" and encounter the world anew. It
was an experiment with "varied ambiance," or contexts.[51] A kind of rhetorical physics, drifting was an attempt to *make strange* one's position in the
Spectacle of commercial propaganda. Distinguishing the drift from the
stroll, which they considered too constructed, the situationists attempted
to drift in such a way that they navigated the city based on their "psycho-
graphic" response to it. The idea was for one to *feel* one's way through the
city by using an unconscious drive that was as yet unaffected by the glit-
tering paths of consumerism.

In a sense, SI advocated a physical response to the problem of an
increasingly brand-saturated world.[52] The situationists, however, did not

Figure 3. Students fend off police in this famous image from the Paris revolts in the spring of 1968. Photograph by Bruno Barbey; courtesy of Magnum Photos.

seem to distinguish, as rhetoricians sometimes do, between the rhetorical effects of *speech* and the rhetorical effects of *bodies in motion.* In any case, I hesitate to perpetuate the problematic distinction between the rhetorical and the corporeal in which the latter—the configuration of bodies within specific material conditions—is relegated to the nonrhetorical. I argue that a practice such as dérive, in which people struggle to navigate the contours of the political, material, and cultural world in which they live, is inherently related to the discourses that, at least in part, construct that world.

In "Theory of *Dérive*," Debord writes that "from the *dérive* point of view cities have a psychogeographical relief, with constant currents, fixed points and vortexes which strongly discourage entry into or exit from certain zones."[53] In other words, the drifter examines and experiments with what is possible in his or her surroundings and, in doing so, discovers blockages, paths, and possible fissures on which to expand. Debord, reflecting his political zeitgeist, wrote "reification is never complete."[54] In other words, the Spectacle is never completely sutured. Something always evades its grasp. Something always exceeds it. The task of the diligent situationist, then, is to find those moments in everyday life in which possibilities for freedom remain. Dérive can be seen as an Aristotelian "discovery" of the rhetorical tools available; one's rhetorical choices are always prescribed by the material and cultural conditions in which one finds oneself. Put another way, you have to start where you are.

For those familiar with Michel de Certeau's work, the drifter likely sounds much like de Certeau's allusion to *Wandersmänner,* "whose bodies follow the thicks and thins of an urban 'text' they write without being able to read it" and prefer making use of "spaces that cannot be seen" to the position of the "voyeur-god" who takes pleasure in judging from on high, but as a result "knows only cadavers."[55] Although they were contemporaries and countrymen, it is unclear whether de Certeau and Debord's situationists were interlocutors. Nonetheless, de Certeau's conception informs my insistence on the rhetorical nature of the drift. He writes, for example, that for the wanderer, "each body is an element signed by many others, [and] eludes legibility. . . . The networks of these moving, intersecting writings compose a manifold story that has neither author nor spectator, shaped out of fragments of trajectories and alterations of spaces: in relation to representations, it remains daily and indefinitely other."[56] De Certeau suggests that, as communicating subjects, we are materially connected to others. Notably, it is precisely this invocation of materiality that disallows an understanding of communication, or rhetoric, that is grounded merely in a system of *representation.*

According to de Certeau, by walking in the city, one escapes the inevitable totalization produced by the voyeur, who attempts to "see the whole," eradicating difference as she does so. In contrast, the wanderer — or in our case, the drifter — allows herself to remain open to the differences she encounters. The drifter's path is unintelligible because she is on the ground, and thus evades the security — and, importantly, the stability — of a predetermined route. Reification can never be complete, because one necessarily engages the production of life in the everyday. Unlike the Kantian subject, who sees objects only in their completion (and not the labor processes that produced them), the drifter cannot so easily engage the world as something that exists merely for her consumption. Like de Certeau, the situationists celebrate the illegibility that drifting provides; "the changing of landscapes from one hour to the next will result in complete disorientation."[57] This disorientation, for both de Certeau and the situationists, is a necessary precursor if one is to be reoriented.

Psychogeography

Psychogeography was a situationist practice, but it was also their overarching goal—for people to peel back the veneer of the modernist city to reveal "the authentic life of the city teeming underneath."[58] In addition to the physical practice of drifting, which pushed the city to the limits of intelligibility, SI members also challenged the Spectacle's rhetoric on the register of its most official manifestation . . . *maps.*

SI mobilized its troupe of artists to fight de Gaulle's government on its own turf, detouring existing city maps in an effort to speak more authentically to the subtleties of urban life. An official map of Paris drawn by Peltier in 1956, for example, provides a cartographic point of view that positions the viewer as a de Certeauian "voyeur god." The map, which borrowed from aerial photography of Paris,[59] allowed one to *consume* the city in toto, without necessarily being affected (or infected) by it. The booklet that attended this map boasted, "no work of comparable importance has been accomplished, for a capital, since the famous Turgot plan published in 1739."[60] Such a confident claim to accuracy made the map a prime target for situationist alteration.

Debord and Jorn responded with *The Naked City: A Psychogeographic Guide of Paris* (Figure 4). Debord and Jorn's piece intended to express "the closeness of areas by feel and not feet"[61] and to identify working-class zones they wanted to see preserved and improved. The image represents their belief that the city was becoming superficially homogenized, while pockets of underdevelopment were being ignored. Situationist map-collages beckoned Parisians to reject renderings of the city and to instead move passionately and spontaneously through Paris's streets. The ultimate goal for SI was to allow the city its dynamism, a quality that was endangered by the functionalist approach of most city planners. Note, for example, the ideal city space presented in 1922 by the famous French architect Le Corbusier (Figure 5).

This image renders time stagnant and people, with all their attendant problems, nonexistent. As Simon Sadler suggests, "In psychogeography, all the struggles were acute again, making nonsense of the Corbusian fantasy of the city as something abstract, rational, or ideal."[62] Although not explicit in situationist writings, I want to point out that one danger of the timelessness of such images is that they seem to imply an

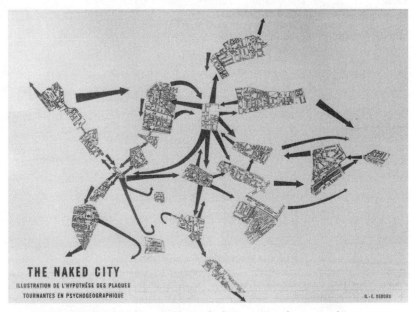

Figure 4. Debord and Jorn's *The Naked City: A Psychogeographic Guide of Paris.*

Figure 5. Le Corbusier's ideal public space (notably sans public). Copyright Artists Rights Society (ARS), New York/ADAGP/Paris/FLC.

end to history. In a society that assumes it lives at the end of history, difference becomes a threat to perfect order—dissent must be eliminated.

In response, a situationist ironically known only as Constant depicted a dynamic city that thrives on difference and change (Figure 6). Unlike in Le Corbusier's image, in Constant's image the perpetual movement of its inhabitants are inextricable from the city. Doors swing frenetically and arrows map rhizomatic motion. Although hardly a blueprint for a more democratic topography, situationist representations such as

Constant's attempted to both document and nurture a city in which history is produced by those who walk its streets.

Conclusion

Echoing components of Adorno and Horkheimer's famous Culture Industry thesis, the Situationist International was highly critical of the effects of industrialization on political and cultural life. Their main themes—alienation of people from mass-produced art, and the standardization of labor and the cultural texts it produced—call attention to a profound shift in cultural production at the middle of the twentieth century. Their critique—that the mass production and standardization of consumer goods required the mass production and standardization of *consumers*—inspired a later generation of activists.

To accomplish the standardization of consumers, it was necessary to to mobilize armies of admen, the advance troops of what would become the most prominent mode of social discourse of the century.[63] The consumer began to replace the laborer as the chief economic engine. Laborers were still important, of course, but they were now expected to fulfill a double role, becoming the market for the things they produced. The situationists recognized this shift and were among the first to actively politicize advertising and consumer culture. They fought against

Figure 6. The situationist Constant's dynamic city.

the homogenization, mediation, and confinement of life under the rule of the Spectacle. They did so by experimenting with alternative ways of being and by trying to protect a space *outside* the Spectacle's reach.

Note, for example, the many situationist-inspired slogans prevalent in the spring 1968 Paris revolts — "Boredom is counterrevolutionary," "No replastering, the structure is rotten," "Those who make revolutions by halves do but dig themselves a grave," "To cede a little is to capitulate a lot," and "Workers of the world, have fun!" These slogans and attendant imagery responded to a mode of power that the worker and student activists saw as confining and oppressive. For many activists, politics amounted to a zero-sum game — one with a clear, monolithic enemy and irreverent heroes who refused to cede even the smallest piece of political ground. The rhetorical themes of these famous 1968 posters by Atelier Populaire[64] clearly articulate a belief in a dissembling official power structure that narcotizes its citizens with false ideologies and treats them like soulless drones in a heavily policed factory-prison (Figures 7–11). The only response was utter refusal to participate: to throw a wrench into the machinery and stop the oppression. Only then, on the ruins of the old model, could the people build a more liberated and egalitarian society.

Although SI tactics may have offered appropriate responses to the historical conditions in which the situationists found themselves, they did so by arguing for a model of the public based on false consciousness. As their antipathy for Charlie Chaplin and others demonstrates, no one who experimented or profited by engaging with the Spectacle was to be trusted. For the situationists, the public was under constant threat of being consumed by the Spectacle. Hence, the public had to be liberated from the ideological conventions of consumption — presumably a blend of fickleness and docility. The role of the critic in relation to this public, then, is always one of the outside observer, the avant-garde scout who sees things as they *really are* and can therefore alert the masses to the truth. This message, scrawled across the walls of a tumultuous Paris, was an understandably attractive alternative to the malaise and boredom upon which the government and commerce thrived.

The proliferation of SI slogans in the May revolts raised Debord's public persona, and the popular appetite for situationist ideas and writings increased. Perhaps not surprisingly, Debord eschewed what he called this "revolting celebrity," and he promised that he and his comrades would

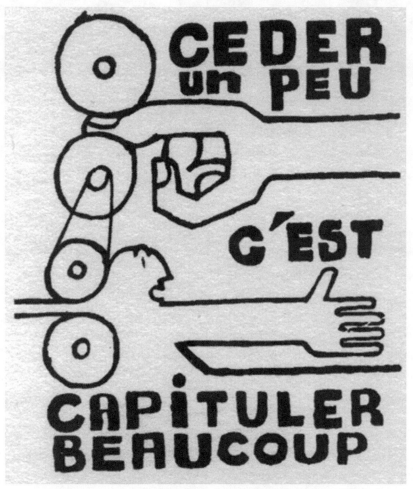

Figure 7. The posters designed by Atelier Populaire (Popular Workshop) are likely the most enduring images of May 1968.

become "even more inaccessible, even more clandestine. The more our theses become famous, the more will we ourselves become obscure."[65] In July 1968, Debord turned over the journal to a committee of editors who ultimately never published another issue. Debord commented that it was just as well, since the journal's popularity had become too "routine." As Brown notes, "Those who used to anxiously await each issue for tips of reality, [Debord] commented wryly, will now have to begin thinking for themselves, in the best situationist tradition."[66]

In late 1994, after years of suffering from alcoholic polyneuritis, Debord ended his life by shooting himself in the heart. As he explained

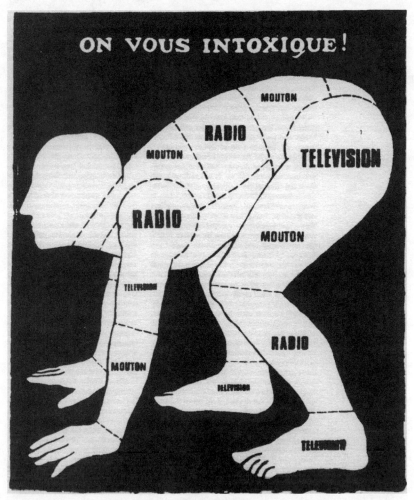

Figure 8. Poster designed by Atelier Populaire.

at the end of a television broadcast on Canal Plus about his work: "This is the opposite of an illness that you contract through an unfortunate lack of prudence. On the contrary, contracting it requires dogged determination over a whole lifetime."[67] It seems that Debord was as committed to dying authentically as he was to living authentically. Avant-garde to the end, he defiantly refused to budge on his principles (or addictions), no matter how costly.

Given his suspicion of hero worship, one wonders how Debord might feel about his renewed popularity among today's anticorporate activists. As I will argue in the next chapter, Debord's assumptions still very much govern the activities of some contemporary anticonsumer activists

Figure 9. Poster designed by Atelier Populaire.

who attempt to keep lit the revolutionary torch of Situationist International. Interestingly, despite SI's complex and often abstract theories, what remains prevalent are the group's catchy slogans and striking imagery. Indeed, the situationist "brand" has become a mainstay of the anti-consumer activist's lexicon. Perhaps this is because, like all good brands, situationism is easily appropriated toward new ends. However, as I argue, by perpetuating the situationist brand, many contemporary culture jammers ignore the fact that the cultural terrain has significantly changed. In today's brand economy, an activist rhetoric of false consciousness may

Figure 10. Poster designed by Atelier Populaire.

cost publics too much, as it demands that individual activists define themselves as outside publics in the hopes that publics will define themselves outside consumption. This political strategy, especially when stripped of the situationists' more ironic sensibilities, depends on the increasingly ineffectual rebel, who demands that one must destroy the consuming public if one wants to save it. Compromising with the logics of late industrial capitalism is, in this model, a form of complicity, and so no position

Figure 11. Poster designed by Atelier Populaire.

that affords critics, activists, and publics a stance from within capitalism can ever produce anything other than failure. Herein lies a self-fulfilling impotency: Given the pervasive ubiquity of late capitalism, the dream of the outsider hero, who sees through the false consciousness of branding and the alleged dissolution of the public that accompanies it, seems increasingly phantasmal.

Anti-Logos

Sabotaging the Brand through Parody

> We will jam the pop-culture marketers and bring their
> image factory to a sudden, shuddering halt.
>
> —Kalle Lasn, *Culture Jam*

In late 2003, *Adbusters,* the activist magazine known for its parodic "subvertisements" and scathing critiques of consumer culture, launched its most ambitious antibranding campaign yet. Its Blackspot sneaker, an unassuming black canvas shoe with a large white spot where one would expect a corporate logo, is intended to uncool sportswear giant Nike by offering an ethically produced alternative to the swoosh. The magazine's first goal was to challenge Nike's controversial CEO by way of a full-page ad in the *New York Times,* declaring: "Phil Knight had a dream. He'd sell shoes. He'd sell dreams. He'd get rich. He'd use sweatshops if he had to. Then along came the new shoe. Plain. Simple. Cheap. Fair. Designed for only one thing. Kicking Phil's ass. The Unswoosher."[1] *Adbusters* also encouraged its readers to help spread the "Blackspot virus" by graffitiing black spots on Niketown windows and displays across the United States and Canada. Although it remains to be seen whether the campaign will, as *Adbusters* hopes, "set a precedent that will revolutionize capitalism,"[2] as I write in late 2006, well over two hundred independent shoe stores and four thousand individuals have placed orders for the shoes, and Blackspot was featured in the *New York Times Magazine*'s special Year in Ideas issue as one of the "Best Ideas of 2003."

The Blackspot now comes in a "classic" sneaker (clearly modeled after Converse's perennially popular Chuck Taylor All Star, which is now, ironically, owned by Nike) and a work boot created by John Fluevog, whose whimsical styles have made his designs a longtime staple of the indie set. Both shoes are made of all-vegetarian materials in a unionized and environmentally friendly factory in Portugal. Although *Adbusters* has gone to great lengths to ensure the Blackspot is made ethically, the shoes themselves are somewhat beside the point. In keeping with the dictates of Nike-style marketing, the sneaker is primarily a vehicle for the brand it distributes. As consumer-culture analyst Rob Walker notes, "Often when a new brand or product is invented, its creators then make an effort to describe (or invent) its deeper meaning or Big Idea. Here the Big Idea came first, and it's the product that's being invented after the fact."[3] It seems *Adbusters* has actually taken Knight's branding strategy to its next logical step, transforming themselves from antibranding activists to brand managers.

Adbusters positions itself as the journal for the advanced troops in the culture-jamming movement. The magazine, published the Media Foundation, a Vancouver, British Columbia, social marketing firm, has made a name for itself primarily through its ad parodies, or subvertisements. Ad parodies, which attempt to serve as rhetorical X-rays that reveal the "true logic" of advertising, are a common way for anticorporate activists to talk back to the multimedia Spectacle of corporate marketing. The so-called subvertisers at *Adbusters* see themselves as the political heirs to the situationists. In a letter to the magazine, for example, a Sioux City, Iowa, high-school student called for "*Détournements,* not football games!" Although most American teenagers are hardly abandoning touchdowns for billboard liberations, many are enthusiastically embracing a do-it-yourself countercultural ethic that has been heavily influenced by situationist practices. *Adbusters* provides them with caustic rhetoric and provocative images meant to fuel homegrown dissent against marketing culture.

Explicitly influenced by the situationist concept of psychogeography, which asked citizens to mine the urban landscape for the authentic life "beneath the paving stones,"[4] *Adbusters* conceives public life geographically, as a topography to be explored and ultimately remapped in more genuine ways. Like the situationists, the Media Foundation challenges clear-eyed activists to dismantle the Spectacular architecture artificially posing as real life. However, the rhetoric of the Media Foundation takes the geographical metaphor further, describing turn-of-the-millennium public life as existing within an organic "media ecology." *Adbusters'* subtitle is the "Journal of the Mental Environment," and its writers frequently decry the polluted state of our "ecology of mind." Kalle Lasn, in his popular book *Culture Jam,* argues that we live in a world polluted by the "infotoxins" spewed by "marketers, spin doctors, and PR agents" and that we are suffocating for lack of "infodiversity."[5] His solution? Lasn argues that just as environmentalists thirty years ago "shocked us into realizing that our natural environment was dying, and catalyzed a wave of activism that changed the world. Now it's time to do the same for our mental environment."[6]

Lasn's call for a cleanup drive of our littered mediascape echoes the arguments of many contemporary media scholars and activists, perhaps the most recognizable of which is the late New York University professor Neil Postman, a founder of the interdisciplinary field of media ecology. Postman argued that "information has become a form of garbage. . . . Our defenses against the information glut have broken down; our information immune system is inoperable."[7] Like Postman, culture-jamming collective Immediast Underground describes the modern mediascape as something of a junkyard:

> We can see how extended exposure to television and mass media
> dulls people with a sense of numbness and nausea. At every turn a
> monologue of coercion penetrates our senses and rapes our atten-
> tion. Wherever we look, wherever we listen, wherever we go: the
> pornography of billboards, bus-side placards, subway cars, glaring
> storefront signs and displays, the glut of junk mail, stupid fly-by
> beach planes and blimps, coupons, obnoxious bumper stickers and
> breast pins. . . . Only the upper atmosphere and the ocean floor offer
> any sanctuary from America's *ecology of coercion.*[8]

Ralph Nader, in his 2000 bid for the U.S. presidency, similarly described a dilapidated public sphere overrun by commercial media telling audiences that they, like most Americans, are likely "overcome by the sheer ugliness of commercial strips and sprawls and incessantly saturating advertisements, repelled by the voyeurism of the mass media . . . feeling that there needs to be more to life than the desperate rat race to make ends meet."[9]

Adbusters, like Postman, Immediast Underground, Nader, and countless other critics of contemporary media, rhetorically constructs the media ecology as an apocalyptic and hermetically sealed dystopia, in which our collective psyche is rotting for lack of fresh air. In his chapter "The Ecology of Mind," Lasn catalogs the multitude of real and constructed psychological disorders rampant in North America, concluding: "More than anything else, it is our mediated, consumption-driven culture that's making us sick."[10] Our communal *dis-ease*, Lasn argues, is a result of our being sold a prefabricated, false bill of goods. Like the situationists before him, Lasn wonders: "Can spontaneity and authenticity be restored?"[11] Lasn's Media Foundation attempts to intervene rhetorically in the inauthentic, unsustainable world brought to us by what he calls "America™".

In this chapter, I explore both the opportunities and limitations of the rhetorical strategies — ad parodies and consumer boycotts — favored by *Adbusters* and other subvertisers. Both modes are meant to interrupt, or sabotage, the endless barrage spewed by the culture industry, which presumably manufactures every aspect of public life. These are strategies responding to corporations' attempts to elevate brands to the level of deities, to make rhetoric the undeniable *logos* of our public life. Here, I intentionally play with the multiple meanings of "logos." In contemporary parlance, of course, "logos" (long "o") are the graphic identifiers of an organization's "personality," the visual shorthand for brand identity. In Greek, however, *logos* (short "o") has multiple meanings — "word," "reason," and "logic," to name a few. For rhetoricians and philosophers, *logos* historically had to do with logical persuasive appeals and also with something more profound — it has been understood as the rational order of the universe, or *truth*. For many Christians, *logos* is understood to be the word of God. Indeed, the Gospel of John opens by foregrounding *logos* (translated in English as "word"): "In the beginning was the Word *[Logos]*, and the Word *[Logos]* was with God, and the Word *[Logos]* was God." So, I want to suggest that in more ways than one, adbusting can be seen as kind of an "anti-logos" — a refusal to accept the brand giants' logos as *logos*.

After I explore boycott and parody, I discuss the characteristics of symbolic sabotage as a political strategy. I then examine what I see as the significant limitations of a rhetorical project that deploys parody as its primary mode of engagement. I suggest that parody, as negative critique, can never offer new responses to the rhetoric of consumer culture, as it provides only a vocabulary for saying "no." It is strictly a rhetoric of repudiation. As I argue, parody derides the *content* of what it sees as oppressive rhetoric, but it fails to attend to its *patterns.* As I detail in the section "Consuming Rebels," the parody of commercial culture is a favored trope of advertising rhetoric and, as such, it may not be as critical an intervention as many subvertisers may hope. I argue that, whereas sabotage may have significant impact in certain rhetorical situations, it should not be seen as a transhistorical strategy that is inherently subversive — primarily because capitalism itself is not a transhistorical system. It is constantly taking new shapes and producing different effects.

Just Say No: Boycotting Consumer Culture

Garnering more attention every year are the international boycotts "Turn Your TV Off for a Week" and "Buy Nothing Day" (the latter of which was strategically set on the Friday after Thanksgiving in the United States, the launch of the annual Christmas shopping season). All U.S. television networks except CNN Headline News refused to air the group's promotions for the boycotts. CBS's Robert L. Lowary claimed, "This commercial [Buy Nothing Day] . . . is in opposition to the current economic policy in the United States."[12] Yet, a groundswell of support on high-school and college campuses demonstrates that the *Adbusters* message is touching a nerve with at least some consumers.

Social activists have long used boycotts to force companies to become better public citizens. For a boycott to work, activists must persuade consumers to refrain from purchasing the products of a particular company. This is traditionally done by making a case for why a company's practices are harmful. In effect, activists persuade other consumers to collaborate in sending a message to a powerful corporation by "hurting them where it counts," by attacking their bottom line. A governing assumption is that average individuals can be persuaded by moral argument, but that companies must be persuaded to act in their own best interests, which is to make a profit. To be successful, a boycott must convince corporate managers that it is more cost-effective to heed the complaints of the activists. So the rhetorical burden of the boycotter is at least twofold: convince consumers to join in the boycott, and send a message to the responsible corporation, explaining the reason for their lost income. Traditionally, the target of the boycott must be made painfully aware of the costs of maintaining the status quo.

The target of Buy Nothing Day (BND) is, however, far more ubiquitous than any individual company with easily identifiable products. It is consumerism itself that the group hopes to thwart, if only for one day. In the years since its inception, BND has steadily grown in force. In 1997, the *New York Times* reported that although BND activities may have been "largely limited to utopia-tinted places like Vermont and Seattle and the handfuls of quixotic counterpropagandists were outnumbered nation-wide perhaps one million to one by glassy-eyed shoppers," the activists' message was clearly striking a chord with consumers.[13] By 2002, BND organizers staged events in the United States, Canada, Australia, New Zealand, Japan, Finland, Mexico, Israel, Holland, Germany, France, Sweden, Belgium, and several other countries. BND events include make-shift barter markets set in popular shopping plazas, helmeted "shopping police" issuing overconsumption tickets to package-laden shoppers, and activists handing out "gift of time" certificates and shopping checklists that ask shoppers to consider questions such as "Do I need it?" and "How will I dispose of it when I'm done?"[14]

Although *Adbusters* initiated and continues to promote BND, one need not belong to a specific group or party to participate in the event. And because it addresses a problem — overconsumption — that is not confined to the practices of specific companies or countries, its message is easily propagated. As Lasn has said, "All I know is that there are these spontaneous outbursts of street theater, of mall invasions, of pranks and shenanigans of all kinds. And this is nothing we're pushing heavily; it's just happening spontaneously."[15]

Like the protests at the WTO's 1999 Millennium Round in Seattle, BND attracts a diversity of activists. Recently, church groups, proponents of "voluntary simplicity," and the Green Party have started to get involved.[16] Overconsumption, like globalization, has become an issue that transcends simple Left or Right alliances. Take, for example, the 2003 anti-SUV television campaign sponsored by conservative socialite Ariana Huffington that suggested SUV drivers are complicit in global terrorism. The ads are a parody of those sponsored by the Office of National Drug Control, in which everyday pot smokers are linked to murdering drug cartels and the terrorists they sponsor. Concurrently with Huffington's ads, a Christian organization launched the "What Would Jesus Drive?" campaign, playing on the familiar "What Would Jesus Do?" (WWJD), which has become something of a Christian brand—featured on T-shirts, armbands, and bumper stickers. The ads urged Christians to embrace their role as "custodians of the earth" and give up their gas-guzzling SUVs. Unlike issues more closely linked to the policies of governmental bodies, or more explicit moral positions (e.g., abortion or the death penalty), over-consumption is not easily coded as a liberal or a conservative issue. Its malleability potentially fosters the conditions for its wide dissemination.

In today's economy of the brand, traditional economic categories such as cost and value are measured differently than even twenty years ago. The economic value of a particular corporation can far exceed that of its actual nuts-and-bolts holdings—factories, employees, sales profits, and so on. A company's "brand equity" can account for as much as half of its worth, and in some cases, *more.* Naomi Klein marks Philip Morris's purchase of Kraft Foods as a watershed in the focus on brand equity. In 1988, Philip Morris paid $12.6 billion for the processed-food manufac-turer—"six times what the company was worth on paper." Klein surmises that the "price difference, apparently, was the cost of the word 'Kraft'"[17] and all that the name meant in the hearts and minds of consumers. It has since become conventional wisdom in the business world that brands are much more than ethereal symbols that put a familiar face on a corpora-tion. Indeed, any savvy businessperson knows that brands generate "cold hard equity" for the companies they represent.[18] *Rhetoric,* then, even in its most traditional sense—the capacity to persuade others to identify with a message—generates real economic value to a degree we have yet fully to realize. To update the Athenian ideal of the agora, our economy is truly a marketplace of desires. Klein thus describes this shift from marketing tangible goods to marketing meaning:

> Overnight, "Brands, not products!" became the rallying cry for a marketing renaissance led by a new breed of companies that saw themselves as 'meaning brokers' instead of product producers. What was changing was the idea of what—in both advertising and brand-ing—was being sold. The old paradigm had it that all marketing was selling a product. In the new model, however, the product always takes a back seat to the real product, the brand, and the selling of

the brand acquired an extra component that can only be described
as spiritual. Advertising is about hawking product. Branding, in
its truest and most advanced incarnations, is about corporate
transcendence.[19]

In response, activists are locking onto brands — in an attempt to bring
corporations back down to earth. Boycott and parody are among their
preferred strategies.

Subvertising: Turning the World of Logos Upside Down

In addition to boycotts, *Adbusters'* uses the strategy of subvertising. Whereas the group's general boycotts aim to discourage everyday
behaviors that characterize consumer culture (watching television and
shopping), subvertisements have slightly different goals. In an effort to
undermine corporations' brand equity, subvertising targets specific companies at the level of their brands through so-called "adbusts," or parodies
of familiar corporate advertising campaigns. Subvertising is a rhetoric of
exposé. It is primarily an attempt to make visible what corporations prefer remain invisible.

If, as cultural historian Stuart Ewen has suggested, "advertising
[is] the prevailing vernacular of public address,"[20] then it is also true that it
can consequently become almost invisible to us. To invoke an analogy that
has become something of a truism for mass-media scholars: Saturated as
we are in the images and vocabulary of advertising, we have become like
fish who cannot perceive the water around them, because ads constitute
the very substance of our environment. As early as 1927, Paris art critic
Louis Chéronnet described the phenomenon thus:

> Advertising is in some way an elastic gas, diffuse, perceptible to all
> our organs. . . . But we have not been aware enough of its beauty,
> latent, profound, scattered, spontaneous. . . . The first domain of
> Advertising was the street. . . . Now it surrounds us, envelops us, it
> is intimately mingled with our every step, in our activities, in our
> relaxation, and its "atmospheric pressure" is so necessary to us that
> we no longer feel it.[21]

It is difficult to think critically about that which we do not see. The tropes,
images, and values espoused by consumer advertising and the commercial media have so profoundly saturated our lifeworld that it is difficult to

imagine ourselves without them. Those who produce ad parodies hope to render opaque a mode of public address that tends toward transparency by virtue of its utter ubiquity.

The defiant stance of *Adbusters* continues a long tradition of industrial sabotage in response to the power of capital. They use the parody mode of "jamming" in order to dismantle the Spectacle of consumerism, at least long enough to display its falsity. Toward this end, they deploy parody in its purest sense: to make "fun of some familiar style, typically by keeping the style more or less constant while markedly lowering or debasing the subject."[22] Literary critic Robert Phiddian suggests that the parodist is "preeminently a *genre-bricoleur,* living off the energies and inadequacies of previous writings, 'borrowing them structurally' and transforming them with a critical eye."[23] He continues, "Parodies *deconstruct* the discourses they invade; they do not blankly *destroy* the discourses on which, parasitically and critically, they live. Instead, both genesis and structure of those discourses appear 'under erasure' (visible but problematized and devalued)."[24]

Ad or brand parodies garner their power from the recognizability of the ubiquitous brands they target. Corporations spend millions of dollars and countless hours of creative energy and legal prowess ensuring that consumers develop an intimate relationship with their logo. As Klein suggests, "Logos that have been burned into our brains by the finest image campaigns money can buy, and lifted a little closer to the sun by their sponsorship of much-loved cultural events, are perpetually bathed in a glow — the 'loglo,' to borrow a term from science fiction writer Neal Stevenson."[25] In contrast, she notes that after social justice movements enjoyed their heyday during the 1960s, their "woefully unmarketable ways no longer held much appeal for energetic young people or for media obsessed with slick aesthetics."[26] In other words, leftist political activism lacked the sexy "loglo" so necessary in today's increasingly hip, colorful, fast, and fun (not to mention well-funded) mediascape.

However, as Klein points out, "From their new 'leech-like' vantage point, the brands' detractors are benefiting from the loglo in an unanticipated way. The loglo is so bright that activists are able to enjoy this light, even as they are in the act of attacking a brand."[27] The strategy of choice for many of those wanting to attack the multinational megabrands is the familiar one of using the master's own very expensive and shiny tools to dismantle the master's house. *Adbusters'* parodies exemplify this attempt to capitalize on a company's "loglo."

As for all parody, for this strategy to work, one must keep the form of the original logo or ad more or less intact while deriding its content. The ad parodies of *Adbusters* and others like them usually serve to make explicit the logic at work in the ad being targeted. "A good jam" for adbusters, writes Klein, "is an X-ray of the subconscious of a campaign, uncovering not an opposite meaning but the deeper truth hiding beneath the layers of advertising euphemisms."[28] Unsurprisingly, *Adbusters'* "Joe Chemo" ad (Figure 12) is an attempt to call attention to the negative health implications of smoking tobacco. The original ads featured Joe Camel, an animated corporate mascot who happily smoked Camels and Camel Lights while shooting pool, riding motorcycles, and hanging out with his friends. The seemingly innocent Joe Camel became a lightning rod for antismoking activism, and ultimately resulted in one of the farthest-reaching government prohibitions on advertising yet created, when Donna Shalalah, secretary of health and human services under former president Clinton, spearheaded a ban against the original ads.[29] *Adbusters'* version of Joe Camel made explicit the easy link between cigarette smoking and cancer.

Figure 12. A poster from *Adbusters'* "Joe Chemo" campaign. Used with permission from *Adbusters*.

"Joe Chemo" was aesthetically similar to his corporate doppel-gänger and was framed by impeccably reproduced fonts and graphics. But unlike the fun-loving Joe Camel, Joe Chemo, gaunt and forlorn, is shown pushing an IV stand down a hospital corridor, laying peacefully in a casket, or in the confines of a windowless hospital room gazing wistfully at his useless sunglasses. The surgeon general's warning at the bottom of the ad reads: "The Surgeon General warns that smoking is a frequent cause of wasted potential and fatal regret." What Joe Chemo "reveals" to consumers is the hidden consequence of Camel's promise that cigarettes accompany good times. By doing so, *Adbusters* intervenes on a brand image—Joe Camel—that R. J. Reynolds spent millions of dollars cultivating; thus performing a kind of rhetorical jujitsu, using the power of the tobacco giant against itself.

The rhetorical effect of the Joe Chemo campaign is essentially one of "flipping" a binary of "health" and "disease." Whereas R. J. Reynolds depicts its character as a young, vivacious good-time boy, *Adbusters* portrays him as sickly and impotent. By foregrounding the potential maladies associated with cigarette smoking, *Adbusters* capitalizes on the dichotomy between the two—health versus disease—to ground their unveiling project. In other words, *Adbusters* tells us "Cigarette smoking does not accompany good times; it lands you in the cancer ward," which presumes, of course, it cannot do both.

Rather than attempt to deconstruct the life promised by Camel ads, Ron English, an accomplished "billboard hacker" altered several Joe Camel billboards for his "Camel Kids" series. One depicted a young Joe Camel as a grade-schooler—a baseball bat in one hand, a cigarette in the other. In another, a familiar slogan means something quite different from what Camel intended when paired with a cuddly "little girl" camel (Figure 13). Under English's paintbrush, a tobacco executive implicitly becomes a smooth character peddling tobacco to innocent children.

Adbusters parodies of two Calvin Klein ads produce a similar effect. The "Fetish" campaign consisted of both print/billboard ads (Figure 14) and a thirty-second television spot. In the television commercial, shot in grainy black and white, images of young, white bodies donning only cotton underwear strike abject poses and cast apathetic gazes. The reference to Calvin Klein's *Obsession* ads of the late 1990s is readily apparent. At the height of their airplay, Klein's *Obsession* ad and, later, his *CK.be*

Figure 13. Artist Ron English "liberates" a billboard. Copyright Ron English, used with permission.

ad were lambasted from both sides of the political spectrum for promoting so-called "heroin chic" to hock trendy clothes and perfume. President Clinton charged in an address to magazine editors: "The glorification of heroin [is not] creative. It's destructive. It's not beautiful. It is ugly. And this is not about art. It's about life and death. And glorifying death is not good for any society."[30] For a time, lampoons of heroin chic were almost as pervasive as the gritty ads themselves.[31] Indeed, "the death blow to drug chic actually may have been struck by a mainstream fast-food chicken chain," surmised one fashion reporter, referring to Klein's use of "black and white images of haunted, waxy-faced, scrawny models bemoaning the emptiness of their existence. 'Eat something!' says the Boston Market guy, set off in robust living color."[32]

While the Boston Market spoof merely poked fun at the heroin chic genre for its mass-produced avant-gardism, the *Adbusters* parody is decidedly more pointed. In the *Adbusters* version, images of a young man who resembles Mark Wahlberg (the actor, formerly known as rapper Marky Mark, who made a name for himself by appearing, along with Kate Moss, in a series of sexy Calvin Klein ads) are spliced together with images of a nude, thin young woman lying facedown on a chaise lounge. A male narrator drones "infatuation" and "obsession" as the young man pulls open the elastic waistband of his shorts, to size up their contents.

Figure 14. A poster from *Adbusters'* "Fetish" campaign. Used with permission from *Adbusters*.

The detached voice-over continues in a whisper: "fetish" and "fascination," as "a sexy, bare-backed woman undulates, alluringly, until you realize she is puking into the toilet bowl. And a Kate Moss look-a-like glares back at the camera, reversing that sadistic gaze."[33] What at first blush seems to be a young woman heaving in sexual ecstasy turns out, as the camera pans back and we are given full view, to be a young woman vomiting.

Such a parody attempts to call attention to the methods women pursue to achieve Calvin Klein's fantasy of the perfect female body. To achieve a figure as slight as model Kate Moss, most adult women would have to continually starve and/or purge themselves. Indeed, starving and purging are the methods du jour for many fashion models who perpetuate this corporeal ideal. In the *Adbusters* Obsession parody, as the young woman wretches, a female voice-over asks soberly: "Why are nine out of ten women dissatisfied with some aspect of their own bodies? The *beauty industry* is the beast."[34] Like the Joe Chemo ad, the Obsession parody attempts to reveal the deceit behind the promises of corporate America. If marketing rhetoric links cigarette smoking to good times and skinniness to sex appeal, then *Adbusters* subvertisements suggest that these versions of the good life ultimately render one's body revolting and malformed.

Implicit in these parody ads' arguments is a reliance on a cause-and-effect relationship between mediated messages and consumer behavior. To the question "Why are nine out of ten women dissatisfied with some aspect of their own bodies?" viewers are offered only one definitive response: the beauty industry is to blame. This is, of course, a controversial assumption. Much scholarly ink has been spilled either defending or challenging the notion that a direct cause-and-effect relationship exists between media images and social ills. Although it is beyond the scope of my argument here to engage the various theories on media effects, I do want to assert that the *Adbusters* spoofs oversimplify the dynamic relationship we have with media images.

However, I also want to suggest that this simplification is not necessarily relevant to the power of their critique. As suggested by feminist media scholar Jeanne Kilbourne, best-known for her Killing Us Softly lecture series,[35] advertising garners its cultural power through repetition. It has been estimated that people in the United States see up to 40,000 commercials each year. Given its ability to repeat over and over an increasingly narrow beauty standard to large audiences, advertising, at the very least, has the power to create a *climate* that greatly affects the way people assess themselves and their bodies. Like the Calvin Klein ads it parodies, the *Adbusters* spoof garners its rhetorical force from images, not verbal claims. The image of the young woman purging into a toilet bowl suggests that the bodies we are conditioned to find sexually attractive are often achieved through none-too-sexy means.

The *Adbusters* Obsession subvertisement is only one in a variety of send-ups of Calvin Klein and Kate Moss. In New York City, feminist activists began scrawling "FEED ME" across posters in bus shelters that featured overly thin models (Moss's ads for Calvin Klein were a popular target). It is unclear who began the graffiti, but like many such "movements" it likely became contagious, providing spontaneous vandals a quick, poignant way to talk back to the advertising machine. In fact, "feed me" has evolved from a graffiti artist's slogan to an adjective in the popular lexicon, used to describe thin celebrities such as Moss, actress Calista Flockhart, vocalist Celine Dion, and actress/singers Lindsay Lohan and Nicole Richie.[36] In another example, a simple game on Urbanemonkey.com inviting visitors to feed Kate Moss generated short-lived buzz in the fashion media. The interactive site features a picture of Moss digitally rigged to grow fatter and fatter as Net surfers "feed" her a selection of high-calorie snacks. "Doesn't she just scream 'feed me!'?" the site asks.

The "feed me" backlash was made most graphically explicit through the practice of "skulling"—another graffiti trend that emerged in the late 1990s. Naomi Klein attributes this particular "visual virus" to Toronto performance artist Jubal Brown, who "taught his friends how to distort the already hollowed out faces of fashion models by using a marker to black out their eyes and draw a zipper over their mouths—presto! Instant skull." As Klein notes, "For the women jammers in particular, 'skulling' fitted in neatly with the 'truth in advertising' theory: if emaciation is the beauty ideal, why not go all the way with zombie chic—give the advertisers a few supermodels from beyond the grave?" It was "simply a détournement to highlight the cultural poverty of the sponsored life."[37] Although they deploy a slightly different strategy, like the ad parodists at *Adbusters*, those engaged in skulling attempt to exacerbate the logic already implicit in corporate advertising. With a few strategic swipes of a magic marker, these graffiti artists offer passersby an X-ray of what the fashion industry is supposedly *really* promoting—unattainable beauty standards.

The Media Foundation has thus far had little luck getting television networks to air their Obsession parody. The Canadian Broadcasting Corporation declined to air the piece during Newsworld's syndicated program *Fashion File*, ironically claiming that the spot violates "CBC's standards of taste policy" because the images "comprise unacceptable exploitation of sex and nudity."[38] Apparently in response to the group's persistence,

CBC/Newsworld changed their guidelines for advocacy advertising: "The content of advocacy advertising cannot relate to the content of the program (i.e., no business advocacy in *Business World,* no beauty advocacy in *Fashion File,* and no sports advocacy in *Game Night*)."[39] An *Adbusters* writer understandably wonders, "Hmmm . . . Could they be trying to regulate away any possibility of public dialogue on television? One set of rules for us, another for the product advertisers."[40] The foundation is waging a legal challenge to Canada's four major networks, utilizing freedom-to-broadcast laws.[41] In an interview, Kalle Lasn explains, "We're willing to pay for the airtime. We just want the same rights as the corporations to buy airtime. But on American television, you're apparently not allowed to speak up against a sponsor."[42] Unless, it seems, you are a competing corporate sponsor.

The antiauthoritarian rebel and the delicate ingénue are both rhetorico-cultural archetypes that have certain "unhealthy" practices woven into their very fiber. The rebel often earns status as such by defiantly smoking a cigarette, government health warnings be damned. And, although her methods are much more discrete, the waifish fashion model earns her keep by maintaining a below-average body weight. By featuring, on the one hand, the toxic chemotherapy of the cancer patient and, on the other, the vomit of the bulimic fashion model, *Adbusters* attempts to call attention to what M. M. Bakhtin would call the "grotesque" elements that constitute these two normalized body types.

Another group that has famously "jammed" the beauty industry is the Breast Cancer Fund. Andrea Martin, founder of the San Francisco–based group, borrowed images from three beauty industry icons in an effort to raise awareness about breast cancer. Parodying Victoria's Secret, Calvin Klein, and the sexy covers of *Cosmopolitan* magazine, the Breast Cancer Fund charges that the beauty industry focuses the public's attention on the aesthetic value of breasts at the expense of women's health (Figures 15 and 16). Martin, who superimposed images of her own mastectomy scars onto images of otherwise voluptuous models, said of the ads: "We wanted to bring the issue into public discussion. We wanted to challenge the cultural treatment of women, their breasts and this disease [breast cancer]. As a society, we are in danger of accepting this disease, which is highly unacceptable. We are an organization that is constantly questioning the status quo and is trying to shake things up."[43]

The breast cancer ads exploited venues such as bus shelters, the sides of buses, and billboards, where the public is used to seeing sexy female bodies. They also borrowed textual and graphic frames — layout, font, color, etc. — that are readily familiar, yet twist the content in somewhat shocking ways. One ad proclaims, in a font mimicking a Victoria's Secret ad: "It's no secret society is obsessed with breasts. But what are we doing about breast cancer?" The Obsession spoof poses the same question. Both conclude with the tagline "Instead of just thinking about breasts, you can help save them," followed by the organization's Web-site address. An ad spoofing *Cosmopolitian*, redubbed *Mastectomy*, replaces the former's usual headline fodder — generally of the "how-to-please-a-man" variety — with reminders and provocations about the dangers of breast cancer.

It was Martin's hope that the ads would start a dialogue about breast cancer and provoke women to schedule regular mammograms. Martin certainly started a dialogue and, as she expected, public response to her ads was mixed. All the Bay Area transit authorities running the ads received calls from people incensed by the ads, and many responded by pulling the ads from city buses.[44] An executive with Outdoor Systems, San Franscisco's biggest bus-shelter company, justified his refusal to post the ads thus: "In good conscience, we just couldn't let these ads through. They're just too tough. You can't force people to look at rough stuff like this. They are very shocking."[45] Even the American Cancer Society was somewhat ambivalent in its support for the campaign. A spokeswoman for the national organization responded: "The point they're making is breasts are viewed as playthings and sexual things, and to deliberately do something so opposite to that is going to be very shocking. I think it's daring and risky, but if it works well, then I congratulate them for doing it."[46] But the spokeswoman noted that the American Cancer Society would not likely deploy such tactics, as it "prefers straightforward educational messages."[47]

Priya Raghubir, professor of marketing at the University of California at Berkeley, argued that the ads had great persuasive potential, as long as people were not overly upset by the images: "A lot of people black out advertising [about health risks] because they simply don't think it will happen to them. What I've found in my research is that [ads that work] get people to recall something that might put them at risk.... These ads might do that. A single ad could trigger a memory or a new behavior."[48]

Figure 15. Models are given digital mastectomies to promote breast cancer awareness. Used with permission from the Breast Cancer Fund.

For some, the ads may have triggered just the opposite. One transit agency executive relayed a conversation she had with a distraught woman who called in to complain about the posters: "Let me tell you what somebody told me this morning. This woman said, 'After I saw that ad, there is no way I'm ever going to have another breast exam because I'd rather be dead than look like that.'"[49]

SOCIETY IS OBSESSED WITH BREASTS

BUT WHAT ARE
WE DOING ABOUT
BREAST CANCER?

Figure 16. Used with permission from the Breast Cancer Fund.

Despite resistance to the parodies, as two editors for *Bitch* magazine point out, such a repulsed response may further justify Martin's cause:

> that the images are shocking and disturbing is exactly why they
> should be seen — then maybe women like the one Krieg spoke with
> wouldn't be so flat-out terrified of the aesthetic results of mastec-
> tomy that she'd risk her health to avoid them. Reaction to the ads
> proved the Breast Cancer Fund's point: that public, sexualized
> displays of breasts are fine as long as they're being used to sell

something—but make a comment that's more relevant to women's lives . . . well, that's just offensive.[50]

Bitch makes a compelling point here. Certainly the protest and censorship resulting from these ads make explicit the cultural hypocrisy that the Breast Cancer Fund was hoping to spotlight. It is difficult for a society inundated with images of an ideal body type—on which full breasts feature prominently—to be confronted with the seeming antithesis of this ideal.

As a political statement against the narrowness of beauty standards, such jarring interruptions of those standards may provide rhetorical moments of powerful critique of a beauty industry that perpetuates those standards. Martin claimed that of the many phone calls she received about the ads, they were "2-to-1" positive responses,[51] offering at least anecdotal evidence of public support for such an approach. However, it may be these more political aspects of the ads that make them so appealing. In other words, the "down with the beauty industry" message may be compelling as cultural critique, but does it get women into the exam room? Ruth Rosen, a historian of the modern women's movement, thinks not: "Sadly the answer is probably no. Most women are terrified of getting a diagnosis of breast cancer. And any campaign that intensifies women's fears, however well-intentioned, is likely to reinforce women's fears of losing their breasts."[52]

Rhetorical Sabotage in the New Brand Economy

Like the situationists before them, the culture jammers described thus far seek to deflate the power of the Spectacle by making evident the implications of its logic. Although their complaints are somewhat similar, the strategies and targets of these contemporary détournements differ in significant ways from those of the situationists. SI activists in the 1950s and '60s were compelled to undermine the capitalist Spectacle, but they did so primarily by attacking the locus of its official power—Charles de Gaulle's Paris. Consumer capitalism as we know it was still in its early stages in mid-twentieth-century France, so it makes sense that those opposing it would focus their attention on governmental control of the market and public discourse about it. Thus, although the situationists had plenty of contempt for the emergence of corporate power, they reserved the bulk of their scorn for the public spaces offered by the conservative Fifth Republic.

In contrast, many modern-day culture jammers wage war within a capitalist society so advanced that it is not uncommon for corporations to have larger operating budgets than entire nations. Although government power is not immune to, say, a well-orchestrated computer hack, most activists recognize that in this age of so-called late capitalism, the Spectacle is generated not from the public sector but from the private. The nay-saying responses exemplified by *Adbusters* and other parodists discussed in this chapter can be loosely categorized as rhetorical *sabotage* that, as I discuss shortly, responds to a different mode of power than did SI's détournement.

In a 1990 interview with Antonio Negri, Gilles Deleuze distinguishes between three modes of power: sovereign power, disciplinary power, and the control over communication. Sovereign societies were organized under the model of feudalism, in which a lord took a cut of what was produced but had no real hand in organizing that production. In disciplinary societies, famously explored in great detail by Foucault in *Discipline and Punish*, the modes of production were brought together, organized, and confined, in order to maximize efficiency and profit. Disciplinary societies operate primarily through the confinement and atomization of individuals (for example, through the familiar models of the prison, the classroom, the military, and the factory). This mode of power was most appropriate to a Fordist world, in which assembly-line-style production was the most efficient way for capital to expand. Fordism required a certain level of standardization to function. Workers were more or less interchangeable and labor practices were repeated with as little variation as possible.

Deleuze suggested that the disciplinary model was under a "passive danger" of withering in entropy, as its maintenance depended in part on clearly defined boundaries between public spheres. These boundaries produced a lack of connectedness between people, technologies, and information that eventually could not be sustained. And, perhaps more importantly for our discussion here, Deleuze suggested that disciplinary societies were under the "active danger of sabotage."[53] The word "sabotage," according to *Merriam-Webster's Collegiate Dictionary*,[54] emerged in Europe around 1910, at the height of the industrial revolution. Indeed, it is a term that is inextricably linked to industrial capitalism. The first definition *Merriam-Webster's* offers is the "destruction of an employer's property or the hindering of manufacturing by discontented workers." The dictionary goes on to explain that the word comes from *sabot,* the name for the wooden shoes worn in many European countries during the nineteenth century. *Saboter* meant "to clatter with sabots" or to "botch," presumably by throwing one's wooden shoes into the machinery. *Sabotage* literally means to "clog" with one's clogs.

A contemporary American synonym for sabotage is "monkey-wrenching," based on Edward Abbey's famous eco-activist novel *The Monkeywrench Gang,* in which a band of environmentalists plot to destroy a hydroelectric dam on the Colorado River. The novel inspired Earth First! in 1981 to symbolically "crack" the Glen Canyon Dam by hoisting a 300-foot plastic ribbon across its facade. Abbey's book has likely also inspired more-violent versions of monkey-wrenching, such as "tree-spiking" — the insertion of metal spikes into trees in ancient forests, which renders the trees too dangerous to be cut.[55]

Sabotage is typically limited to the destruction of property. For example, in 2001 a group calling themselves the Anarchist Golfing Association broke into two greenhouses owned by an Oregon biotech firm, destroyed more than $300,000 worth of experimental grasses, and spray painted messages such as "Nature Bites Back." According to the *Oregonian,* in 2001 alone there were more than twenty such attacks against North American biotech companies that experiment with plant and food crops.[56] Companies in the weapons, textiles, petroleum, and pharmaceutical industries have been the targets of similar actions in recent years. In keeping with the tradition of sabotage, these instantiations block or jam an industrial machine, in an effort to impede its ability to function.

Although sabotage is often characterized as senseless vandalism, its potential effects as a political strategy are at least twofold. First, sabotage can cost corporations a lot of time and money, damaging their ability to run efficiently. Second, if the saboteurs are media savvy (which increasingly seems to be the case) and if they embrace the potential *rhetorical* force of sabotage, they destroy property in a way sensational enough to warrant coverage in the twenty-four-hour news cycle. Consider the black-clad anarchists who shattered the windows of the Gap, McDonald's, Starbucks, and Niketown when protesting the WTO's Millennium Round in

Seattle. Of course, the actual property damage to these storefronts was probably minimal: the price of a few panes of glass. However, when images of, say, America's corner coffee shop standing vulnerable and tattered in what amounted to a "free trade" war zone were sent around the world via international media, such public places became more explicitly *politicized* than ever before. As Kevin DeLuca and Jennifer Peeples argue, it was the rhetorical impact of the *images* of sabotage that enabled their widespread dissemination. In contrast, the many *speeches* made by anti-globalization activists during the three-day WTO protests went largely uncovered by the media. As DeLuca and Peeples write: "Global democratization and fair trade activists recognize the TV screen as the contemporary shape of the public sphere and the image event designed for mass media dissemination as an important contemporary form of citizen participation."[57]

The media's fascination with the striking images of the "Battle in Seattle" was cultivated, in large part, by the image rhetoric of advertising. Marketers know, perhaps far better than rhetorical scholars, that compelling images can insinuate themselves into the public's psyche in such a way as to almost escape rational scrutiny altogether. As one of the characters (an incredibly successful owner of an international "guerrilla marketing" firm) in Gibson's *Pattern Recognition* explains: "You 'know' in your limbic brain. The seat of instinct. The mammalian brain. Deeper, wider, *beyond language and logic.* That is where advertising works, not in the upstart cortex. . . . all truly viable advertising addresses that older, deeper mind, beyond language and logic."[58]

Tellingly, it was not at random that particular storefronts were targeted by activists. The same smooth "borderless" terrain that allowed the targeted companies to expand and enjoy international recognition (indeed, the "new world order" that the WTO promotes) is what made them susceptible to attack. Because of their own carefully crafted global profiles, a few well-aimed bricks transformed these companies and their logos into symbols of voracious globalization run amok. An *Adbusters* writer claimed after the events in Seattle: "Let's remember November 30 and the days that followed as the launch of the Seattle Rebellion, the anti-corporate resistance that will reshape society in the next 10 years. It wasn't a skirmish or an opening salvo, but a manifesto etched in the streets by tens of thousands of people."[59]

This claim that the Seattle WTO protests were a collective *manifesto* captures nicely the *material* component of the rhetoric of culture jamming. The bodies and images of protestors were as much a part of their rhetoric as their words. In one of the more clever and controversial acts of vandalism that weekend, a handful of protestors wrenched the letter "T" from the façade of the Seattle Niketown megastore, momentarily leaving the phrase "NIKE OWN" in large letters above the shoe giant's doors. The impressive storefront Nike had recently spent so much money to construct was, with the easy removal of one letter, transformed into a conspicuous indictment of the company's monopolizing business practices. As activists assess the available means of persuasion with which to etch their arguments in the streets, they find handy and powerful tools indeed: corporate logos, superstores, brand names, slogans, and jingles. The ubiquity of marketing rhetoric and its familiarity to the public makes it easily appropriated for alternative uses.

The events at the WTO's Millennium Round illustrate a pivot point in what Deleuze diagnoses as the transition from disciplinarity to control. As the Western economy moves from one based on North American factory production of goods to one that primarily purchases goods from elsewhere, the important site of production is the selling of those goods. One of the corporate targets in Seattle knows this well. As Naomi Klein and others have demonstrated, Nike CEO Philip Knight's focus on brands rather than products now functions as the prevailing philosophy of the contemporary marketplace. Of course, many activists have taken on Nike at the level of goods production—for example, protesting its labor practices in its factories in Indonesia and the Philippines—but these activists have achieved only limited success. Perhaps having learned from these limitations, activists are now beginning to challenge Nike and other image-dependent companies at the site of their most treasured product—their brand. These activists operate under the assumption that, as Deleuze suggests, "marketing is now the instrument of control."[60] The site of action for today's industrial saboteur may be less the factory than the marketplace.

Importantly, today's marketplace is a space, a rhetorical space, composed primarily of images. Stuart Ewen points out that "today's ascendant businesses are those that traffic in highly profitable, if mostly transient, representations: news and entertainment products, digital information technologies, marketing and opinion management, and—perhaps the quintessential image-hawking enterprise—the securities market."[61] Compare, for example, the companies that make up the Dow Jones Industrial Average today versus those in the early twentieth century. Almost across the board, corporations dealing in tangible goods and raw materials like steel, petroleum, and automobiles (U.S. Steel, Standard Oil, General Motors) have given way to those brokering less-tangible cultural products such as films, software programs, and lifestyles (Walt Disney, Microsoft, and Coca-Cola). So, although contemporary powerhouses such as Microsoft, Viacom, and AT&T deal strictly in information and communication "intangibles," even those companies producing "real product"—hamburgers, carbonated beverages, khaki pants—rely primarily on image-based rhetoric for their share in the marketplace.[62]

Because the actual products of this new communication economy are often very similar to one another, their market share is subsequently based on their ability to differentiate themselves through the production of unique images, information, and values. Take, for example, a somewhat mundane illustration I use with students in my course "Rhetoric, Resistance, and Consumer Culture": khaki pants. In the age of mass production, khaki pants, a staple product of the Gap, Dockers, Ralph Lauren, FUBU, and Dickies, differ superficially in terms of style, design, and fabric. What allows these products to appeal to vastly different consumer groups is the *brand* and the attitude each represents: mainstream trend-watchers, business casual, New England bluebloods, urban hip-hoppers, and blue-collared everymen, respectively. Consumer goods, like khaki pants, SUVs, and even computers, are increasingly marketed as vehicles to a particular kind of lifestyle: "I get to be _____ kind of person if I buy _____ brand of product."

As Deleuze argues, we are now in the midst of a capitalist society that is "no longer directed toward production but toward products, that is, toward sales or markets. Thus it's essentially dispersive, with factories giving way to businesses."[63] Factories *make* things, whereas businesses *sell* them increasingly through brand expansion. It is with this power of branding in mind that the culture jammers at *Adbusters* seek to undermine corporations' control over their own brand identity. *Adbusters* articulates the position clearly in their "Culture Jammer's Manifesto": "We will jam the pop-culture marketers and bring their image factory to a sudden, shuddering halt."[64] *Adbusters* here defines "jamming" much like monkey-wrenching, rendering "jam" akin to the creation of a logjam (in order to stop the flow of water) or to the throwing of one's clogs into machinery (in order to stop the flow of production). *Adbusters* explicitly hopes that their ad parodies and boycotts will thwart the flow of corporate-sponsored mind control long enough for consumers to elude its grip.

Consider again *Adbusters'* declared goal to "bring the image factory to a shuddering halt." Certainly, we can acknowledge that adbusting tactics such as parody are also versions of critique that rely on appropriation, an alternative to sabotage I discuss in chapters 3 and 4. Joe Camel becomes "Joe Chemo," calling attention to the "real logic" behind tobacco ads. Such critique appropriates advertising tropes and the public's familiarity with popular brands in order to be effective. It only makes sense because audiences quickly recognize the images associated with Camel cigarettes. However, this approach is really designed with a disciplinary society as its target. It is an attempt to free information otherwise hidden behind glossy images. Tellingly, adbusters maintain the trope of an image *factory*, connoting a disciplinary model of power. However *factory*, and, hence, sabotage as a mode of resistance, is an inadequate model for understanding today's brand economy. Ultimately, as I argue in the following section, the strategy of ad parody, grounded as it is in negative critique, fails to take the image rhetoric of advertising seriously *enough*. That is, the adbusting mode of engagement does not address the shift Deleuze rightly identifies — the shift from a factory mode of production to the protean business of branding. *Adbusters* clearly wants to thwart the business of branding, but it does so by perpetuating metaphors and rhetorical tools traditionally used to sabotage the factory.

The Limitations of Sabotage

The culture jammers at *Adbusters* are facing a backlash. If the magazine's letters-to-the-editor section is any indication, many of its own readers are growing impatient with *Adbusters'* continued insistence on negative critique. For example:

> It seems like all you are really doing is making people feel bad about themselves and hopeless about the world, without giving them any real alternatives. (Josh Adams, Shoreview, Minnesota)[65]

Any hope of building a cultural revolution on the back of such resentment [as promoted by *Adbusters*] is ill-founded. (Joshua Mostafa, via e-mail)[66]

You self-righteous, self-important wretches! You high-and-mighty crapmongers! . . . What precisely would you suggest we all do? Any helpful suggestions at all? (Michael Hugh Anderson, Vancouver, British Columbia)[67]

Ironically, for many readers the contrarian rhetoric of *Adbusters* resembles the preachy "just say no" asceticism advocated by Nancy Reagan in the 1980s — by all accounts a miserably unsuccessful campaign to curb teenage drug use. As the letters above attest, part of the problem is an inability of such rhetoric to affirm any alternative beyond endless critique. It can only negate, only repudiate the status quo. This is not a bankrupt rhetorical strategy per se, but in the face of advertising, the seductive mobilization of images and desires, a message that merely urges us to avert our eyes from the mesmerizing Spectacle. It is a weak one indeed.

Perhaps more significantly contributing to the backlash against *Adbusters* is its attempt to simultaneously deploy and escape the tropes of advertising. Its self-righteous outsider stance inevitably sets it up for charges that the organization has sold out. James Harkin of the *New Statesman* wonders after an interview with *Adbusters* founder Kalle Lasn: "If the raison d'etre of *Adbusters* is to combat the white noise of the messaging industry, how does Lasn justify a special claim on our senses for its anti-branding propaganda? Or, to put it another way: what exactly is it that distinguishes an anti-brand from a mainstream commercial brand?" Because much like its commercial counterparts, Harkin notes, *Adbusters* is "beautifully produced, has created its own distinctive aesthetic and boasts a global circulation of 100,000."[68]

Carrie McClaren publishes *Stay Free!* an impressive low-budget 'zine that offers critiques of consumer culture and occasional adbusts of its own. She shares Harkin's suspicion of *Adbusters*' credibility as a leader on the antimarketing front. Unlike its early days, when the magazine's "newsprint sometimes rubbed off," McClaren complains that *Adbusters* is now "glossy, full color everything, a graphics fetish . . . and a cover price, $5.75, that pretty much prices out the masses/students it's designed to reach."[69] More problematic for McClaren is that everything in *Adbusters* is "reducible to a catchy, meaningless slogan like 'Economists Must Learn to Subtract.'" "Particularly disturbing," she notes, "is how the latest issue seems to be ushering in an even bolder new phrase for anti-adland. And with it, naturally, a slogan: Culture Jamming."[70] *Adbusters'* branding of the antibranding movement is a hard pill for many activists to swallow. Mark Hosler of Negativland, the band credited with coining the phrase "culture jamming" in "Jamcon '84," tends to resist the label for his group's film and music collages of copyrighted material.[71] "I don't want to be a member of any 'culture jamming club,'" he said, referring to what he sees as *Adbusters'* degradation of the strategy to yet another countercultural trend.[72]

Even Naomi Klein, perhaps the best-known anticorporate critic of recent years, voices suspicion about the effectiveness of the *Adbusters* brand of negative critique: "At times *Adbusters* magazine feels like an only slightly hipper version of a Public Service Announcement about saying no to peer pressure or remembering to Reduce, Reuse and Recycle. . . . Mark Dery, author of the original culture-jammers' manifesto and a former contributor to the magazine, says the anti-booze, -smoking and –fast-food emphasis reads as just plain patronizing — as if 'the masses' cannot be trusted to 'police their own desires.'"[73] Media pranksters Guerilla Media, in an explicit dig at *Adbusters'* retailing enterprises, assure visitors to their Web site: "We promise there are no GM calendars, key chains or coffee mugs in the offing. We are, however, still working on those t-shirts that some of you ordered — we're just looking for that perfect sweatshop to produce them."[74]

Art critic Sven Lütticken, in his analysis of culture jamming for *New Left Review,* questions *Adbusters'* commodification of an anticonsumer stance. Like McClaren and Guerilla Media, he notes that "*Adbusters'* commercialism (one can buy culture-jamming merchandise from them) makes them seem like another — hip, progressive, 'critical' — brand." But, like Klein and Dery, he argues that "a further, more substantial problem is that their message often merely consists of politically correct truisms in graphic form: smoking and alcohol are bad for you, etc."[75] In the United States today, the notion that cigarettes cause cancer is hardly a contestable position. One understandably wonders who it is *Adbusters* hopes to persuade by making this argument. Most Americans *know* that smoking is unhealthy, yet many do it anyway. Perhaps understandably, a number of critics are charging that this brand of culture-jamming rhetoric tends toward smug self-satisfaction. As Aristotle has taught us, the realm of persuasion is the *contingent*. The only messages that are potentially persuasive are those advancing positions that are still contestable.

Although the above comments are drawn from readers and activists who might be expected to be sympathetic to *Adbusters'* goals, they focus on what are perceived as the magazine's frustrating tendencies: nay-saying without alternatives, grumpy asceticism, self-righteous elitism, and a hypocritical interest in promoting *Adbusters* as the "next big thing." These critiques in part emerge out of *Adbusters'* own claims about its importance and integrity. Indeed, on the first page of *Culture Jam*, Lasn writes that his band of culture jammers see themselves as "the advance shock troops of the most significant social movement of the next twenty years."[76]

Lütticken suggests that the work of *Adbusters* remains so dissatisfying for many of its comrades in anticorporatism because it relies on "conventional satire," a mode of critique he describes as "more Alfred E. Neuman than Guy Debord."[77] Lütticken's comparison of the freckle-faced "What, me worry?" cover boy for *MAD* magazine and the situationist leader is instructive. Referring to SI's detailed treatises on détournement, discussed in chapter 1, Lütticken reminds us that the situationists adamantly wanted to distance détournement from "mere parody for the sake of 'comical effects.' Traditional parody still presupposes the notion of an original—*MAD* magazine parodies remain dependent on the films and TV shows they mock—whereas the Situationist regards his 'sources' as null and void."[78] Lütticken's explanation for *Adbusters'* taking a somewhat safe route compared with the situationists it seeks to emulate is that while the latter could afford a certain arrogance in late-1960s Paris, today's activists cannot be nearly so sure history is on their side.

Unlike the militant SI, then, the culture jamming promoted by *Adbusters* "starts from the presupposition that even the smallest changes have to be fought for, and most other changes will be for the worst and, what's more, highly unlikely to provoke an insurrectionary uprising against the system." As a result, "the impulse seems to be less to destroy current capitalist culture than to curb its excesses."[79] If, in the heyday of Situationist International, the primacy of consumer capitalism was very much under contest, it seems that today it has undeniably edged out any competition as *the* economic model of the new global order. In response, Lütticken points out, *Adbusters* engages in a politics of incremental reform, ostensibly trying to place a parodic finger over the flimsy dike protecting us from drowning in commercially saturated culture.

I suggest that while such a strategy is not without some rhetorical value, it is insufficient as a strategy for addressing the mode of power it faces—a mode of power that is quite happy to use subversive rhetoric and shocking imagery. I discuss this further in the following section. Here, I suggest that parody, or turning the world upside down, perpetuates a commitment to rhetorical binaries—the hierarchical form it supposedly wants to upset. That is, although its practitioners often describe parody as a tool for deconstruction, the parodic form stops short of observing the kind of rhetorical play that Jacques Derrida, the primary theorist of deconstruction, describes.

As Jeffrey T. Nealon explains in *Double Reading*, "Time and time again Derrida warns of the metaphysical and political danger of simply neutralizing oppositions in the name of deconstruction. Derrida emphasizes that deconstruction involves a *double* reading, a neutralization *and a reinscription*."[80] He points to Derrida's assertion that deconstruction must "practice an *overturning* of the classical opposition *and* a general *displacement* of the system. It is only on this condition that deconstruction will provide itself the means with which to *intervene* in the field of oppositions that it criticizes."[81] The frustration expressed by *Adbusters'* critics implies that being told what is best for them is no more welcome from *Adbusters* than it is from advertisers. The parodic form neglects what Nealon calls the "crucial operation" of deconstruction—that is, the *reinscription* of oppositions back into a larger textual field.[82] Hence, parody, as negative critique, is not up to the task of undermining the parodist's own purchase on the "truth."

As Michel Foucault suggests in his essay "Nietzsche, Genealogy, History," critique is often in the name of a telos, or some perceived "should" that demands ratification. Further, it presupposes that correct values exist somewhere under the radar of the discourses that speak them. Indeed, this is the mode of critique most favored by ad parodists. Foucault points out that Nietzsche demonstrated how a search for origins is mistakenly "directed to 'that which was already there,' the image of a primordial truth fully adequate to its nature, and it necessitates the removal of every mask to ultimately disclose an original identity."[83] As such, this form of critique ignores the function of *discourse* in the creation of truth. Critical discourse less *uncovers* truth than *produces* it.

Parody's insistence on an outside knowable truth becomes a problem for a couple of reasons. First, as the letters from *Adbusters'* readers seem to indicate, it disallows a forceful response because it can only *react*. It is a rhetoric that resentfully tells its audience "things are not as they should be," without affirming possible alternatives. Saying "no" is itself often a productive alternative, but it is hardly one on which to build a lasting political movement capable of providing an alternative to commercial culture. The nay-sayer is, in essence, yoked in a dialectic tug-of-war with the rhetoric it negates. Second, because one has not challenged the essential form of the binary, one can never adequately negate. A rhetoric that is defined by negation must always encounter more boundaries that must be overcome. More transgression is always required, which inevitably produces more cynicism and resentment. Importantly, by ardently pursuing the authentic realm *out there,* the individual plays her role as *consumer* in the fullest possible sense, endlessly chasing after something just beyond reach.

Further, despite complaints to the contrary, the problem is not that the ad parodists at *Adbusters* have sold out. Rather, I argue that they do not take the rhetoric of advertising seriously *enough.* Instead, they utilize an *instrumental* version of rhetoric, which, depending on who wields its power, either dissembles or uncovers the truth. In the face of a marketing (control) society that operates largely through the affective mobilization of emotions and *desire, Adbusters* deploys a rhetoric that admonishes people to resist those false desires by relying on their ability to eschew desires and think *rationally.* Ironically, Dery, in his criticism that *Adbusters* ignores the masses' ability to "police their own desires," advances an appeal to rationality; celebrating the autonomy of the free-choosing masses over the admonishments of *Adbusters.* This appeal perpetuates a binary between our animalistic desires on which advertising preys and the firm hand of reason that must corral those desires within appropriate boundaries. This faith in the rationality of the marketplace leaves unproblematized one of the governing tropes of capitalism. For publics who want to critique marketing culture, it reduces persuasive opportunity to a simple encouragement of consumers to finally see clearly and resist the marketing charlatans. It does not offer a new locus for the desires the market currently seems to satisfy—desires for community, identity, and beauty, for example.

Certainly, thinking rationally has its own affective appeal. But at its best, the rhetoric of *Adbusters* appeals to activists because it offers a desirable "cool" alternative, albeit an alternative that derides consumers' hunger for cool. Unlike the many critics of *Adbusters,* I do not want to suggest that *Adbusters* should adhere *more* rigorously to the promises of its authentic outsider posture, rather that it adhere less so. Given that "thinking outside the box" and authenticity constitute the marketer's credo as much as the subvertiser's, *Adbusters* might be better advised to heed its own suspicions about the marketplace. A 2003 *New York Times* article argues: "Over the last fifty years the economic base has shifted from production to consumption. It has gravitated from the sphere of rationality to the realm of desire: from the objective to the subjective; to the realm of psychology."[84] Perhaps a way to rework consumption is not through an ascetic repudiation of desire in favor of rationality (a celebration of the objective), but through experimentation *within* the "box" of the market—to see where else its desires and resources might lead.

Or, perhaps more significantly, a different approach to consumption might entail abandoning altogether a notion of a "box" that either traps or excludes otherwise-free consumer publics. The most successful marketers, for example, have long abandoned the traditional relationship between product and brand, advertisement and audience, favoring instead more amorphous strategies such as "viral" and "guerilla" marketing. *Adbusters* does often deploy, for example, the rhetoric of "memes"—a basic unit of information that travels distributively across publics. However, it does so within a modernist framework that ignores the viral character of memes. In *Adbusters* parlance, memes become a human-controlled instrument of "communication warfare" rather than a self-transmitting unit of information for which humans are merely hosts. If one follows carefully the logic of memes, it becomes clear that they, like viruses, do not propagate through a logic of negation or repudiation, but through mutating and even intensifying components of their host environment.

While negative critique, as détournement, had a certain amount of rhetorical success in late 1960s France, culture jamming emerged from and must respond to a very different political environment. Whereas SI practiced its détournement primarily within Paris, the unequivocal nexus of French politics and culture at the time, culture jammers face an enemy that has no clear center, nor any set rules governing its flow. That is, although national governments remain important to economic forces as *regulatory* mechanisms, it is increasingly the needs of markets — primarily global in nature — that determine the geopolitical landscape.

Furthermore, at a speed impossible for governments to match, the market, as Spectacle, is able to mutate in response to adversity. Structural breakdowns and reconfigurations are consubstantial with this flexibility, as capital requires ever more novelty for its force. Following Deleuze and Guattari, Hardt and Negri argue that when confronting "Empire," the only way out is *through.* Resistance, say Hardt and Negri, should not be conceived as an opposition to Empire, but as simultaneously productive of and different from it: "The creative forces of the multitude that sustain Empire are also capable of autonomously constructing a counter-Empire, an alternative political organization of global flows and exchanges."[85] As an astute reviewer of Gibson's *Pattern Recognition* puts it, there is an "inherent tension between the monoculture and the emergence of novelty. On the one hand, the monoculture lives by assimilating originality. On the other, new art has nothing but the monoculture to launch itself from. It's one of the happy paradoxes of modern life."[86] The situationist goal of allowing the people to talk back is possible, but that back talk is never the final, revolutionary word. Whereas SI's collage work *confused* its audiences by radically recontextualizing fragments of familiar images, *Adbusters* offers clear-cut arguments housed in a traditional parodic form. *Adbusters'* rhetorical message is usually quite explicit and not particularly challenging to viewers.

The subvertisers at *Adbusters* largely position themselves as the torchbearers of situationism, but their rhetoric seems even more yoked to the logic of disciplinarity than that of their Dada-inspired predecessors. As I suggested in chapter 1, the situationists' arguments about what they thought they were doing and why were quite pointed. They wanted to free "authentic experience" from the shackles of the Spectacle. Like *Adbusters'* theories, SI's theories about their work suggest a deceitful enemy that must be exposed as a sham. But I am suggesting that the respective rhetorical projects that evolve out of those theories are quite different. *Adbusters* largely relies on parodies, which attempt to reveal the

Truth behind advertising images. In contrast, the situationists embraced the unique rhetorical power of images and *capitalized* on their ability to provoke awe, bewilderment, and unpredictable affect.

Put simply, a consumer viewing an *Adbusters* "jam" confidently says to herself, "Ah ha, the tobacco industry is making false promises that can be harmful to my health," while a consumer engaging an SI détournement may instead merely utter a confused "Huh?" Although SI was politically committed to fighting a disciplinary mode of power—the homogenizing factory of the Spectacle—many of its strategies anticipated the mode of power characterized by "control." That is, their endless cutting and pasting of cultural imagery did not lend itself easily to judgment in the same way as verbal arguments. The rhetorical power of images is not dependent on their "truth" or "falsity" but on the responses they provoke. Nor do these images representationally stand in for words that are simply absent.

Consuming Rebels

The market may consume (or contain) rebellion, but it also turns us into "rebels" who consume. The writers featured in *Commodify Your Dissent,* a retrospective collection of essays from the *Baffler,* a vibrant and angry cultural-commentary 'zine, launch scathing critiques of consumer culture's exploitation of subcultural resistance. Published in 1997, the essays in *Commodify Your Dissent* not surprisingly focus on the commodification of the so-called "Generation X." The basic premises of the analyses are all the more relevant in this first decade of the twenty-first century, when the selling of "individual authenticity" has intensified.

In "Why Johnny Can't Dissent," *Baffler* editor and neo-Adornian cultural critic Thomas Frank captures beautifully our current cultural zeitgeist, in which rebellion is always entangled in the rhetoric of the market:

> Consumerism is no longer about "conformity" but about "difference."
> [Advertising] counsels not rigid adherence to the tastes of the herd
> but vigilant and constantly updated individualism. . . . This impera-
> tive of endless difference is today the genius at the heart of American
> capitalism, an eternal fleeing from "sameness" that satiates our thirst
> for the new with such achievements of civilization as the infinite
> brands of identical cola, the myriad colors and irrepressible variety
> of the cigarette rack at 7-Eleven.[87]

Grunge, the neo-Beatniks, postmodern business literature, techie-bible *Wired* magazine, and even Quentin Tarantino (whom writer Gary Groth describes as "today's feel-good movie director, the Frank Capra of the nineties"!)[88] are all decried as loci of counterfeit rebellion, as neatly packaged examples of the market's love of all things "edgy" and "alternative." The *Baffler*'s suspicion of commodified dissent clearly echoes the situationists' rejection of the work of many of their avant-garde contemporaries, such as Charlie Chaplin and Jean Luc-Godard. For contributors to the *Baffler*, like those of *Adbusters* and *Situationist International*, real rebellion is a scarce commodity indeed, one enjoyed by only a precious knowing few.

Frank and others at the *Baffler* also have little use for scholars of cultural studies (sometimes derisively called "Madonna Studies") who celebrate the subversive potential of, say, William S. Burroughs' participation in a Nike ad. For example, *Village Voice* writer Leslie Savan argues that Nike's use of the elderly, gay, heroin-addicted (accidental) wife-killer proves that *nothing* is outside the reach of corporate marketing's insatiable hunger for subversive street-cred. The issue is not, Savan argues, that Burroughs "sold out"; rather, any gap between subcultural rhetoric and corporate rhetoric has long since been sutured. "What's changed," writes Frank, "is not Burroughs, but business itself. As expertly as Burroughs once bayoneted American proprieties, as stridently as he once proclaimed himself beyond the laws of man and God, he is today a respected ideologue of the Information Age.... His inspirational writings are boardroom favorites, his dark nihilistic burpings the happy homilies of the new corporate faith.[89]

Frank and his *Baffler* colleagues' approach is decidedly one concerned with cultural *production.* As such, Frank notes in his book *The Conquest of Cool,* his approach may "seem antiquated to many" cultural studies scholars.[90] Whereas the dominant trend in many academic circles has been to focus on cultural *reception* and *consumption* — see, for example, Dick Hebdige's Barthian analysis of British punks,[91] John Fiske's celebration of resistant reading practices,[92] Camille Paglia's enthusiasm for the feminist pedagogy offered by Madonna videos,[93] or the myriad studies of the role of polysemy in subversive interpretations of mainstream messages — Frank wonders if such optimism too readily neglects the often dazzling inventional expertise of those who craft cultural messages.

Frank's position, "antiquated" or not, reminds us that seeing resistance only in a Burroughesque "cutting up" of dominant discourse eclipses the ways in which parody, pastiche, and wordplay *are* the preferred tools of even the most mainstream Madison Avenue hucksters. As Frank's argument implies, if Jerry Rubin's mantra "Amerika says: Don't! The yippies say: Do it!" and Burrough's pursuit of a "constant state of kicking" are now the advertising motif of corporate-monolith Nike, then the old strategies of rhetorical resistance must surely be recalibrated.

Frank argues: "Capitalism, at least as it is envisioned by the best-selling management handbooks, is no longer about enforcing Order, but destroying it. 'Revolution,' once the totemic catchphrase of the counter-culture, has become the totemic catchphrase of boomer-as-capitalist."[94] Frank here anticipates Hardt and Negri's Empire thesis. As Hardt and Negri illustrate in great detail, calls for revolution from the Left, however unintentionally, run the risk of providing the very "crises" on which Empire thrives. Global markets respond to challenges by differentiating themselves and, ultimately, intensifying their control over social life.

Calls for revolution, the argument implies, committed as they are to a dialectical progression from one political structure to another, actually provide the conditions for capitalism's endless quest for "the new." Indeed, as Frank points out, "Marx's quip that the capitalist will sell the rope with which he is hanged begins to seem ironically incomplete. In fact, with its endless ranks of beautifully coiffed, fist-waving rebel boys to act as barker, business is amassing great sums by charging admission to the ritual simulation of its own lynching."[95] Madison Avenue culture jammers make every effort to subvert traditional advertising tropes — selling edgy brands as tickets to the rhetorical lynching of consumerism.

I want to be clear here that neither Hardt and Negri nor Frank describe a totalitarian brand of capitalism in the face of which the Left must resign itself to defeat and hoist a collective white flag in surrender. Rather, each project, in its own way, simply reports that leftist calls for revolution and resistance fail to acknowledge the current political terrain and instead march, in lockstep with their enemy, chanting, "Appreciate diversity" and "We demand change." While challenges to hierarchical order and homogeneity may have been effective, say, during the cold war, today these demons primarily remain in the form of a rusting political exoskeleton. Global capital is as interested in deconstructing modernist bureaucracies as are its opponents.

As Frank points out, "We live in what [new business guru Tom] Peters calls 'A World Turned Upside Down,' in which whirl is king and, in order to survive, businesses must eventually embrace Peters' universal solution: 'Revolution!'"[96] This notion of a world upside down, what literary theorists Peter Stallybrass and Allon White refer to simply as WUD, has received much scholarly attention in recent years.[97] Partly following Paul de Man's Americanization of deconstruction, many scholars optimistically mine for kernels of subversion rhetoric that overturns social and political hierarchies — rhetoric that privileges, say, the body over the mind, the feminine over the masculine, or the "subaltern" over the colonialist. However, if we accept that one of the characteristics that defines these so-called "postmodern" times is a breakdown of the old vertical cultural distinctions, then we must wonder, with Frank, how subversive such inversions of hierarchies really are. If Tom Peters, one of the best-selling business writers of the 1990s, enthusiastically claims successful corporate managers are those *Thriving on Chaos,* then perhaps the language of hierarchy subversion does not pose the challenge to the rhetoric of corporate America that many might hope.[98]

Indeed, culture jammers must now share some of their favorite strategies and venues with advertisers. For example, a recent automobile billboard campaign featured "spray painted" comments to create the appearance the billboards had been "liberated" by a graffiti artist. Not surprisingly, the comments were unmistakably benign: "Hi" and "Nice car." Sony hired graffiti artists to spray-paint ads in city parks for a PSP handheld game, and megacorporations Coca-Cola and Clear Channel have both staged "pirate" radio stations. While Coca-Cola's 2004 campaign was an obvious attempt to piggyback on the indie spirit of youth culture (as I write, the company is regularly running ads that feature a pair of young men making a "shoestring" documentary film as they road-trip across the United States, encountering extreme skateboarders and pirate radio operators along the way), Clear Channel's project was much more surreptitious. In May 2005, Radio Free Ohio, broadcasting out of Akron, lambasted the takeover of corporate radio conglomerates like Clear Channel:

Radio in Ohio sucks. We know, We've listened.

Radio has changed. Gone are the days of big name personalities who weren't afraid to play what they wanted. Gone are the days when we could hear a newsman deliver the news about what was happening in my town without follow-ups on runaway brides or stories about a Game Show host bedding a contestant.

Most importantly, gone are the days of multiple viewpoints and opinions. Instead we get corporate mandated opinions from talking heads. Corporate controlled music playlists, and so on.[99]

Turns out, Radio Free Ohio was owned, ironically, by Clear Channel itself. Apparently the company that had made its fortune piggybacking off the grunge explosion and mainstreaming indie rock needed a way to continue to make money off "sticking it to the Man" now that Clear Channel had become, in the world of rock radio, "the Man." The stunt was short lived, however; when, after little more than a week of operation, audiences learned of the fake indie channel, Clear Channel promptly pulled the plug, acknowledging the stunt was an attempt to attract progressive listeners to one of its AM stations that was changing its format.[100]

Perhaps these corporations took the advice of the savvy marketing consultants at Westhill Partners, who tell clients: "Once you know that people are parodying your TV ads with self-made ones, you don't sue them. You invite them to make your next ad. Then you pitch a story about that to a reporter. That's what's happening at the edge of your brand — *the reality of brand politics* — and it's what Westhill Partners is ideally suited to address."[101] Culture jamming, it seems, sells.

A caveat: Although I believe these and other examples corroborate Frank's excellent description of the market's "commodification of dissent," his rhetoric is ultimately unsatisfying as a corrective to marketing culture. The world he paints is one in which any attempt at intervention is instantly commodified, repackaged, and sold back to a public duped into false rebellion. Such a position too easily perpetuates a cat-and-mouse avant-gardism in which one must always stay one step ahead of "the Man." Simply daring capital to "Commodify this!" strikes this rhetorician as a hopelessly dead-end game. It might make individuals feel edgy and authentic, but if I understand Frank's argument, it is our own self-satisfied "uniqueness" that is the problem. And as Clear Channel's dilemma illustrates, this cat-and-mouse avant-gardism seems to be the precise model, or posture, favored by contemporary marketing. Where

Ezra Pound's rallying cry of the modernist revolution — "Make it new!" — demanded artists stay one step ahead of the factory production of culture, it sounds today like the latest campaign for this season's widget.

Ultimately, Frank's argument seems much like a more sophisticated version of Lasn and *Adbusters'* arguments. To wit, in "Alternative to What?" Frank offers Lasn-style culture jamming as a response to the marketer's commodification of youth subculture: "As they canvass the college radio stations for tips on how many earrings and in which nostril, or for the names of the 'coolest' up-and-coming acts, they will find themselves being increasingly misled, embarrassed by bogus slang, deceived by phantom blips on the youth-culture futures index, anticipating releases from nonexistent groups."[102] Frank's position, attractive as it may be, relies on a knowing in-group of rebels so hip they're beyond appropriation, rebellious to the bone. Echoing a popular situationist sentiment, Frank argues that whereas parasitic music executives "manufacture lifestyle; we live lives."[103] Such lives can only be lived, it seems, on the most avant-garde islands of authenticity, what Internet guru Hakim Bey describes as "temporary autonomous zones," the "pirate utopias" known to cyberanarchists simply as TAZ.[104] I contend that responding to the marketing of rebellion by simply declaring *"We're* the real rebels! We *get* it!" is to cede important argumentative terrain. Such a posture does not question the viability or desirability of the authentic, uncontaminated self as a productive goal for democratic publics.

Adbusters' parody of a Tommy Hilfiger ad makes a similar argument to the *Baffler's* about the standardization of rebellion (Figure 17). Hilfiger's ads — the most relevant of which features an image of Peter Fonda from the 1960s cult classic *Easy Rider,* an American flag emblazoned across his back as he speeds down the open road on his chopper — capitalize on Americans' hunger for outsider cool. In the company's typical rhetorical style, Hilfiger borrows a familiar icon from countercultural rebellion to sell its brand — in the Peter Fonda case, sunglasses — as a vehicle for those wanting to identify as an independent American spirit. Hilfiger ads exemplify Frank's notion of the commodification of countercultural dissent. *Adbusters,* echoing Frank's rhetoric, exposes the inherently flawed logic of Hilfiger's claim, by insinuating that mass-marketed rebellion produces conformist sheep that, despite intentions, do nothing more than follow the flock.

Figure 17. Mass-produced rebels follow the flock in this *Adbusters* spoof. Used with permission from *Adbusters*.

The Gap's infamous appropriation of the likenesses of counter-culture heroes Jack Kerouac and James Dean to sell khaki pants inspired a similar response from the adbusting community. To the Gap's claim that "Kerouac wore khakis," one group of subvertisers responded with the likeness of Adolf Hitler, another twentieth-century icon known for wearing khakis. As such, Gap khakis were recoded as a symbol not of rugged individuality but of genocidal totalitarianism — the conformist impulse writ large.

Despite an unmistakable knowing pleasure that the consuming rebellion critiques provide to marketing-weary publics, I have tried to suggest here that arguments and images that purport to turn the world upside down are advanced as often by the advertiser as they are the jammer. Not only is WUD the language of the market, but so is its goal: difference. As Fredric Jameson has famously argued, the cultural logic that accompanies this era of late capitalism is defined by a codification of the eccentric modernist style of resistance. Faulkner's long sentences or Pollack's distinctive paint blobs, for example, may have carried a powerful rhetorical punch when responding to forces during the factory age, when "authentic" art was seen to be under imminent threat of becoming yet another mass-produced cultural commodity. Faulkner, Pollack, and their contemporaries were ostensibly daring the industrial capitalists to "Mass produce this!" by offering highly individualistic styles intended to thwart easy appropriation.

However, as Jameson points out, these flagrantly rebellious styles "ostentatiously deviate from a norm which then reasserts itself, in a not necessarily unfriendly way, by a systematic mimicry of their willful eccentricities."[105] In other words, parody becomes one of many social codes; codes that are as available to the capitalist as they are to the artist. Jameson writes, "If the ideas of a ruling class were once the dominant (or hegemonic) ideology of bourgeois society, the advanced capitalist countries today are now a field of stylistic and discursive heterogeneity without a norm. Faceless masters continue to inflect the economic strategies which constrain our existences, but they no longer need to impose their speech." Consequently, he concludes, "In this situation *parody finds itself without a vocation*; it has lived, and that strange new thing pastiche slowly comes to take its place."[106]

Conclusion

In significant ways, the situationist strategies of collage and pastiche, subversive as they may have been in their original time and place, are now quite at home in the vernacular of advertising. The contemporary subvertiser's goal of uncovering the truth behind the images makes much less sense in our contemporary world, a world in which, as Jameson points out, consumers have an "appetite for a world transformed into sheer images of itself and for pseudo-event and 'spectacles' (the term of the situationists)." He continues:

> It is for such objects that we may reserve Plato's conception of the 'simulacrum,' the identical copy for which no original has ever existed. Appropriately enough, the culture of the simulacrum comes to life in a society where exchange value has been generalized to the point at which the very memory of use value is effaced, a society of which Guy Debord has observed, in an extraordinary phrase, that in it "the image has become the final form of commodity reification."[107]

If, as Jameson argues, we live in a cultural landscape where one can no longer distinguish between originals and copies, then what are the inventional resources for creative publics? Gibson's heroine in *Pattern Recognition* complains about branding boy-wonder Tommy Hilfiger,

"Simulacra of simulacra of simulacra. . . . There must be some Tommy Hilfiger event horizon, beyond which it is impossible to be more derivative, more removed from the source, more devoid of soul."[108] In what ways can publics engage this seemingly endless plane of sourceless simulacra? What are the tools for response made available in this specific rhetorical moment?

It seems that the *Adbusters* Blackspot sneaker campaign is an attempt to address their critics' charges that they are all complaint and no action. Of course, they now face charges that they have sold out and become just one more lifestyle brand, but I am unconvinced that selling out is necessarily a problem in this instance. Heath and Potter open their *Nation of Rebels* (a project they acknowledge is an extension of the ideas Frank outlines in *The Conquest of Cool* and *Commodify Your Dissent*) with a snide description of Blackspot as proof positive of their thesis that the counterculture was never anything but a sellout:

> September 2003 marked a turning point in the development
> of Western civilization. It was the month that *Adbusters* maga-
> zine started accepting orders for the Black Spot Sneaker, its own
> signature brand of "subversive" running shoes. After that day,
> no rational person could possibly believe that there is any ten-
> sion between "mainstream" and "alternative" culture. After that
> day, it became obvious to everyone that cultural rebellion, of the
> type epitomized by *Adbusters* magazine, is not a threat to the
> system — it *is* the system.[109]

Heath and Potter mock *Adbusters'* claim that the Blackspot might revolutionize capitalism, reminding us that "'fair trade' and 'ethical marketing' are hardly revolutionary ideas, and they certainly represent no threat to the capitalist system."[110] Heath and Potter's easy dismissal of the Blackspot is unfortunate and unfair, *especially* given that their ultimate thesis is that countercultural calls for revolution distract people from more valuable incremental reforms. Their book is so set on disabusing the masses of the countercultural "myth" that they fail to see that, in this case, *the myth sells valuable incremental reform.*

Adbusters' Blackspot campaign deploys a rhetoric that appeals to people, and it directs that appeal toward what Heath and Potter should themselves consider good ends — fair wages, environmentally sound production practices, and sustainable materials. However, they end up throwing the baby out with the bathwater, rejecting *Adbusters'* experiment with ethical branding as counterproductive, because it doesn't also do away with the language of rebellion. Ironically, like the countercultural rebels they so abhor, Heath and Potter insist on an all-or-nothing politics, in which the faintest whiff of revolution is grounds for wholesale rejection. Mired as it is in "authenticity" and absolute Truth, this position fails to recognize the rhetorical value in the countercultural appeal. As I have argued, subvertising alone is problematic as a nay-saying critique of consumer culture, because it sees itself as outside the world of marketing. However, Blackspot is a good-faith attempt to say "yes" to the logic of branding, and to see what else it can do. Although Heath and Potter are too constrained by their own puritanism to grant it, *Adbusters* deserves credit for updating their political strategies for the new brand economy.

In chapters 3 and 4, I engage the strategies of publics I describe as "pranksters" and "pirates." Both emerge out of and in response to the rhetoric of commerce. Instead of attempting to expose or dismantle the image rhetoric of consumerism, these activists and artists *appropriate* current lines of power. As I argue, unlike the saboteur, pranksters and pirates do not *jam* consumer culture, in the sense of thwarting its flows. Rather, they engage in interpretive, impromptu *jams* as musicians would with a piece of music. They jam *with* culture rather than against it. For these publics, the "media ecology" is not a hermetically sealed dystopia contaminating an otherwise pristine public sphere, it is a complex and fertile ground for spontaneous and tactical appropriation.

Intermezzo

And Now a Word from Our Sponsors

On a flight to Atlanta a few years ago, I was engaged in my favorite fear of flying distraction, flipping through the pages of a glossy fashion magazine. Suddenly, there among the beauty tips and perfume samples was an image of several angry young women, fists in the air, carrying picket signs and shouting protests on the steps of some anonymous, white-columned hall of the establishment. My interest was instantly piqued. After all, this was Jane, *not the* Nation; *the cognitive dissonance was ticklish, if not jarring. I looked closer—what social ill drove these denim-clad beauties to take to the streets? The impending war in Iraq? The increasing infringement on civil liberties? Racism? Famine?*

No, these protesting pretties were urging the powers-that-be to "free the goldfish." Yes, that's right, "free . . . the . . . goldfish." I had to learn more about this movement. When I got home, I visited the Web site for Diesel Jeans, the brand behind this movement that was seemingly causing such a frenzy.

When I got to the site, I was dizzied by the cool, progressive graphics—they appealed to the hip, edgy dissident inside me. The Web site encourages young, disaffected Web surfers to take "ACTION! For Successful Living." The welcome page featured two screaming punks, in sunglasses and mohawks. Beneath their belligerent scowls, inked in the collage font of a ransom note: "This is a wake-up call for the rebel inside you." By clicking on an arrow labeled "act," I was channeled into a web of pages expressly designed for the burgeoning social protestor. "It doesn't matter what you protest against," the site assured me, "the cause can be big or small. Serious or fun. Use these tools to speak up for what you believe in and start your own personal protest now." Diesel offered fifteen sample social protests seemingly started by other angry young rebels, propelled by such radical resolutions as: "Hold more hands," "Believe in the #13," "Marry young," and "Legalize the 4 day weekend." By clicking on a slogan, netizens can view images and QuickTime movies of hip urban protestors, like the ones I had seen in Jane, carrying picket signs and shouting defiantly into bullhorns. Diesel even provides you with the tools to get involved, offering the "Action! Placard Printer," a program to help you "take your protest out into the street." And a page of "protest tips" offers golden nuggets such as: "Before you start shouting, use some mouthwash."

Furthermore, one can become an "active member" of the "movement" by signing up for Diesel's mailing list. "Becoming an Active Protestor might require a few more of your details, but you'll get more Diesel for your data," the site promises. I decided to "join the cult" and become what Diesel calls a fully active "protestor" by giving the company a detailed list of my demographic stats. I also took advantage of Diesel's offer to submit for public display my own protest, heeding their suggestions to "go for short, positive slogans for maximum publicity." I was thrilled to see my dissident impulses take root as my own pithy slogans were immediately posted to the Diesel Web page alongside those of my comrades in fashionable politics. Diesel had given me a venue through which my voice could finally be heard, and in a stylish, edgy context to boot! I was now engaged in a dialogue with other fed-up activists! Together, we were no longer aging Gen-X sellouts, we were fighting for our collective causes, committed interlocutors in the marketplace of ideas!

Or were we? I became suspicious about whether my subversive slogans were really reaching my militant brothers and sisters in the Diesel brand public sphere. The company's causes—goldfish, bowling, the number thirteen—are clearly radical and inclusive, but I wondered, would they embrace even my "protests": "Up with phony denim whores!" and "Say 'yes' to fake politics"? Sure enough, when I ran down the hall and called up the Diesel site on a colleague's computer, my clever slogans were nowhere to be seen. My voice, it turned out, longing to ring through cyberspace expressing all my Diesel-inspired outrage, could be heard only by me, displayed on *my computer screen alone. You see, my own personal protests were simply that: solitary signifiers visible only to me, serving only my self-satisfaction. My Diesel-sponsored activism, it seems, was a sham. And my comrades? Advertisers, not activists.*

Now, my first inclination was to shake my head in disgust at the blatant corporate appropriation of my rebellious political posture. But, as Thomas Frank reminds me, "the problem with cultural dissent in America isn't that it's been co-opted, absorbed, or ripped-off. Of course it's been all of those things. But it has proven so susceptible to such assaults for the same reason it has become so harmless in the first place . . . It is no longer any different from the official culture it's supposed to be subverting."[1] Could Frank be right? Has my defiant, authentic 'tude become no different from a rebellious brand of blue jeans?

And, is it possible that my investment in my own personal individualized radicality is what made Diesel's pitch so seductive in the first place? Perhaps Nietzsche was right when he famously argued that the desire for uniqueness is the defining characteristic of herd mentality. Or, to cite another, perhaps more convincing, source: Maybe we are not so different from the teeming mob of townspeople in Monty Python's Life of Brian, *enthusiastically echoing the charismatic rabble rouser: "We are all individuals! Yes, we are all different!" If individual autonomy is now an ad for, irony of ironies, the U.S. military ("I am an army of one"); Nike makes millions selling mass-produced rebellion; and Diesel Jeans urges us all to launch our own "personal protests," then how rebellious can a politics of personal expression be? Even my temptation to join that lone voice in* Life of Brian—*the one who, in response to the claim that "We are ALL individuals!" ventures: "I'm not!"—offers me no way out. I can only wonder: Is the rhetoric and imagery of rebellion bankrupt?*

Pranks, Rumors, Hoaxes

"Dressing Up" and Folding as Rhetorical Action

> A prank can be a multi-functional tool like a hammer — you
> can hit somebody over the head with it, or pound nails
> with it. Pranks are techniques to change life with; they're
> based on principles that are not widely known
> or recognized. . . . The point is to discover and
> get familiar with the principles that apply.
>
> — Monte Cazazza, performance artist

> Illusion is a revolutionary weapon.
>
> — William S. Burroughs, "Electronic Revolution"

n the third essay of *On the Genealogy of Morals,* Nietzsche argues that the ascetic ideal, the resentful nay-saying of the first order, "has at present only *one* kind of real enemy capable of *harming* it: the comedians of this ideal — for they arouse mistrust of it."[1] Unlike the ascetic, with whom we can affiliate the negative critics described in chapter 2, the comedian is uninterested in "bringing the people to consciousness" as if she can use her comedy to expose the Truth or push the limits of power until they reveal their true logic. These are the goals of the parodist, not the comedian. To *reveal,* one must stand in a familiar place and know just what she will find behind the Spectacular curtain. In contrast, the comedian is something of a surfer; she has no firm, knowable ground on which to stand. Rather, she learns to navigate a force that is already in motion and will continue in motion long after she has passed. Whereas the parodist attempts to change things in the name of a presupposed value, the comedian diagnoses her situation and *tries* something to see how people respond.

In this chapter, I examine the rhetorical strategies of comedians, pranksters, and explorers of the commercial cultural landscape. Comedians make manifest Foucault's observation that one need not be "sad in order to be militant." Rather than using political action to discredit a line of thought (as the parodist might have it), Foucault urges his readers to "use political practice as an *intensifier* of thought, and analysis as a multiplier of the forms and domains for the intervention of political action."[2] In this spirit of intensification, the pranksters, media hoaxers, and performance artists in this chapter resist less through negating and opposing dominant rhetoric than by playfully and provocatively folding existing cultural forms in on themselves. Pranksters prefer affirmation and appropriation to the adbuster's strategies of opposition and sabotage. The prankster performs an art of rhetorical jujitsu, in an effort to redirect the formidable resources of commercial media toward new ends.

In what follows, I first discuss why the prankster's ethic may offer a more compelling response than parody to contemporary cultural and economic forces. Second, in an exploration of pranking, I offer six case studies of radical and mainstream efforts to hijack, or appropriate, popular media forms. I conclude by suggesting that although pranking strategies do perform the Aristotelian notion of exploiting "available means of persuasion," for them to be fully imagined as rhetoric, "rhetoric" itself may have to be somewhat recalibrated in its role as a mass-mediated political art.

Perhaps the best-known media prankster is legendary New York performance artist Joey Skaggs. Since 1966, Skaggs has been putting people on, using the news media's own insatiable appetite for sensational images as his canvas. Skaggs says of his work: "I had concepts that I thought would make a statement. *I was using the media as a medium.* Rather than sticking with oil paint, the media became my medium; I got involved with the phenomenon of the media and communication as my art."[3] Skaggs's most famous and widely disseminated "image event" (to borrow Kevin DeLuca's phrase[4]) was his 1976 "Cathouse for Dogs," a phony doggie brothel where one could supposedly have one's dog sexually "serviced." To begin,

Skaggs simply issued press releases and ran the following advertisement in the *Village Voice:*

> *Cathouse for Dogs*
>
> Featuring a savory selection of hot bitches. From pedigree (Fifi, the French Poodle) to mutts (Lady the Tramp). Handler and Vet on duty. Stud and photo service available. No weirdos, please. Dogs only. By appointment. Call 254–7878.

He explains: "If your dog graduated from obedience school, if it was his birthday, if you were embarrassed to come home and find him humping a pillow, or fearful of having a party because your dog would mount your company's legs . . . now for the first time for fifty dollars you could get your dog sexually gratified."[5] Skaggs set up a storefront and hired actors to play the "doggie pimps" for his phony cathouse. On its face, this silly prank hardly seems the kind of thing that would garner much reaction beyond a few perverts and thrill seekers. However, Skaggs's "Cathouse for Dogs" received more attention than even he imagined. Several New York television stations sent camera crews, the *Soho News* ran a piece, and the ASPCA, the Bureau of Animal Affairs, the NYPD vice squad, and the mayor's office all campaigned to put Skaggs out of business. His greatest exposure came by way of ABC:

> I refused to allow [ABC] to see the cathouse for dogs because I didn't want to go through the *production* problem again. Every hoax I do is like doing a film or a theater piece or a commercial. It's conceived, written, produced, directed, staged, acted; there are locations, props — it's very complicated. Rather than do that every time some other media source wanted to see the Cathouse, I provided them with a videotape of the dogs humping.

So, with little more than some footage of mating dogs and an interview with Skaggs, ABC produced a standard wraparound news piece — interview–footage–interview — and aired it in a larger story about animal abuse. Skaggs's hoax quickly spread, earning him international media attention as well as a lawsuit from the ASPCA. Skaggs is careful to point out that his production was purely rhetorical: "I didn't want customers — it was never my intent to defraud or deceive people for money. Deceit — yes, fraud — no. . . . An artist is much different from a con-man. I am a con-man, but I'm a con-fidence, con-ceptual, con-artist. That's different."[6] Artistic intentions aside, Skaggs was subpoenaed by the attorney general's office for "illegally running a cathouse for dogs." Meanwhile, ABC's documentary piece featuring Skaggs's Cathouse was *nominated for an Emmy* as "best news broadcast of the year."[7] Facing criminal charges, Skaggs publicly revealed his Cathouse as a hoax. Facing professional humiliation, the ABC journalists never retracted their story, despite Skaggs's revelation.

Skaggs's hoax illustrates an important characteristic of the media. It functions, in his words, as something of a "telephone game" in which meaning and content mutate with each repetition:

> In this day and age, with electronic telecommunications instanta-
> neously darting around the globe and people feeding off everyone
> else's network of nerve endings, a misspelled word or a misplaced
> explanation mark can totally change what is being said. And it's
> almost impossible to determine where the accidental change came
> from. And that's on a mild level. It's even *intentionally* done. Gov-
> ernments are doing it, corporations are doing it. Individuals within
> the media itself are doing it, and people like myself are doing it to
> make sociopolitical commentaries [about the irresponsibility of the
> news media].[8]

As Skaggs suggests, his strategy is not uniquely his own, the domain only of the political subversive. Rather, he observes that unpredictable differentiation is an unavoidable effect as texts are disseminated across the mediascape. Messages and images mutate as they migrate across the vast variety of media outlets, until questions of source and original intent cease to matter. As he notes, governments and corporations often sponsor disinformation campaigns, using the media to start rumors or to deflect the public's attention from potential scandals. Indeed, thanks to ABC's professional constraints, Skaggs's "Cathouse for Dogs" remains on the record as historical "fact."

Definition of Terms: A Station Break

Skaggs's "Cathouse for Dogs" event—as well as his many other events, which have included "Celebrity Sperm Bank" and a Thanksgiving world-hunger performance piece—is noteworthy because it exemplifies pranking as a strategic mode of engagement with commercial media and consumer culture in general. Skaggs's project clearly functioned as a prank in its most familiar sense: a trick, a practical joke, or a mischievous act. This is "prank" in the mundane sense of tying a classmate's shoelaces together under the desk, or short-sheeting a bed. A prank affords the prankster a certain "Gotcha!" pleasure at having pulled one over on an unsuspecting party. But more importantly for our purposes here, Joey Skaggs's prank—as well as the others I discuss in this chapter—illustrates two alternative senses of the word:

Alternative one: In Middle English, "to prank" was to add a stylistic flourish, as to one's dress: "to deck, or adorn," as in "to dress, or deck in a gay, bright, or showy manner; to decorate; to deck oneself *out*, dress oneself *up*."[9]

Alternative two: Prank can also mean "a fold," or a "pleat, as in the figurative sense of 'wrinkle.'"[10]

These alternative senses of "prank" are imperative for this discussion of the mode of culture jamming in this chapter. In neither alternative is prank an act of dialectical opposition. In the first alternative sense, as in to "deck in a showy manner," a prank is a stylistic exaggeration. It is a kind of *layering up* of adornment in a conspicuous way that produces some sort of qualitative change. Prank, in this sense, is an *augmentation* of dominant modes of communication that interrupts conventional patterns. In the second alternative sense, a prank is a wrinkle, or a fold. Like a fold, a prank can render a qualitative change by turning and doubling a material or text. This qualitative change is produced not through the addition of novelty, but through reconfiguration of the object itself.

Even in its traditional sense, exemplified by my mundane examples of shoelaces and bedsheets, pranking works through the rerouting of existing and expected patterns. Shoelaces are untied and retied to make the unsuspecting target stumble over his own feet. Sheets are folded over in order to stop a sleepy victim from climbing into bed. In both cases, the movement of bodies is interrupted—tripped up or blocked—not by the introduction of an outside element, but through a reconfiguration or a repatterning of existing material conditions and expected reality.

For analytical purposes, let us continue to stretch and layer the meaning of "prank" to include a folding over of the rhetorico-cultural field. Dominant texts are *wrinkled,* they are *folded,* they ravel and unravel as a result of these stylistic layerings. Furthermore, let us recall the etymological roots of "text" itself. A "textile" is something that has structural integrity; it has a shape and a texture. Yet, the "weave" of texts come in varying degrees of density; they can be loose or tight, embellished, or cropped. In what follows, I will play with these alternative senses of prank—"adornment" and "folding"—in an attempt to describe the rhetorical effects of media and brand pranking.

While we are playing with definitions, let us consider another: I propose an alternative sense of "jamming" itself. Ultimately, if marketing is, as Deleuze suggests, a new instrument of social control, then perhaps engaged publics must better learn to play and manipulate that instrument. Rather than approaching jamming as simply a monkey-wrenching or *opposition* to marketing rhetoric, as *Adbusters* rhetoric might have it, perhaps activists might approach the market as well-trained musicians approach music—as a familiar field within which to improvise, interpret, and experiment. In chapter 2, I discussed the roots of "sabotage" (literally, throwing one's clogs into the machinery) during the industrial revolution. Importantly, in what is little more than a side note in its definition of "sabotage," *Merriam-Webster's* states that, in addition to referring to wooden shoes, "sabot" (the etymological root of "sabotage") also denotes "a thrust transmitting carrier" or a kind of "launching tube."[11]

This second definition of "sabotage," as a "launching tube," provides a compelling alternative sense of the concept. As we have seen in its monkey-wrenching version, sabotage implies destruction, or the stopping and hindering of flows through the introduction of an outside element. Put simply, it is a *clogging.* However, as a "launching tube," sabotage implies a channeling or a transmission of energy or resources through a conduit. This implies that "resistance" can enable and direct energy flows rather than merely thwart them. With this in mind, one's rhetorical tools need not come from *outside* at all, as an oppositional model might insist. Furthermore, as the invocation of "tube" and "carrier" imply, and as we have seen from the previous examples of culture jamming, sabotage is not a chaotic, shapeless, anarchic practice, but one that is restrained and shaped by the machinery from which it emerges; without the "transmitting carrier," it has no thrust. In other words, constraints can be seen as immanent to those flows that seek to transform them.

Jamming, in this *interpretive* sense, requires both practice and knowledge of one's instrument as well as a dynamic exchange within a community of agents. Jamming, although it often implies a free-form chaos, requires knowledgeable and disciplined players in order to work. Recall, for example, Joey Skaggs's description of the work he put into his

"Cathouse for Dogs." He painstakingly set up an image event that would appeal to the needs of the televisual news media. He employed the strategies of a television producer in an effort to *fold* the medium over on itself. As Skaggs suggests, the broadcast media itself is his canvas. Skaggs knows the contours of his canvas well: "First there's the hook, when I do the performance; next, I document the process of miscommunication, or how the media twists the content and meaning of the message; finally, I talk about the serious issues underlying the performance piece. The media often trivialize the third stage by saying 'Oh, he's a hoaxter, he has an ego problem, he wants attention, etc.'"[12] Skaggs's strategies do not oppose dominant modes of power, they utilize them. As he suggests, "You're already being pranked every day. If you think *I'm* the prankster, you are sadly mistaken. I'm just ringing the bell."[13]

To jam as a musician does is to *interpret* an existing text. I do not mean here "interpret" as in trying to make one word correspond directly to its equivalent, as one does when translating a text from one language to another, and for which the interpreter is obligated to get the translation as "correct" as possible. Rather, I mean "interpret" in its sense as *appropriation*, as when a group of jazz musicians appropriate an existing piece of music or a set of chord progressions and, in doing so, produce a new interpretation. This interpretation does not necessarily correspond to anything outside itself. It does not fail or succeed at representing an original. However, it does contain familiar textual residues. Jamming as appropriation, in this way, differs from jamming as sabotage.

And Now, Back to Our Program. Hacking Gender: The Barbie Liberation Organization

In 1989, a group of culture jammers known only as the Barbie Liberation Organization (BLO) pranked the infamously litigious Mattel Corporation by means of its most prized brand: Barbie. Barbie and G.I. Joe, Hasbro's military action figure, are notorious for reinforcing unrealistic, even dangerous, gender stereotypes. But for the BLO, Mattel's Teen Talk Barbie "proved to be the last straw."[14] The doll, enhanced with a computer-chip voice box, was programmed to giggle random phrases when a button on her back was pressed (Figure 18). Mattel's chosen phrases included:

Math is hard!
I love shopping!
Will we ever have enough clothes?[15]

In response, the Manhattan-based BLO organized a prank that continues to generate discussion at feminist and culture-jamming Web sites. The BLO claims to have inspired similar hacks in Canada, France, and England.[16] Taking advantage of the mechanical similarities between Teen Talk Barbie and her male counterpart, Talking Duke G.I. Joe, the BLO purportedly purchased thousands of each doll from local stores, took them home, and switched their voice chips. At the height of the Christmas shopping season, they returned the dolls to stores, so they could be resold to unknowing shoppers. When children opened their toys on Christmas morning, instead of Barbie chirping cheerful affirmations of American girlishness, she growled in the butch voice of G.I. Joe: "Eat lead, Cobra!" "Dead men tell no lies!" and "Vengeance is mine!" Meanwhile, Joe exclaimed: "Let's plan our dream wedding!"

The rhetorical message of the Great Barbie Hack may be somewhat obvious. The sheer dissonance created by hearing gender-inappropriate voices and sentiments may have rendered absurd otherwise normalized gender norms. As one BLO operative put it: "Our goal is to reveal and correct the problem of gender-based stereotyping in children's toys."[17] Another BLO member told the *New York Times:* "We are trying to make a statement about the way toys can encourage negative behavior in children, particularly given rising acts of violence and sexism."[18] Political goals aside, the reprogrammed dolls have become something of a collector's item. As another BLO member jokingly told National Public Radio's Scott Simon, the BLO is good for business: "Nobody wants to return [the dolls]. . . . We think that our program of putting them back on the shelves [benefits] everyone: The storekeepers make money twice, we stimulate the economy, the consumer gets a better product and our message gets heard."[19] It also may have confused and upset some children on Christmas morning. But not seven-year-old Zachariah Zelin, who received one of the altered G.I. Joes. When asked "whether he wanted Santa to take back the feminine Joe, he responded sharply 'no way. I love him. I like everything about him,'" reports one Associated Press writer.[20]

What was truly inspiring about the BLO during this particular event was their *media savvy.* Each "hacked" doll had a sticker on its

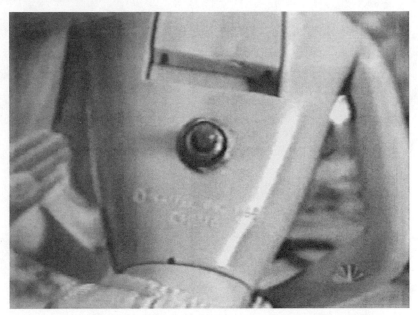

Figure 18. The push of a button starts Barbie talking.

back urging recipients to "Call your local TV news," ensuring television journalists would have actual disgruntled families to interview for their reports.[21] The BLO later utilized the new medium of the Internet to disseminate detailed instructions on how to perform comparable hacks, complete with pictures and diagrams, thus enabling others to perpetuate the practice. Finally, utilizing a strategy that has become increasingly popular with media activists, the BLO produced its own prepackaged news pieces to be distributed to content-hungry local television stations. The video documentaries showed doll hackers at work, "post-op" Barbies and Joes, and interviews with BLO members explaining their project (Figure 19). The videos were sent out to television stations, complete with press releases explaining what the BLO had done and why.

When reporters asked the toy manufacturers for their reaction, one Hasbro spokesman simply called the attack "ridiculous."[22] Another was amused but nonplussed: "This will move us to have a good laugh and go on making more G.I. Joes. . . . Barbie dolls and G.I. Joes are part of American culture."[23] Mattel officials only downplayed the attack, saying they had received no complaints from consumers.[24]

The BLO was among the first and most prominent culture-jamming project funded by ®™ark (pronounced "artmark"), something

Figure 19. A call to future Barbie liberators: "I was forced to say things that I didn't want to. Luckily, we checked ourselves into a special hospital and had the damage reversed. You can help us! Give us new voices. Liberate us!"

of a culture-jamming clearinghouse, which has modeled itself after a corporation. ®™ark was also behind the popular Bush-campaign parody site www.GWBush.com, which sought to display the "real" goals of a Bush presidency, such as helping the rich and repealing environmental regulations. For a time, the site received up to a million hits a day. The Bush campaign tried in vain to shut the site down by sending cease-and-desist orders and by complaining to the Federal Election Commission. George W. Bush himself even responded, calling the site's creator a "garbage man," and, in one of his more infamous gaffs, telling a reporter who asked about the site, "There ought to be limits to freedom."[25]

®™ark exploits a corporate luxury that rankles many culture jammers — an ability to skirt certain legal restrictions that *individuals* are obliged to heed. According to the ®™ark's Web site:

> ®™ark is a brokerage that benefits from "limited liability" just like any other corporation; using this principle, ®™ark supports the sabotage (informative alteration) of corporate products, from dolls and children's learning tools to electronic action games, by channelling funds from investors to workers for specific projects grouped into "mutual funds."[26]

A private corporation, the group enables activists and investors to participate in illegal product tampering without much personal risk. As the group describes its mission: "®™ark is indeed just a corporation, and benefits from corporate protections, but unlike other corporations, its 'bottom line' is to improve culture, rather than its own pocketbook; it seeks *cultural* profit, not financial." The most recent version of the group's Web site — a hilarious send-up of contemporary biz-speak and graphics — promotes "Veneer™," which "when paired with RTMARK's flagship product, Protester™ — the first software platform for real-time Cultural Capital™ trends analysis — companies can harvest activist-donated intellectual property without expensive and unreliable surveillance mechanisms."[27]

®™ark spokesperson Ray Thomas argues that many people still think of power in "the old terms," that is, government power. His group seeks to make explicit the increasing power of corporations: "They are so adaptable, and they're so organic that it's hard to speak of any one corporation as the enemy. It's more the system that allows tremendous abuse."[28] Rather than attempt to dismantle the corporate power system, Thomas and other activists at ®™ark exploit it; they observe the "adaptable" and "organic" nature of corporations and approach it as fertile soil for rhetorical and political appropriation. As one journalist for the Australian Broadcasting System notes, ®™ark has "cleverly aped the structures and jargons of a financial institution, even down to a smarmingly corporate-sounding promotional video."[29] Opening with warnings from Abraham Lincoln about the unfettered corporate power, this promotional video — *Bringing It to You!* — offers viewers a history of the corporation and rehearses ®™ark's style of intervention. In the spirit of "pranking," as I conceive it in this chapter, ®™ark folds and augments the corporate model in a way that offers new dimensions for political innovation.

The BLO is but one of about twenty pranks ®™ark has funded. Others include the popular "Mash Up" CD, *Deconstructing Beck*, and The Yes Men's impersonation of World Trade Organization representatives (I discuss these pranks later in this chapter). Some of the BLO's comrades in anti-Barbie politics were disgruntled by the group's popularity with the press. The Barbie Disinformation Organization (BDO), for example, charges, "[The BLO has] even been on 'Sixty Minutes,' for chrissakes, as sure a sign of polite applause by the bi-coastal media axis as anything short of a guest spot on 'Friends.'"[30] Like *Adbusters*, the BDO prefers its rhetorical message to be unambiguous and untainted by the enthusiastic buzz of commercial media. The BDO executes pointed parodic strikes at Barbie by placing mock stickers on the doll's packaging. For example, they replace graphics for Barbie's Stylin' Salon with "Barbie Lesbian Barber Shop," including instructions on how to give Barbie "Dyke Haircut nos. 1 & 2"; Barbie's Best Friend Betty becomes "Lipstick Lesbian Betty"; and so on. It is unclear how pervasive the work of the BDO has become. The group claims to have executed Barbie box hacks in New York, Boston, and Philadelphia.[31] But given the simplicity of their strategy — quickly placing stickers on boxes — it has the potential to spread in ways the more complicated voice-box hacks of the BLO cannot.

Pie Crimes and Misdemeanors: The Biotic Baking Brigade

In 1998, Nobel Prize–winning economist Milton Friedman (along with conservative California governor Pete Wilson, multimillionaire Steve Forbes, and George Schultz, former secretary of state under Ronald Reagan) was attending a conference on the benefits of privatizing public education. As Friedman was greeting well-wishers, a young man emerged from the crowd, exclaiming, "Mr. Friedman, it's a good day to pie!" and heaved a coconut cream pie into Friedman's (Figure 20). face. With that, the Biotic Baking Brigade (BBB) executed the first of what would become many successful missions of publicly delivering "just desserts" to what they call "pompous people." Since the BBB's inception, its targets have included Microsoft founder Bill Gates; Robert Shapiro, CEO of genetic-engineering giant Monsanto; Kenneth Derr, Chevron CEO; Willie Brown, San Francisco mayor; and Renato Ruggiero, WTO chief.

When reporting the public pieing of Willie Brown (who had just mandated a citywide "sweep" of the homeless), a confused San Francisco anchorman asked, "Is it funny? Is it some kind of statement? A physical assault?"[32] The BBB is consistently ready with pointed answers to journalists' inevitable question "Why?" In the case of Milton Friedman, for example, BBB "special agent" Christian Parenti says:

> Milton Friedman is the chief architect of neo-liberal economics.
> [His] particular brand of economics further allows multi-national
> corporations to rape the land, to plunder social systems . . . to pre-
> vent any type of popular resistance to occur. So, even though Milton

Friedman may seem like a strange target, like just some fuddy-duddy old geek, the man is like a purveyor of an ideological poison that is central to the kinds of policies and politics that are threatening the health of the planet and threatening the interests of common people all over the planet.[33]

A pie in the face of Milton Friedman becomes what rhetoricians call a "synecdoche"; the pieing stands for a whole host of grievances against globalization's prevailing economic ideology.

The BBB's Rahula Janowski explains the logic behind the group's choice of weapon: "Pie is an example that you don't have to revere someone just because they're more powerful than you . . . Pie is the great equalizer. How wealthy and powerful are you with pie dripping off your face?" Janowski points out that many CEOs and other powerful people do not often put themselves in situations where they hear dissent. So the BBB seeks them out in public forums, often where the target is giving a speech in some controlled, formal environment: "It's a message of 'we know who you are and we don't agree with what you're doing.' And it also puts a face on that dissent. Here's this person and they're willing to come right up and put the pie in your face. Like, 'we *really* don't like what you're doing.'"[34]

Figure 20. Scene from the front lines of the pie wars: Milton Friedman falls victim to the Biotic Baking Brigade.

Although the BBB's *message* is clearly one that opposes the ideologies and practices of their targets—genetic engineering, neoliberal economics, clear-cutting of the redwoods, corporate monopolies, etc.—their *tactic* of choice, pie throwing, expresses their opposition in a way that makes it difficult for targets to respond using conventional methods, or for audiences to understand. As BBB agent Rosie Rosebud explains: "A clown, a comedian, is someone who can laugh at themselves, they can laugh at society, and their rulers."[35] The BBB's rhetoric, when its agents speak to reporters, is clearly oppositional in nature, but it is their *comedic* posture and their creation of Spectacular images that get them the interviews in the first place.

The BBB understands well how to get their agenda in newspapers and on television broadcasts. Unlike *Adbusters,* the BBB does not remain resentfully on the outside, denied access to the "public screen"[36] by the commercial media. Instead, they hijack events that are already orchestrated for television—public speeches, rallies, meet and greets, and so on. They know that the image of a famous politician or captain of industry getting a pie in the face is so striking that the image-hungry media cannot help but cover it. Bill Gates with meringue dripping from his nose *will* make the five o'clock news. Unlike their more ascetic counterparts, the BBB does not condemn the news, it *makes* it; by cooking up tasty images for the Spectacle to consume. As San Francisco prankster Mark Pauline puts it in another context: "The media can never deny coverage to a good spectacle. No matter how ridiculous, absurd, insane or illogical something is, if it achieves a certain identity as a spectacle, the media has to deal with it. They have no choice. They're hamstrung by their own needs, to the extent that they're like a puppet in the face of such events."[37]

Again, BBB agents are always on hand to offer journalists a quick interpretive sound bite, such as "Monsanto CEO Robert Shapiro is the Pinochet of the food world [so] he's gotten his just desserts!" But it is the *image* of the powerful being pied that says more than a spoken message ever could. As Janowski explains: "The American public understands the impact of the message that is put forth by a pie. I mean, I think of Three Stooges. Think of the Marx Brothers. It's *very, very plain* what's happening when a pie is delivered."[38] A pie in the face becomes a powerful rhetorical symbol that requires little explanation. Agent "Salmonberry" puts it most succinctly: "I think the history of pie throwing shows that it's a form of *visual esperanto.* It's a universal language. Everyone understands the pie in the face. [It's about] taking their spectacle and just spinning it around. It allows people to have a laugh at the expense of the rich and powerful and otherwise unaccountable."[39] The BBB, then, mobilizes two familiar but dissonant visuals — a sober public speaker and a pie in the face — and by joining them, produces a kind of political jujitsu. Like rhetorical martial artists, they use the power of the broadcast media and deploy it toward their own ends.

To ensure its images make the news, the BBB sends its own camera operators on missions. In some cases, as with the pieing of Chevron CEO Kenneth Derr, the news media cannot be counted on to capture the moment on video. Like the BLO, the BBB happily provides budget-strapped local news stations with ready-made video packages, complete with interviews and images. This is a strategy often used by corporate advertisers hoping to create buzz around a new product. Advertisers offer preproduced PR stunts packaged as news features, which local news stations can easily queue up for broadcast. The result is free content for the station and free advertising for the corporation. Culture jammers such as the BLO and the BBB borrow this strategy, turning the media's love of images over on itself and creating a venue for issues the commercial media often ignore. Furthermore, BBB agents, despite their somewhat militant politics, are always clean-cut, articulate, and wear a sly smile. Hence, they are not easily dismissed as militant hippy radicals creating anarchy. They realize that they too must look the part for broadcast television if they are to gain access to it (Figure 21). As BBB agents often tell reporters, civil disobedience is "as American as apple pie."[40]

The Yes Men: Performing Globalization

In August 2000, Tampere University of Technology in Finland was hosting a textiles industry conference. The conference organizers, wanting to invite a representative from the WTO to address the attendants, instead stumbled onto www.GATT.org, the WTO-parody Web site maintained by The Yes Men, an activist group that seeks to challenge the WTO's abolition of labor rights and environmental regulations. The Yes Men's Mike Bonnano and Andy Bichlbaum were already beginning to make a name for themselves and for their cause by accepting a number of invitations to serve as free-trade "experts" at conferences and on news

Figure 21. The BBB's Al Decker takes advantage of the media spectacle.

programs. For example, Bonnano and Bichlbaum posed as WTO representatives at an international trade-law conference in Salzburg, Austria, where they "proposed a free-market solution to democracy: auctioning votes to the highest bidder."[41] On CNBC's *Marketwrap Europe*, on the eve of the Genoa Group of 8 (G8) conference, Bichlbaum, again posing as a WTO representative, announced that "might equaled right . . . that there ought to be a market in human rights abuses."[42]

Taking advantage of a mistake made by Tampere University of Technology as well as funding from ®™ark, Bonnano and Bichlbaum accepted an invitation to speak at the textile conference. Bichlbaum, posing as phony WTO representative Hank Hardy Unruh, delivered a speech that not so subtly mocked industrial impositions on civic values. Surprised that their supposed shocking satires of the WTO had yet even to raise eyebrows, despite their ludicrous assertions, Bonnano and Bichlbaum decided to step up their tactics, as "these people clearly need something more visual that will demonstrate without words what the WTO is about."[43] The Finland hoax is captured in the film *The Yes Men*, and the text of Unruh's (i.e., Bichlbaum's) speech was reprinted in its entirety by *Harper's* in November 2001.

The details of this oratorical prank merit some discussion here, as the prank borrows a familiar form (the academic conference address), yet, because of the anonymity offered by the Internet, Unruh's speech hijacks the situation and takes it in an unexpected direction.[44] Unruh greeted his naïve audience of textile industry chiefs, academics, and free-trade proponents: "I see members of the European Commission, Euratex, and other important political bodies that aim to ease rules for corporate citizens. I also see professors from great universities walking into a prosperous future hand in hand with industrial partners, using citizen funds to develop great textilic solutions to be sold to consumers for profit and progress." His speech detailed what he called (using the bureaucratic-speak of management literature) the "history of the worker/management problem"; that is, capitalism's exploitation of workers from early industrial England forward.

Unruh's section titles displayed in his PowerPoint presentation, beginning with "From Involuntarily Imported Workforce (IIW) [read: slavery] to Remotely Located Workforce (RLW) [read: Southeast Asian sweatshops]," outline a tongue-in-cheek pro-globalization argument suggesting that slavery was simply financially inefficient and that exploiting third-world labor makes much more sense. Showing a slide of Gandhi sewing, he described India's "main rabble-rouser" as "a likable, well-meaning guy who wanted to help his fellow workers along but did not understand the benefits of open markets and free trade." Ultimately, Unruh told his audience, the people's uprising in India was simply a failure of proper *management:* "By making only small adjustments, British management could have kept India on the path to modernity."

Unruh concluded his speech by essentially making the case for an intensification of what Deleuze describes as the cultural shift from "discipline" to "control." "To avoid another India," he said, "we must ensure that management is *constantly* in touch with workers — and not just intellectually but viscerally." He began his final section, on the WTO's proposed solutions for remote-worker inefficiency, by showing a "clip of a guy in a panopticon," referencing Foucault's central image of a disciplinary society, telling his audience that the WTO's new, more efficient technology "enables a lot more rapport with remote workers." At this moment in the speech, according to *Harper's,* an assistant (Bonnano) "grabs [Unruh] by the tie and belt and rips off his suit to reveal a golden spandex unitard underneath." Unruh exclaimed, "Ah! That's better! This is the Management Leisure Suit. *This* is the WTO's answer to the problems of maintaining rapport with distant workers ... Allow me to describe the suit's core features." With this, he "unzips the front of the suit, then pulls on a rip cord that inflates a three-foot-long golden phallus. The audience claps." He then revealed that this "Employee Visualization Appendage" (Figure 22) contained an electronic device for detecting exact amounts of employee output by communicating with "small unobtrusive chips" implanted in workers' bodies. Unlike the British Empire, which suffered from lack of technology, the new world order enabled by the WTO allows "the corporation to be a corpus, by permitting total communication within the corporate body on a scale never before possible."

Finally, referring to the leisure suit, Unruh explained, "In the United States, leisure — another word for freedom, really — has been decreasing steadily since the 1970s. The MLS permits the manager to reverse this trend by letting him do his work anywhere." He added that the device had nonwork-related uses as well: "With the MLS, officials of the WTO

Figure 22. The Yes Men's Andy Bichlbaum, posing as a WTO representative, reveals the "Employee Visualization Appendage," supposedly designed to allow executives to keep tabs on remote workers. Photo courtesy of The Yes Men, http://www.theyesmen.org.

will be able not only to see protests but to *feel* what's going on in the hot spots of the world. What will the danger level be when the first protestor is beheaded? I'm against beheading, but they do that in Qatar, where we're holding our next meeting." He concluded by repeating his first slide featuring corporate logos and smiling faces.

The Yes Men's public address hoax pranks the tropes of contemporary managerial rhetoric. *It performs the shift from disciplinarity to control.* Under what Foucault described as a disciplinary society — perhaps most readily recognized through the example of the prison panopticon — a centralized "eye" governed and disciplined subjects through constant observation. As Foucault describes it: "The major effect of the Panopticon" is to produce "a state of conscious and permanent visibility that assures the automatic functioning of power."[45] This was also the main model of discipline in factories: workers were kept in line through the assumption of constant supervision by an omniscient foreman. However, as Deleuze has pointed out, in our current economy "we're in the midst of a general breakdown of all sites of confinement — prisons, hospitals, factories, schools, the family."[46] The old mode of controlling people through direct observation has given way to remote control, enabled in part by digital technologies. Since the time of Deleuze's writing, in the late 1980s, this shift toward increasingly "open" control mechanisms has only intensified.[47]

As Deleuze suggests, control, like discipline, is a mode of power that operates through *surveillance.* By hijacking the venue of a public address, The Yes Men highlight the function of control and hype and intensify it, potentially rerouting the discussion. This is public address as appropriation art. The hijacking attempts to illustrate that increased communication, increased access, increased *talk* is not necessarily always in the best interest of workers' rights. As Deleuze argues, "Maybe speech and communication have been corrupted. They're thoroughly permeated by money — and not by accident but by their very nature. We've got to hijack speech. Creating has always been something different from communicating. The key thing may be to create vacuoles of noncommunication, circuit breakers, so we can elude control."[48] The marketplace, functioning through the logic of control, tells workers, "You can work anywhere!" However, even given this new flexibility, the worker is still (and perhaps more so) *monitored.* With the ridiculous visual of their

Management Leisure Suit, The Yes Men simply exaggerate the increasing *control* that accompanies new freedom for workers, challenging any comfortable assumptions that today's economy is more humane than its slavery predecessor.

As The Yes Men put it, "The goal of this performance, of course, is to clarify how dangerous it is to equate human freedom with a free market. Demonstrating visually the logical conclusion of neoliberalism."[49] Despite this less-than-flattering portrayal of the history and future of industrial capitalism, the audience responded with "a healthy round of applause," and *Harper's* reported that the speech was "well received, and the master of ceremonies praised it three times during the day."[50]

INFKT Truth: Pranking Big Tobacco

One of the most successful models of media pranking comes in the form of an institutionally sanctioned public service campaign: the American Legacy Foundation's public service campaign "INFKT Truth." Funded by more than $100 million in tobacco money per annum[51] after the 1998 "Master Settlement" agreement between tobacco companies and forty-six states, the impeccably produced television, print, radio, and Web campaign seeks to mobilize young people against Big Tobacco. The campaign visuals are distinguished by a bright orange background and a cyber-style font and graphics popular in both rave and video-gaming culture. As its use of the phonetic device "INFKT" implies, the Truth campaign encourages young people to infect their peers with knowledge about how the tobacco industry markets to children.

Unlike Nancy Reagan's 1980s "Just say no" campaign, which was, by most accounts, a dismal failure, the Truth campaign invites young people to assume a subversive posture that is far more active than just impotently saying "no" to tobacco. An underlying assumption of INFKT Truth is that Nike's provocation to "Just do it" has proven far more compelling to young people than Reagan's message of abstinence ever could. In an article about teen antismoking campaigns, one Scottish newspaper sarcastically asked: "Would you embrace a drug-free lifestyle on the advice of an emaciated former actress with concrete hair and a designer clothes habit many times more expensive than the average teenager's dope habit?"[52] Whereas the "Just say no" admonishment came from the first lady, an unmistakable symbol of the establishment, the Truth campaign takes seriously young people's antiauthoritarian attitudes and positions itself *with* them. Rather than asking teenagers to correct their own *individual* behavior, the Truth campaign encourages a critical analysis of tobacco as an *industry*.

Before the American Legacy Foundation launched its Truth campaign in 2000, the most prominent voice against underage smoking was the tobacco industry itself, forced by a series of courtroom battles to sponsor antismoking public service announcements (PSAs). At first blush, these tobacco-sponsored PSAs seemed well-intentioned, but their rhetoric was so out of touch with the tropes of so-called "Generation Y" that they seemed *purposefully* ineffective. Take, for example, tobacco giant Lorillard's "Tobacco is Wacko (if you're a teen)" campaign that supposedly sought to discourage kids from picking up the habit. First, let us assume that for most of today's teens and 'tweens (as the market so cleverly has labeled preadolescents), "wacko," and its nerdy sister "wacky," is probably not on the slang radar. More importantly, Lorillard neglected the fact that being "outside the box," "on the edge," "Xtreme," or, okay, even slightly "wacko" is precisely what is understood as cool for today's kids. As I discussed in chapter 2, everyone else pursuing the volatile teen market has known this for some time. Although even the most cursory analysis of market-produced rebellion demonstrates that kids are encouraged to symbolically "rebel" in a mass-produced way — that is, by purchasing the latest "edgy" product — kids at least want to *feel* they are choosing not to run with the herd when buying this or that brand of widget.

On its face, then, it might seem that Lorillard missed the boat of what has proven effective with the youth market, by implying that it is "wacko" (read: edgy) to smoke cigarettes. Although it hopelessly fudged the vernacular of today's teens, it perpetuated the aura that makes smoking so sexy to kids in the first place. Smoking is what distinguishes you from the pack. It is what makes you a rebel. In this light, Lorillard's choice of the outdated "wacko" was clearly not misguided at all. In fact, it is likely that the company's court-ordered antismoking campaign was *ineffective by design*. As one antitobacco Web site puts it:

> The tobacco industry favors only measures that are known not to
> work well and may even be counter-productive — such as age-related
> restrictions, retailer schemes, exhortation from parents and teach-
> ers, and "finger wagging" messages that smoking is only for grown

ups. These methods deflect attention away from the industry, are difficult to enforce, and present cigarettes as a "forbidden fruit" reserved for adults — exactly what most young people aspire to be![53]

Indeed, the outdated choice of "wacko" makes the "Don't smoke" message all the more unhip, which leaves tobacco products untainted by any odor of unfashionability. In the end, the tobacco industry spent millions to tell kids that more than anything else their product makes you a rebel, which is precisely the message every other successful advertiser sends to kids.

In contrast, the Truth campaign does not just tell kids not to smoke. In fact finger-wagging messages never appear in its literature at all. Instead, the Truth campaign encourages young people to themselves become culture jammers or pranksters; it even provides them with the tools to do it. In light of the discussion in chapter 2 about "consuming rebels," it becomes clear that the Truth campaign seems to be successful because it maximizes a truism in contemporary marketing to teens: kids want to *feel* like they are sticking it to the Man even if the Man provides them the tools with which to do so. Whereas the tobacco industry's pseudoattempt to curb teen smoking continues to afford the smoker the rebellious subject position, the Truth campaign flips that equation. In the Truth campaign, the *nonsmoking* teen is the rebel and the tobacco executives, rather than parents and teachers, represent the Man. By rehearsing a series of culture jams, pranks, and détournements instigated by ordinary teenagers, the Truth campaign offers kids a new subject position in relation to tobacco advertising. It is an agency born of engaged mischief and hip rebellion rather than nay-saying and abstention.

For example, one series of magazine ads provides kids with an incredibly simple way to become antitobacco activists. In several popular teen magazines, the group took out double-page spreads featuring the Truth campaign's trademark orange background and bold white letters. One spread read "Cigarette Smoke Has Arsenic," and the other, "Ammonia Is Added to Cigarettes." On the following page was a picture of bookstores, magazine stands, and grocery-store checkouts with magazines opened to Truth "billboards." The demonstrative ads urge readers to "Spread the knowledge. Infect truth." Not only did the Truth campaign provide mini billboards inside teen magazines, it showed contexts in which those billboards might be displayed. In doing so, it provided young people with a quick and easy way to protest, to feel as if they were committing a subversive act, however small and temporary.

In another magazine ad campaign, Truth provided stickers in the shape of blank "conversation bubbles," as in a comic strip. Next to the free stickers was a picture of the Marlboro Man advertisement, on which someone added a bubble and wrote in his or her own message (Figure 23). In this case, the text within the bubble read: "When I get tired of counting cow patties, I like to count the 4,000 chemicals in cigarette smoke." The bubbles are outlined in the familiar Truth orange but are otherwise just blanks slates, ready for kids to contribute their own messages to the vast sea of advertising. In short, these Truth ads demonstrate an easy way for kids to hijack the ads that so saturate their landscape.

As tobacco giant R. J. Reynolds is aware, the visual vocabulary of comic books appeals to kids. In a 1973 memo on how to better market its Camel cigarettes to young people, an R. J. Reynolds executive wrote: "Comic strip type copy might get a much higher readership among younger people than any other type of copy."[54] The tobacco industry put this wisdom to use years later with the hugely successful Joe Camel campaign. In response, the Truth campaign launched its "bubble" campaign, folding big tobacco's enthusiasm for the rhetorical power of comic-book imagery over on itself and, in doing so, allowing kids to participate in the construction of a new narrative.

The Truth bubble campaign borrows from a common situationist détournement strategy: revising the dialogue in popular comic strips as a venue for its own rhetorical messages (Figure 24). As situationist René Viénet argued, "Comic strips are the only truly popular literature of our century."[55] As such, comic books were a potentially powerful vehicle for rhetorical intervention. The situationists detourned existing comics, but they also borrowed the familiar dialogue bubbles that had become part of the popular vernacular as vehicles for détournement in other venues. Viénet writes: "It is also possible to detourn *any* advertising billboards—particularly those in subway corridors, which form remarkable sequences—by pasting over pre-prepared placards."[56] Anticipating the terminology later made famous by Marshall McLuhan, Viénet described the practice as "guerrilla media" warfare.[57] In this spirit, the Truth campaign in effect *trains* young people to practice their own brand

Figure 23. The Marlboro Man is subjected to a détournement.
Copyright American Legacy, used with permission.

of situationism, by confiscating a small space from commercial advertising and using it as a site for rhetorical invention. The goal to reclaim public space from the increasing "contamination" by commercial messages is shared by many culture jammers—billbard liberators, graffiti artists, hackers, etc.—but these practices usually require a criminal act: defacing private property. The Truth bubble strategy is no different; it encourages young people to, in effect, vandalize a corporation's property. But unlike culture jammers who readily embrace their role as cultural "guerrillas," the Truth campaign's suggested "hijack" is noteworthy in that it comes from a government-regulated organization working with legally granted tobacco money.

The Truth campaign has also aired a series of PSAs that rehearse culture-jamming strategies and feature young people participating in a variety of pranks on the tobacco industry. A series of radio spots, for example, featured teenagers making prank phone calls to tobacco giants. In one, a young man wanted to know if the company would purchase his dog's urine, as urea is a common tobacco additive. One television ad, "Body Bag," begins with a white "Truth" van pulling up outside a tall office building. A subtitle tells the viewer we are "outside a major tobacco company." A group of teenagers in heavy coats and stocking caps hop out and frenetically begin pulling from the back of the van heavy sacks stenciled

Figure 24. Comic strip characters became Marxist revolutionaries after situationist détournements.

with "body bag" in big black letters. A young African American man pulls out a bullhorn and shouts, "Excuse me! Excuse me!" as the camera cuts to suited executives turning away from the windows. "Sorry to bother you, but we have a question. Do you know how many people tobacco kills every day?" Meanwhile, at the entrance to the building, the other teenagers build a stack of weighted body bags on the sidewalk. The young man on the bullhorn continues: "You know what? We're gonna leave this here for you, so you can see what twelve hundred people actually looks like." The ad ends with a long-haired young man postering the street with signs for "Truth" as the camera zooms back to offer a bird's-eye view of the scene. A massive stack of white body bags blocks the sidewalk for a full city block.

The teenagers in the "Body Bag" ad are essentially staging an event much like those of the yippies in the United States and the situationists in Europe in the 1960s. Although their rhetorical venue is that of the public service announcement, the mode of engagement that these ads deploy is that of the politically charged, yet playful, media event. Like Abbie Hoffman and his comrades who staged a "levitation" of the Pentagon and wreaked havoc on the stock-market floor by raining buckets of dollars down on the heads of greedy stockbrokers, or like Ken Kesey's Merry Pranksters, who sought to make psychedelic the Kafkaesque, machine-like world Kesey described in *One Flew Over the Cuckoo's Nest,* the Truth campaign uses compelling visuals to poke fun at dominant modes of power.

When the Truth campaign launched its INFKT campaign (exemplified by the magazine ads discussed above), its television spots took on a more surreal tone. In one ad, for example, a group of teenagers release a swarm of mechanical babies in Times Square. The ad captures the faces of puzzled New Yorkers as the babies crawl across sidewalks, emitting an eerie, electronic cry. Only at the end does the ad remind viewers that cigarette smoking causes birth defects.

To be sure, the "Body Bag" ad is only a small cry from the *Adbusters* strategy of negative critique. What differentiates the INFKT Truth campaign from *Adbusters* is the *form* of their rhetorical strategy. Unlike the Joe Chemo parody, which critiques cigarette smoking and the ads that promote it, the Truth campaign unabashedly *uses* the rhetorical tropes of branding; it taps into the language of the market. Its signature color orange, its use of white asterisk pop-ups to connote a spreading virus, and its digital font are consistent across its magazine, television, and Internet campaigns. In effect, the Truth campaign is an excellent example of good brand management.

The Truth campaign's ubiquitous 2002–2003 "Behind the Curtain" ad, in which one teenager pulls back an orange curtain to reveal another reading damning quotes from tobacco industry documents, follows a similar revelatory *logic* as the parodies described in chapter 2, but its strategies position its audience much differently than *Adbusters* does with its resentful stance. By modeling public pranks, the Truth campaign offers young people something to do that is fun, active, and plays on their desire for rebellion. It is a *comedic* subject position. Importantly, young people pulling pranks and wild stunts in public has become a prevalent part of teenage vernacular, thanks to shock radio and popular television shows like MTV's "Tom Green Show" and "Jackass," and Comedy Central's "Crank Yankers" and "The Man Show." Truth taps into a certain mood or posture with which teenagers are already familiar, and redirects that mood toward a political engagement with the tobacco industry.

Contemporary consumer culture tends to promote what Arthur Asa Berger describes as a culture of "privatism," in which "the focus is upon personal consumption, not social investment for the public good."[58]

Powerful self-help gurus such as Oprah Winfrey and Tony Robbins reinforce this privatism by promoting a psychoanalytic gaze that consistently asks people to "look inward" to solve their problems, precluding any critique of systemic and institutional causes. In such an era, the Truth campaign to turn the analytical microscope away from the individual and the "correctness" of his or her *choices* and toward industrial institutions and the logics of profit and advertising is considerably refreshing. And thus far it has been highly successful. According to a study conducted by the American Legacy Foundation, the number of high-school smokers has declined by 18 percent since 2000, when the ads began.[59] In another study conducted by the foundation in tandem with the Center for Disease Control, students exposed to the Truth campaign ads "were much less likely to smoke than those who did not see the anti-smoking television ads."[60]

The INFKT Truth campaign experiments with a mode of rhetoric that is not grounded in the proclamations of any individual speaking subject, but still affords teenagers that all-important posture of the rebel outsider. Indeed, the group's Web site beckons visitors to "Join Truth now! But, don't think of it as 'joining' something." Truth promotes a kind of word-of-mouth dissemination of arguments against the tobacco industry. As such, it capitalizes on what may be two favorite pastimes of many teens: rebelling against authority, and *gossip* . As I discuss in the next section, gossip, or rumors, can have powerful persuasive effects — despite any identifiable origin or any verifiable truth value.

Pssst... Pass It On: Rumor Rhetoric

It may be surprising that one of the most enthusiastic media pranksters in American history was none other than Benjamin Franklin. Franklin published, in his own newspapers or in other newspapers in England and colonial America, a series of fabricated stories that illustrated his position on various social and political issues. Franklin, a published journalist since the age of twelve, printed hoaxes addressing his disdain for witch trials, slavery, and religious intolerance, among other issues.[61] His most successful hoax was a fictional public address supposedly given by a young mother in a New England courtroom. The "Speech of Polly Baker" told the tale of a young woman who challenged laws mandating the corporal punishment of unwed mothers. The London *General Advisor* published the "transcript" of Baker's speech in 1747, apparently having picked it up from colonial newspapers. Other European and colonial newspapers subsequently printed the address, and it helped shape the public's thinking on the hypocrisy of a legal system that held unmarried women solely responsible for their "illegitimate" pregnancies.[62]

Franklin early on knew the power of the commercial media in the shaping of public opinion. He also understood that rhetorical effects could be produced as effectively through rumor and deceit as through sound argument and verifiable truth. His Polly Baker address was accepted as fact for more than thirty years (until Franklin himself dispelled it), and even "scholars quoted the hoax, treating it as a serious sociological document."[63] As the story disseminated through an emerging network of print media, the wording and facts of the story changed somewhat. However, like many stories that find "legs," Polly's story was *necessarily* embellished, commented on, and revised. Its mutability enabled it to move more easily, picking up details here and there as it traveled from England to France and so on. One thing that was not necessary for the story's dissemination or its effectiveness, however, was its *truth value.*

Joey Skaggs, following in Franklin's footsteps, describes his strategy for spreading a hoax: "get someone from an out-of-state newspaper to run a story on something sight *unseen,* and then *Xerox* that story and include it in a second mailing. Journalists see that it has appeared in print and think, therefore, that there's no need to do any further research. That's how a snowflake becomes a snowball and finally an avalanche."[64] In his book *Media Hoaxes,* Fred Felder concurs: "The media are easy to fool because they depend upon other people. Reporters cannot find, investigate, and write every story by themselves. Instead, they rely upon a variety of tipsters to inform them about stories that seem to be newsworthy."[65]

As William S. Burroughs put it, "The control of the mass media depends on laying down lines of association. When the lines are cut the associational connections are broken."[66] Burroughs envisioned breaking these lines of association by modifying his experimental literary practice of the "cut/up" for the electronic age. He advocated an "electronic revolution" in which activists would use the malleability of analogue tape to deploy illusion "as a revolutionary weapon." For example, one might blare a "parody of the President's speech up and down the balconies" until it spread like fire through the networks of urban life: "messages passed along like signal drums . . . in and out open windows, through walls, over courtyards, taken up by barking dogs, muttering bums, music, traffic down windy streets, across parks and soccer fields."[67] Burroughs considered the spread of rumors as one of the many revolutionary strategies afforded by new technologies: "Put ten operators with carefully prepared recordings out at the rush hour and see how quick the word gets around. People don't know where they hear it but they heard it."[68]

The work of Skaggs and Franklin, unlike the work of some of the jammers discussed in chapter 2, depends on rumor rather than parody. Questioning whether the content is true or false is relatively inconsequential to the effectiveness of rumor. Unlike parody, rumor does not depend on producing that "aha!" moment in one's audience. In contrast to consciousness-raising rhetoric, which depends on faithful interpretation, rumor acts directly on the discursive field. Indeed, rumor can generate huge amounts of capital, as it did in the late 1990s for many dot-com start-ups, with little more to offer investors than a young, hip CEO and "next-big-thing" status on cable news channels. Whispers on Wall Street or a CNN interview with an "edgy" entrepreneur was often all that was needed to send a company's stocks through the roof. A well-placed rumor can also *siphon* capital, as can attest any public relations professional who has had to squelch rumors of product tampering or imminent stock crashes.

The material effects of rumor are just an exaggerated example of the logic of branding and advertising itself. Since the inception of market economies, the success of products and services has at least partially depended on good word of mouth. More than ever, contemporary advertising functions by generating an affective buzz around a particular brand. Indeed, viral marketing firms, like BzzAgent, who enlist everyday people to generate buzz around their clients' products are reporting huge successes. (If the growing influence of Malcom Gladwell's best-selling book on the subject, *The Tipping Point*, is any indication, the trend is only beginning.) Nike can charge upward of $150 for a pair of sneakers only by attaching to those sneakers spiritual values, lifestyle fantasies, and that indefinable but most important category: cool. As we know, it is not workers' wages that warrant the high price of Nikes, it is the added value provided by marketing rhetoric. And since the rhetoric and imagery of advertising does not depend on categories like "truth" to function effectively, neither does the counter-rhetoric of a culture jammer's rumor campaign. Nonetheless, a well-placed, "catchy" rumor campaign can wreak havoc on the corporate brand identity it targets. As Fredrick Koenig argues in *Rumors in the Marketplace*, "Next to an act of terrorism, what corporations fear most is that they may be targeted with an outlandish tall tale."[69]

One of the most successful brand projects of the last decade has been that of Tommy Hilfiger. Hilfiger made a successful career out of blending New England preppy couture with an urban hip-hop posture. As Naomi Klein puts it, Hilfiger "turned the harnessing of ghetto cool into a mass-marketing science" and became a model for "clothing companies looking for a short cut to making it at the suburban mall with inner-city attitude."[70] Around the turn of the new millennium, Hilfiger's famous logo (resembling a nautical flag) was something of a floating signifier, linked both to popular rap stars and to middle-class white kids hoping to purchase a bit of cool. The Hilfiger brand, for a time, was a quintessential case study in how a brand could successfully navigate the race and class dynamics of twenty-first-century America.

Klein explains that Hilfiger's winning formula was a result of his savvy response to countercultural reappropriations of his brand:

> Tommy Hilfiger started off squarely as white-preppy wear in the tradition of Ralph Lauren and Lacoste. But the designer soon realized that his clothes also had a peculiar cachet in the inner cities, where the hip-hop philosophy of "living large" saw poor and working-class kids acquiring status in the ghetto by adopting the gear and accoutrements of prohibitively costly leisure activities, such as skiing, golfing, even boating. Perhaps to better position his brand within this urban fantasy, Hilfiger began to associate his clothes more consciously with these sports, shooting ads at yacht clubs, beaches and other nautical locales. At the same time, the clothes themselves were redesigned to appeal more directly to the hip-hop aesthetic.... He also plied rap artists like Snoop Dogg with free clothes and, walking the tightrope between yacht and the ghetto, launched a line of Tommy Hilfiger beepers.[71]

After he had successfully insinuated his brand into the vernacular of urban ghetto style, Hilfiger could all the more effectively tap into that most coveted consumer demographic: middle-class white kids, who in the late 1990s embraced all things hip-hop. Klein reports: "Company sales reached $847 million in 1998 — up from a paltry $53 million in 1991 when

Hilfiger was still, as [cultural critic Paul] Smith puts it, 'Young Republican clothing.'"[72]

Beginning in 1996, the Hilfiger brand became the target of an e-mail rumor campaign that, as I write, has yet to fully disappear. A product of the most prolific rumor mill in history—the Internet—the so-called "Hilfiger-Oprah Hoax" goes something like this: Apparently Tommy Hilfiger, while a guest on the *Oprah Winfrey Show*, told Oprah he was outraged that his clothes had become so popular with black youths in the inner city, prompting Oprah to kick the designer off her show. A few versions of the hoax e-mail, usually under the heading "Tommy Hilfiger hates us!" continue to circulate. The least offensive version reads:

> Subject: FWD: Tommy Hilfiger hates us . . .
>
> Did you see the recent Oprah Winfrey show on which Tommy Hilfiger was a guest? Oprah asked Hilfiger if his alleged statements about people of color were true—he's been accused of saying things such as "If I had known that African-Americans, Hispanics and Asians would buy my clothes, I would not have made them so nice," and "I wish those people would not buy my clothes—they were made for upper-class whites." What did he say when Oprah asked him if he said these things? He said "Yes." Oprah immediately asked Hilfiger to leave her show. Now, let's give Hilfiger what he's asked for—let's not buy his clothes. Boycott! Please—pass this message along.[73]

According to the most prominent Web sites that track Internet rumors—Snopes.com and TruthorFiction.com—the Hilfiger-Oprah rumor is among the most enduring in the history of the Internet. It has been actively circulating via e-mail forwards and discussion boards for years. Despite its staying power, the rumor has no factual basis. Hilfiger's own Web site prominently featured this disclaimer on its home page: "I am deeply upset that a malicious and completely false rumor continues to circulate about me. I create my clothing for all different types of people regardless of their race, religious or cultural background. I want you to know the facts so that you are not the victim of a classic 'urban myth' that perpetuates untruths and has no basis in reality. Please read further to learn the truth."[74] Oprah Winfrey also announced on her show that there was no truth to the rumor and that she had never even met Hilfiger.

Brendan O'Malley, who follows urban legends for America Online, observes it is nearly impossible to quash an interesting story on the

Internet: "The speed and ease with which lies, rumors, innuendo and old-fashioned folklore can travel over the Internet is starting to spook corporate America and other organizations whose reputations and public goodwill are threatened by fast-spreading lies."[75] Despite, or perhaps *because of,* the rumor's outrageousness (some versions have Hilfiger spouting vicious racial epithets at Oprah and her studio audience), participating in the rumor's spread may afford many a certain subversive satisfaction. Regardless of its factuality, the Hilfiger rumor (and the subsequent call for a boycott) foregrounds a burgeoning suspicion toward the successful designer on the part of ethnic minorities. Keeping the rumor going may be one small way to "talk back" to a designer whose intentions, for many African Americans, are somewhat suspect.

Hilfiger built a corporate empire capitalizing on the intangible "cool" of urban street culture. He did so by picking up on its countercultural use, repackaging it accordingly, and selling it back, sans irony. The strategy made Hilfiger a multimillionaire, but it ultimately seems to have cost him his credibility with American youth. As I write, Hilfiger's cultural and financial capital has taken a nosedive. The company's stock, once trading at over $40 a share, in early 2003 dropped to just under $6 a share, and in early 2005 the company reported that it had suffered a nearly 59 percent plummet in its third-quarter income, before taxes.[76] In 2003 Hilfiger began the process of closing all but seven of his forty-four specialty shops.[77] It seems that young African Americans, important barometers of cool, have moved on to brands that seem less exploitative. Among the most popular brands are the Afrocentric FUBU (For Us, By Us), Phat Farm, and Sean John, all conspicuously owned and promoted by black designers. As the *New York Times* reports, Hilfiger is trying to address his company's financial hemorrhage by pulling out of the black market altogether: "Now the dreadlocks are gone from the advertisements — and the big red, white and blue 'Tommys' are pretty much gone from the streets. The Tommy Hilfiger Corporation has announced that it is moving away from its logo after many of the company's earlier urban constituencies abandoned Tommy for designers they call more 'authentic.'"[78] "As a company," reports Todd D. Slater, a financial analyst, "Tommy has to reinvent itself,"[79] and is doing so by attaching itself to the less controversial (and decidedly white) surfer culture popularized by shows like FOX's *The OC* and MTV's *Laguna Beach.*

Certainly the Hilfiger-Oprah Internet rumor cannot be credited with single-handedly bringing the Tommy brand to its knees. However, the rumor's popularity, despite well-publicized repudiations, may stem from its articulation of underlying suspicions about Hilfiger and mass-marketed fashion brands in general. By piggybacking on popular subcultural styles, big-brand campaigns necessarily play out whatever appeals those styles have for participants, forcing a migration to the next big thing. The rumor's subject line, "Tommy Hilfiger hates us!" does not have to be *true* to have an effect. Hilfiger likely does not hate ethnic minorities. But, for many, he did exploit them through a kind of cultural colonization, mining their communities for nuggets of street cool, and then, after processing them through the Tommy brand factory, selling them back at high prices.

Importantly, the rumor was likely not the work of any organized movement. In the age of the brand, the old and powerful force of the urban legend has become in the age of the Internet almost impossible for corporations to inoculate themselves against. Internet rumors have no identifiable source. The ability to splice and disseminate digital texts takes Burroughs's visions of an electronic revolution to new levels. The Hilfiger-Oprah rumor, which seems to have started from a disparaging comment Hilfiger made about Tommy knockoffs made in Southeast Asia and sold in U.S. inner cities, took on a life of its own, like a virus. The rumor helped undermine Tommy's essential street cred, and exacerbated a sentiment that cost him his most valuable asset: brand equity.

Again, the truth or falsehood of marketplace myths does not necessarily affect their rhetorical force. As French sociologist Jean-Nöel Kapferer points out in his intensive study *Rumors:* "Generally speaking, any definition of rumors involving the criterion of truth or falsehood is doomed from the outset, hindering as it does the explanation of rumor dynamics. A logical examination of the opposition between truth and falsehood shows that the dividing line between information and rumor is particularly vague."[80] Furthermore, the mobilization and endurance of a particular rumor is usually grounded in genuine public sentiment. As Brian Boling argues in his essay "Corporate Myths": "Folklore doesn't spring into existence *ex nihilo;* it responds to and reflects people's attitudes about the world. . . . These stories demonstrate popular suspicion of big business."[81] Hence, large corporations, especially those dependent on public affinity for their brand, take rumors and myths very seriously; so seriously that the effectiveness of anticorporate rumor campaigns is questionable.

Sociologist Gary Fine, whose research on rumors includes *Whispers on the Color Line* and *Manufacturing Tales*, argues that marketplace myths are ultimately politically impotent: "It is very easy for people to be critical of business in the context of these stories. But at the end of the day, they are no better off. These myths do not lead to large-scale social changes."[82] Although Fine acknowledges that electronic mail has enabled the increased dissemination of rumor campaigns such as that launched against Tommy Hilfiger, he notes that Internet technology *diminishes* the rhetorical power of rumors as well. When asked in an interview whether forwarded e-mail messages "remove the *folk* somewhat from folklore [since] unlike oral stories forwards are in a set form and passed along in an identical way," Fine responded, "What these forwards do is kind of freeze claims. People have to go out of their way to retype it rather than simply passing it on. This technology allows for rumors to be spread fast but also to fade or be denied more quickly."[83] In other words, the *mutability* that often allows texts to disseminate is, at least in the form of email forwards, somewhat undermined.

Conclusion: Pranking Rhetoric

This chapter has been about pranking rhetoric. On one hand, pranking rhetoric names a category of rhetorical action: pranking. On the other, it articulates an underlying premise of this analysis: in order to consider pranking as rhetoric, rhetoric itself must be, well, *pranked.* Here I mean "prank" in all its forms: "to trick" but also "to fold" and "to adorn." The practices discussed in this chapter — pranks, hoaxes, rumors — are not explicitly persuasive. As I suggested, they do not necessarily rely on that "aha!" moment when an audience becomes *conscious* of some new insight. And their effectiveness does not depend on the ethos or charisma of a specific political actor. Hence, they fall outside expectations of what conventionally qualifies as effective rhetoric. Clear arguments often do follow pranks — as in the Biotic Baking Brigade's critique of neoliberal economics — but such arguments are *translations* of pranks. They do not account for the power of the prank itself. One might even argue that such translations dilute the rhetorical power of pranks to confuse and provoke.

In other words, attaching an explicit argument or making a prank make sense may undermine what is unique about pranking's asignifying rhetoric in the first place.

The pranks, hoaxes, and rumors discussed in this chapter do not oppose traditional notions of rhetoric, but they do repattern them in interesting ways. Media pranksters undermine the authority of rhetoric by hijacking its sanctioned venues, as did The Yes Men's WTO imposter. Hoaxes challenge rhetoric's relationship to Truth (either its misuse as a tool for propaganda, or its correct use in revealing facts to audiences), because they produce rhetorical effects that have little to do with facts or evidence, as in the case of Benjamin Franklin's Polly Baker hoax. Rumors unravel rhetoric's continued reliance on individual auteurs (be they presidents, protestors, or filmmakers), because their source is impossible to locate and is ultimately irrelevant to their rhetorical and political impact.

Traditionally, communication has largely been conceived in industrial, Fordist terms. Arguments are systematically and rationally assembled. Messages move teleologically toward an end product: persuasion. Perhaps the strategies of pranking and branding (pranking's commercial counterpart) may have something to teach observers of media and culture. As North America moves into an economy driven as much by information and marketing as by the production of tangible goods, it becomes all the more crucial that scholars attend to the battles being waged over commercialization. A basic tenet of both the marketing and prankster worlds is that ideas and innovations spread less like widgets coming off an assembly line than like viruses in an ecosystem.[84] Indeed, viruses *communicate* diseases, yet they cannot be said to possess intentions nor to progress teleologically, as a factory model might imply.

In *Pranks!* Vale and Juno acknowledge that pranking can often be funny, even trivial. But they remind us that pranks can also pose a "direct challenge to all verbal and behavioral *routines,* and their undermining of the sovereign authority of words, language, visual images, and social conventions in general."[85] Contemporary commercial culture is dependent on consumers having somewhat routine responses to words and images; however, these responses need not be completely homogenous. Indeed, it is the protean, polysemic nature of brands that allows them to be disseminated globally, across individuals, publics, and cultures. For example, the Nike swoosh may signify self-discipline to one person, and liberty to another; and it is likely that the Nike corporation does not much care how people interpret it, as long as they keep buying Nike products. This is the viral power of the brand — its ability to provoke through sheer replication of form.

Pranking — as appropriation, intensification, and folding — is conceptually and practically quite different from how we often consider rhetorics of social protest. Pranking is often comedic, but not in a satirical, derisive sense that prescribes a "correct" political position. It takes the logic of branding seriously. As illustrated by the rallying cry of contemporary marketing — "Brands! Not products!" — successful brands are not limited to a closed system of representation. The swoosh has the capacity to signify much more than sneakers, and that is just the way Nike wants it. Nike understands that in an age when the factory has largely been moved overseas, it is now in the business of producing something much more profitable than sportswear: its product is seductive imagery and the loyal consumers it attracts.

As I have argued throughout this chapter, pranking repatterns commercial rhetoric less by *protesting* a disciplinary mode of power (or clogging the machinery of the image factory), than by strategically augmenting and utilizing the precious resources the contemporary media ecology affords. In doing so, pranksters, those comedians of the commercial media landscape, make manifest Foucault's observation that one need not be sad to be militant. Culture jamming, at its best, multiplies the tools of intervention for contemporary media and consumer activists. It does so by embracing the viral character of communication and culture, a quality long understood by marketers. So-called "cool hunters," for example, employ the tools of anthropologists, who engage in "diffusion research" to determine how ideas spread through cultures. These marketers, like their anthropologist counterparts, have learned that people tend to adopt messages less in response to rational arguments than through exposure and example.[86] Activists with a prankster ethic, such as those promoting the INFKT Truth campaign, capitalize on this capacity of ideas to multiply and disseminate like viruses.

Whereas the ad parodies discussed in chapter 2 offer up alternative interpretations of marketing rhetoric, pranks potentially upset the obligation of rhetoric to *represent* at all. As Vale and Juno write, pranks "attack the fundamental mechanisms of a society in which all social/verbal intercourse functions as a means toward a future *consumer exchange,* either of goods or experience. It is possible to view *every* 'entertainment' experience marketed today either as an act of consumption, a prelude to an act of consumption, or both."[87] Pranks, rumors, and hoaxes — precisely because they border on the nonsensical — reconfigure the very structures of meaning on which corporate media and advertising depend. Although *Adbusters'* campaign to "spread the Blackspot virus" may still promote oppositional *content* — "kicking Phil's ass" — its embrace of the viral form indicates the group's advertising savvy. Tellingly, the magazine's focus on advertising parodies has waned in recent years.

The next chapter explores the culture-jamming work of what I describe as *pirates* — artists and activists who, like pranksters, *appropriate* owned cultural property in their process of invention. Rather than try to stop production of the mass media, pirates instead "hijack" the so-called tools of control to produce different rhetorical effects. If we are indeed, as Deleuze (and, following his lead, Hardt and Negri) suggests, moving into a political terrain that permits rather than denies access to information, then rhetorical responses seeking to liberate speech from the hands of the market may be less effective than many hope. In the next chapter, I also explore the ways in which pirating and hijacking, as practices, encourage a reconfiguration of how publics conceive authorship, property, and invention.

Intermezzo

A Sequel

In the early stages of this project on contemporary protest rhetoric, the United States was teetering on the brink of "war" with Iraq. I knew that long before these textual musings would ever see the light of day, this country would have violently invaded a sovereign nation and the television personalities of CNN would never utter such unfashionable words as "occupation" and "imperialism" (both so twentieth century) in their reports. After all, we live in the society of the post, *do we not? But, despite my misgivings about this war, and they are vast, the strategies of resistance historically deployed by baby boomers in the face of that other controversial war—picketing, chanting, marching—somehow feel so dated, worn-out, much like the gaucho pants and wooden clogs I remember on my mother. That is, although these strategies of resistance, like sixties fashions in general, continue to make their rounds in the retro-vortex that has made politics and fashion nearly indistinguishable from one another, they somehow fail to fit me. They're intended to offer a kind of "one size fits all" democratic vibe, yet they too often end up feeling shapeless and cumbersome.*

I was at an academic conference held in that beautiful city of rebels, New Orleans, Louisiana (well before the natural and bureaucratic horror known as "Katrina"). Following a compelling debate over the merits of waging war on Iraq, a group of my colleagues planned to march down the streets of the Big Easy, inviting passersby and tourists to join them. As they gathered outside the plush lobby of the big-brand hotel in which I stood, shifting my weight uncomfortably and shamefully from foot to foot, I felt simultaneously drawn to and repelled by their growing numbers. I chastised myself for my vacillation. Was I such a poster child for the Generation X media construct that I could muster little more than a bemused interest in my impassioned colleagues? I braced myself against my slacker guilt by striking ironic and sarcastic postures with likeminded friends behind the safety of the Hilton's revolving doors. Who were we to tell the good people of New Orleans what to think about the war, we said. Of course, we hated our administration's cold-war bravado as much as our boomer colleagues did. After all, despite the return of Rumsfeld and rubber bracelets, I prefer to deny that the eighties are back. Despite our shared politics, something about joining a group of fist-pumping liberal academics somehow felt too earnest, too sixties.

But what alternatives had my *generation offered? Irony and sarcasm? I can confidently call myself a popular-culture savant, well versed in the wink-and-nod cultural criticism of* The Simpsons *and* The Daily Show. *But is that activism? A potent and equal mix of guilt and curiosity propelled me through the revolving door of cynicism, er, the Hilton, and out onto the sidewalk to join the swarm of protesters that was now taking the shape of a slow beeline toward the county courthouse (the nearest, and hence most convenient, "Hall of the Establishment"). As the small swarm began its swarming, hoisting handmade placards and shouting "No blood for oil!" I was hit with a profound sense of embarrassment and exposure, like it was the first day of seventh grade and I didn't quite know where to stand, what to say, how to walk. Using a strategy I developed early in junior high school, I immediately turned on my heel and rushed back into the hotel lobby, where I quickly translated my vulnerability into a series of self-deprecating one-liners that earned me the validating laughter of my peers.*

I have to clarify. I genuinely admired and respected my colleagues' intentions. They, like myself, believed that the invasion of Iraq was wrong, that it was an unjustified violence and a vulgar show of arrogance. And they were willing to voice that opinion and challenge the status quo by confidently puncturing the silencing tendencies of blind patriotism. It was not the activists' intentions that made me suspicious, but the pattern formation *they assumed. Ironically, it is a sixties icon that best articulates my misgivings about much protest rhetoric. As Tom Wolfe reports in* Electric Kool-Aid Acid Test, *that classic of new journalism (arguably the iconic literary form of the sixties generation), Ken Kesey, leader of the legendary Merry Pranksters, tells a crowd at Berkeley: "You can't stop a war by marching and fighting. You have to say 'fuck it' and walk away." But, as we know, Kesey did not walk away in apathy or cynicism, but into a long career of writing and activism. As Kesey suggests, marching and chanting simplistic slogans is what the* military *does. For that reason alone, we must at least be* reflexive *about their effectiveness as an antiwar strategy.*

Thanks to Kesey, I let myself off the hook a bit. It is not that I'm so cowardly or "hip" that I am impotent in the face of war. Indeed, I even participated in a few local protests, because they offered the only public assemblage of those of us who, for a while at least, were underrepresented by public opinion polls. Yet, marching and chanting somehow don't fit me. I find the prankster's ethic more compelling than the protestor's. Pranking addresses the patterns *of power rather than its* contents. *And, ultimately, if I give myself over to the prankster strategies of folding and layering, I realize it's really not about* me *at all. Maybe "I" am just an* effect *of a series of foldings; just layers of various cultural styles. Perhaps "I" am a prank.*

Pirates and Hijackers

Creative Publics and the Politics of "Owned Culture"

> I played hip-hop mix tapes for my professors and they said,
> "Oh, I don't think this deconstruction stuff applies to urban
> youth culture." I was like, "Yo, they're taking fragments and
> it's no longer about the original authorial presence and
> it's a direct aural parallel with Literary Theory."
>
> — Paul D. Miller, aka DJ Spooky, That Subliminal Kid

> It's not that I think that we were somehow brilliant, it's
> just that I'm a kid, I've grown up in a media saturated
> environment and I'm just tuned into it . . . when I
> started messing around with sounds there was
> no conceptual pretense at all.
>
> — Mark Hosler, founding member of Negativland

Whether they came to it with theoretical/conceptual models in mind, or organically from personal experience, a generation of "appropriation artists" is seeing its preferred style of rhetorical invention hit the mainstream, although not without significant legal controversy. Legal scholar William Landes describes appropriation art thus:

> Appropriation art borrows images from popular culture, advertising, the mass media, other artists and elsewhere, and incorporates them into new works of art. Often the artist's technical skills are less important than his conceptual ability to place images in different

settings and, thereby, change their meaning. Appropriation art has been commonly described 'as getting the hand out of art and putting the brain in.'[1]

By unabashedly using copyrighted and trademarked material in their work, appropriation artists, or intellectual property pirates, attempt to call attention to the asymmetrical control over our cultural materials. In doing so, many have — sometimes strategically, sometimes unwittingly — provoked major corporations into high-profile legal battles that directly affect the future shape of what counts as "public domain."[2] Art scholar Sven Lütticken argues that such artistic "theft" is not an anomaly to healthy publics, but the rule. In the face of our current proprietary culture, he suggests:

> Perhaps a counter-attack against the dominant legal perspective could take the form of an ironic appropriation of its vocabulary. Why not maintain that theft is an essential part of any culture that wishes to remain dynamic? An evolving and self-critical culture is unthinkable without an art of theft as one of its constituent elements: quoting and appropriating is a way of manipulating material and introducing new meanings.[3]

Illustrating this art of theft are those who pirate and hijack owned material, attempting to free information, art, film, and music — the rhetoric of our cultural life — from what they see as the prison of private ownership. They exploit the double bind that culture owners find themselves in as they attempt to disseminate their products across the mediascape. As Kembrew McLeod puts it: "Intellectual property owners attempt to bind a sign to its originary source, the commodity, but when it leaves the owner's corporate orbit and is distributed to a wide audience, the property faces reinterpretation and rearticulation."[4] In turn, these reinterpretations are increasingly the subject of high-profile lawsuits.

Hip-hop, to cite the most recognizable current example of appropriation art, regularly samples existing musical texts in its compositions. But the popularization of sampling as an art form has caused seemingly equal parts resentment and enthusiasm in musicians and fans. Sean Combs (aka Puff Daddy and P. Diddy), for example, has made millions borrowing from famous pop riffs, but he has also earned the scorn of many who see the rapper/producer/entrepreneur/menswear mogul as little more than a rip-off artist siphoning the talents of others. At the same time, funk legend George Clinton has released two original CDs, *Sample Some of Disc,*

Sample Some of D.A.T., volumes 1 and 2, which he composed expressly as fodder for a generation of DJs, many of whom were already sampling Clinton's vast body of work (mainly with his bands P. Funk Allstars, Parliament, and Funkadelic).[5] DJs who use Clinton's music need only follow a few instructions, carefully detailed in the liner notes: they must send Clinton a copy of their CD (so he can keep up with what the younger artists are doing) and they must pay the minimum industry standard for each copy sold ("a few pennies," says Clinton).

Clinton's democratic take on copyright enables anyone from marquee rap acts to adolescent upstarts to use his work in theirs. In 1994, when Bridgeport Records, the label that produced Parliament's music, used Clinton's name in a suit against Sony and Public Enemy's DJ Terminator X for copyright infringement, Clinton felt obliged to speak out on the issue: "I called [Public Enemy founders] Chuck [D] and Flava [Flav] and we got on CNN and I told 'em I didn't care. I did it for Chuck and Flava. I did it for hip hop." For Clinton, the increasingly sharp teeth of copyright law are decidedly political in nature and not without a racial component. As he told *Wired* magazine (August 1994): "That old way's like sharecroppin'. . . That's Snidely Whiplash shit. Some guy laughing and saying, 'But you must pay the rent.'" Clinton twirls an imaginary handlebar mustache. "I love the new stuff, and I want to see what people do with my music." Clinton's position, that music ideally does not *belong* to anyone, articulates a dominant attitude held by many musicians, artists, and software designers who see intellectual property law as a seminal issue in contemporary cultural politics. Indeed, a mantra that governs the politics of software pirates, "hacktivists," and so-called "techno-socialists," who try adamantly to defend the Internet from commercialization, is: "Information just wants to be free!" This sentiment is inspired by John Perry Barlow's 1996 manifesto "A Declaration of Independence of Cyberspace," which, following William Gibson, declared cyberspace the world of the mind, relegating the encroaching governments to the archaic media of "flesh and steel."[6] Barlow's manifesto gave voice to a movement that is still alive and well, most effectively through the work being done by the Electronic Frontier Foundation, a kind of ACLU for the Web that Barlow helped found.

However, in an age when entertainment is one of the United State's most profitable industries, only a small minority of copyright holders shares Clinton's egalitarian view on intellectual property. The most stark example of the culture industry's militant protectionist stance is Disney's and the Motion Picture Association of America's heavy lobbying efforts to promote the 1998 Sony Bono Copyright Term Extension Act (named after the late pop star and congressman, who was fond of saying "Copyright should be forever minus a day"), which extended the life of copyrights for songs, films, books, and cartoon characters by twenty years, marking the eleventh extension of copyright since 1960. Not coincidentally, the bill was drafted shortly before the copyright was to run out on Disney's most profitable character and most recognizable ambassador of the Disney brand: Mickey Mouse (Donald Duck, Pluto, and Goofy's protection would have expired just three years later). In early 2003, the U.S. Supreme Court assessed the constitutionality of the Bono Act in response to a vigorous campaign spearheaded by then Harvard law professor Lawrence Lessig, who urged the Court to overturn the law on grounds that it unconstitutionally undermines freedom of expression. Nevertheless, the Court decided seven to two to uphold the Bono Act, making Mickey safe from the public domain for another twenty years (Figure 25).

Lessig (now at Stanford), the leading scholar of Internet politics and the law,[7] made a name for himself when in 1997 he was recruited by a U.S. district court judge to help with the "mother of all tech litigation": *Department of Justice v. Microsoft.* Before that historic case went to court, Microsoft fought hard against Lessig's participation, arguing that the scholar's first book, *Code and Other Laws of Cyberspace,* was, as one journalist put it, "an anti-Redmond rant." Microsoft's complaints were ultimately heeded and Lessig was dismissed from his role as judicial advisor. Six years later, in Lessig's Supreme Court challenge to the Bono Act (what he and others refer to as the "Mickey Mouse Protection Act"), Lessig argued that corporations are choking the life out of our public culture through the unchecked abuse of intellectual property law. He lays out his critique in great detail in his influential 2002 book *The Future of Ideas,* which *Wired* calls "the bible of intellectual property monkey-wrenchers,"[8] and he envisions alternatives in his book *Free Culture.*[9]

In his books, public lectures,[10] and blog (www.lessig.org/blog/), and through the Creative Commons project (www.creativecommons.org; I discuss this project at length in chapter 5), Lessig makes a case for a robust intellectual commons, which he believes provides the only con-

Figure 25. Artist Andrew Baio's détournement of a Disney cartoon satirizes the Eldred case. Copyright Andrew Baio, http://www.waxy.org, used with permission.

ditions in which innovation and ideas can thrive. Lessig does not argue for the abolition of intellectual property, and is even, in his own words, "fanatically pro-market," albeit "in the market's proper sphere."[11] Lessig and others question the adoption of contemporary market values in every sphere of communal life. Ultimately, for Lessig, the question of copyright is "best described as a *constitutional* question: it is about the fundamental values that define this society and whether we will allow those values to change."[12] In response, Lessig wants, in the face of the increasing encroachment of commercial imperatives, to preserve the Enlightenment civic virtues that ground the American political tradition.

Those who pirate and hijack owned material attempt to challenge our tendency to treat cultural material as *property*. This chapter, in an attempt to assess appropriation art on its own terms, explores the values and its strategies of appropriation art. I look at the work of a variety of artists who practice the "art of theft," which many suggest is the only way to maintain a folk-art tradition in which the artist utilizes existing cultural content to comment on her world. I discuss the ways in which appropriation art both foregrounds and attempts to trouble an Enlightenment conception of authorship, a fundamental tenet for rhetorical and cultural scholars; and also how appropriation art resists corporate attempts to hoard intellectual material as property. Ultimately, I suggest that much appropriation art, despite providing a justified critique of our proprietary culture, runs the risk of grounding its resistance in the very assumptions it seeks to undermine. Doing so maintains a notion of the public as something *outside* consumption and the tools of invention and relies on the individual rebel auteur as the locus of political action.

Illegal Invention: Pirates, Hijackers, and Rhetoric as Appropriation Art

A few years ago, I attended a New York City art exhibit/conference titled "Illegal Art," curated by independent magazine publisher Carrie McLaren of *Stay Free!* magazine.[13] The legendary Bowery rock venue CBGB hosted a small exhibit of artwork that included, in a variety of novel contexts, images of Barbie, Kentucky Fried Chicken's Colonel Sanders, Mickey Mouse, and other American icons. An underground magazine cover depicted Binky (a rabbitlike creature from *Simpsons* creator Matt Groening's comic strip *Life Is Hell*) punching out General Mills mascot, the Trix rabbit. A computerized graphic titled "the Symbolic Lotus of a Thousand Colonels" offered a dizzying kaleidoscope of Colonel Sanders forming a psychedelic lotus flower. A Gap parody by Dyke Action Machine featured two lesbians kissing. One photographer's "Food Chain Barbie" series cast the all-American girl in blenders, sans clothes and in compromising positions. Another showed *Sesame Street*'s Bert hanging from a noose. Etcetera. Etcetera.

Little of the work on the walls of CBGB was what most would consider great art, nor was much of it explicitly political in a way that made it obviously "activist." Judged by either of these typical standards, these works would likely not have merited public exhibition, let alone their own show at CBGB. What made these works notable was that each of their creators had either been taken to court or barraged with cease and desist orders from the lawyers of copyright and trademark holders. Ironically, the pieces I found to be the most interesting of the bunch were not by the target of a trademark suit, but by the trademark holder himself. To be precise, the "artist" was not the artist at all. Rather, the "work" was orchestrated by Kembrew McLeod and produced by a combination of the

United States government, an attorney, and a few Massachusetts journalists. McLeod (now associate professor of communications at the University of Iowa), while a graduate student at the University of Massachusetts, applied for *and was granted* the trademark for "Freedom of Expression." That's right: Kembrew McLeod, a mere scholar of communication studies, *owns* "Freedom of Expression."[14]

McLeod's contribution to the "Illegal Art" exhibit was his certificate (trademark number 2,127,381) from the commissioner of patents and trademarks, ensuring him exclusive rights to use the phrase on printed matter such as magazines and newspapers. McLeod also showcased a series of framed letters and newspaper articles documenting his experiment. As an exercise in communal performance art, McLeod had a friend pose as the publisher of a punk-rock fanzine called *Freedom of Expression*. McLeod then hired an attorney, without letting her in on the joke, to send a cease and desist order to the friend. The wording of the letter took on an unintentional satiric quality, issuing McLeod's accomplice a "demand that you refrain from all further use of Freedom of Expression." Finally, McLeod issued press releases that included both his trademark certificate and the letter, sparking a short-lived controversy in the local media.

In *Owning Culture*, McLeod explains that he wanted the irony of the trademark to emerge somewhat organically:

> The point of this particular media prank was to "play it straight" and never let on to a reporter my intention to engage in social commentary — I would let the news story itself be the social commentary. That is, rather than someone reading a quote from me stating "I'm concerned with the way intellectual property law facilitates the appropriation of significant aspects of our culture by corporations . . . blah blah blah," I wanted to orchestrate the story in a way that newspaper readers would come to that conclusion on their own.[15]

In *Owning Culture* and his more recent *Freedom of Expression*, however, McLeod allows himself to indulge more explicitly in an analysis of intellectual property. Among his chief concerns is that intellectual property is increasingly deployed ideologically, strategically shutting down public dissent from corporate culture. He writes, "In this environment, the obvious question to ask is how in the world are people supposed to critique the ubiquitous, privately owned texts that help shape our consciousness without being able to reproduce them?"[16]

While McLeod's "art" was an attempt to tweak rhetorically the restrictive tendencies of trademark law by trademarking what many might consider the unthinkable, other artists challenging corporate rhetoric often find themselves on the wrong side of a lawsuit. In 1999, for example, Utah-based artist Tom Forsythe received a complaint from Mattel, which claimed that his "Food Chain Barbie" photography series infringed on its Barbie copyright and trademark. Although Forsythe was not making money from the works, he decided to fight the case, obtaining legal aid through the American Civil Liberties Union (ACLU). In 2004, both the U.S. Court of Appeals and the U.S. Circuit Court of Appeals found in favor of Forsythe, and even ordered Mattel to pay the artist $1.8 million for his legal fees in what one judge called "an objectively unreasonable and frivolous case."[17] Many in the copyright movement are understandably encouraged by the victory.

Another of the artists showcased at the Illegal Art exhibit was not so lucky. Kieron Dwyer, a former cartoonist for Marvel and D.C. Comics, created a Starbucks parody in a solo comic project and on his Web site (Figure 26). The parody, which turned Starbucks' familiar green and white mermaid logo into a symbol of unbridled consumerism, features an anatomically embellished mermaid with stars in her eyes wearing a dollar-sign tiara and holding a steaming latte in one hand and a cell phone in the other. Random symbols such as @ ? * #, usually connoting expletives, float from the receiver and over her head. The words "Consumer Whore" and dollar signs replace "Starbucks Coffee" and the stars of the original logo. The image, in Dwyer's words, captures the "crass, rampant commercialism in this country."[18]

In the controversial case, Starbucks was able to stop Dwyer from distributing his lampoon in any way, despite the fact that it fell under the traditionally recognized fair-use protections for parody of copyrighted material. How is it that Dwyer's piece, an obvious political commentary through the parody of a recognizable image, was not protected under the rules of fair use? After all, "criticism" and "comment" are explicitly listed in "Section 107: Limitations on Exclusive Rights: Fair Use" (17 § U.S.C. 107) as protected speech. The lawyers representing the latte empire sued for trademark and copyright infringement, unfair competition, and trade-

Consumer Whore Parody Logo ©2000 Kieron Dwyer   www.LCDcomic.com

Figure 26. The parody at issue in *Starbucks Corp. v. Dwyer.* Copyright Kieron Dwyer, used with permission.

mark dilution via tarnishment. The latter, trademark dilution via tarnishment, was the only claim not readily dismissed by the federal district court hearing the case.

Trademark dilution is a relatively new restriction in trademark law that is intended as a way for companies to discourage other logos, slogans, or imagery that may "water down" a brand's impact on consumers.[19] Legal scholar Sarah Mayhew Schlosser explains:

> The Trademark Dilution Act enables owners of famous trademarks to sue unauthorized users of their trademarks for lessening the capacity of the mark to identify and distinguish goods or services,

regardless of the presence or absence of competition between the
owner of the mark and the secondary user, or a likelihood of confusion, mistake, or deception. Thus, owners of famous trademarks are
entitled to nationwide injunctive relief against uses that would tend
to 'dilute' the mark.[20]

By invoking a trademark clause that was supposedly created to preclude
confusion between corporate brands, Starbucks was able to wipe from
public existence Dwyer's parody. A long-cherished rhetorical strategy —
one deployed by political commentators from Aristophanes to Benjamin
Franklin to Jon Stewart — seems to be in jeopardy under the current climate of corporate protectionism. Given that, as Schlosser writes, "Today's
political hot buttons are often corporate in nature," corporations' ability to
shut down voices of dissent is significant. The lobbying for and invocation
of increasing trademark protection, Schlosser notes, "act to chill meaningful criticism of corporations" and "silence otherwise legitimate parody."[21]
At present, artists and activists wanting to comment on our increasingly
corporate world must weigh the risk of exercising their freedom of expression with that of facing a team of lawyers in a trademark case.[22]

Starbucks essentially did an end-run around copyright, with its
cumbersome fair-use restrictions. The company did so by declaring that
a kind of physical damage had been done to its trademark, that its integrity was being corrupted through a dilution process. Although fair-use
restrictions allow citizens to use others' property for certain purposes,
the law, through trademark, can prohibit the boundaries of that branded
property from being blurred. I have already discussed how the necessity for brands to disseminate is both their strength (as they corner more
and more of the "mindshare" market) and their weakness (as they spread,
they become more vulnerable to interlopers and misinterpretations). The
appeal to trademark dilution is in some ways a confession as to the tenu-
ousness of a brand's hold on the property to which it lays claim. Dilution,
after all, comes from the Latin for "to wash away" — if these spurious legal
battles are the only thing preventing the erosion of a brand, then brands
are precarious commodities indeed.

McLeod's possession of "Freedom of Expression" both metaphor-
ically and materially illustrates the at least superficial ease with which
copyright holders can "own" the fodder for rhetorical engagement in civic

life. Dwyer's experience with Starbucks demonstrates the risks artists and activists face when daring to challenge that ownership. In response to this current state of affairs, many activists have sought to challenge the two basic tenets on which contemporary intellectual property law is founded — authorship and property.

The Rhetoric of the Copyleft: Intellectual Property Law and Freedom of Expression

Originally, after careful consideration by the drafters of the U.S. Constitution, copyright protected works of art for only fourteen years. Today, however, copyrights can protect a work for up to seventy years beyond the life of the author, and for ninety-five years for corporate copyright holders. Although the original intention of copyright was to *inspire* creativity by insuring the livelihood of artists and writers, Lessig and others argue that repeated legal extensions and the public's seeming impotence to stop them may result in a total privatization of culture and no space for novel and noncorporate creative projects. Whereas previous legal challenges to federal extensions of copyright merely argued over the *definition* of "limited" in the founding fathers' assertion that copyright shall secure "for limited times to authors and inventors the exclusive right to their respective writings and discoveries," Lessig argues that the perpetual extension of corporate-owned copyright undermined the *reason* the drafters codified copyright in the first place: "to promote the progress of science and useful arts."[23]

This became the crucial point in Lessig's argument in front of the Supreme Court and it continues to govern much of the debate around copyright and the privatization of culture: by grandfathering existing copyrights, the "cause of 'art and science' actually suffers under retroactive extensions, because works that otherwise would have been returned to the public are kept in private hands."[24] Siva Vaidhyanathan, a scholar of information and culture at New York University, puts it simply: "[Copyright law] rewards works already created and limits works yet to be created," which is precisely what copyright was supposed to *avoid.* Copyright "rewards the established at the expense of the emerging."[25]

Copyright law is a major growth industry, and fair use, the legally protected space for "purposes such as criticism, comment, news reporting, teaching, . . . scholarship, or research,"[26] is continuously under threat of erosion. Due in part to the diligence of a 1990s rap act, fair-use limitations on the exclusive rights of copyright holders have been upheld — so far. The controversial hip-hop group 2 Live Crew, best known for its hypersexual (many say misogynist) lyrics, won a landmark court case when the U.S. District Court of Appeals deemed that the group's parody of Roy Orbison's "Pretty Woman" was obviously a racially charged spoof and thus made fair use of the original material.[27] Although Vaidhyana-than optimistically describes the 2 Live Crew case as "the case that made America safe for parody,"[28] media law scholar Edward Samuels explains that what constitutes fair use of copyrighted material is, in its legal appli-cation, still very much in play. He likens efforts to quantify fair use to those "magic eye" posters popular in the 1990s, from which, depending on one's focus, very different pictures emerge:

> Fair use was of course codified for the first time in the 1976 Copy-right Act, and one might have expected that the codification would result in a certain amount of clarification and uniformity in the application of the doctrine. However, fair use has remained an elu-sive, if not enigmatic, doctrine. One can stare at the fair use factors described in the statute, and apparently still not know how to bring them into focus in any particular situation.[29]

It is within this shifting and somewhat fuzzy realm of fair use that many activists are struggling over the very meaning of "author," "property," and "public." By defiantly pirating copyrighted or trademarked cultural prop-erty, these activists hope to call attention to the ways in which these cate-gories have served increasingly to deny public access to the imagery and rhetoric that shape public life.

The Ontology of Authorship

Consider the following two statements:

> A person is he, whose words or actions are considered, either as his own, or as representing the words or actions of an other man. When they are considered as his own, then is he called a *Naturall Person:* And when they are considered as representing the words and actions of another, then is he a *Feigned* or *Artificall person.* (Thomas Hobbes, *Leviathan*)

[I do] not consider it as any part of my charge to invent new ideas altogether, and to offer no sentiment which had ever been expressed before. (Thomas Jefferson, to James Madison when charged with plagiarizing the Declaration of Independence)

It is hopefully clear why I might begin a discussion of the relationship between authorship and ontology with the distinction offered by Hobbes in 1660 between "natural" and "artificial" persons. Hobbes's distinction, positioned squarely within his understanding of the integrity of one's *word*, foregrounds the logocentrism that has defined Western conceptions of language and ontology at least since Plato. Hobbes echoes Plato's assumption that the truth value of a claim is judged based on its correspondence to an essential reality (in this case, the identity of the individual speaking subject). One's words are either a true representation of an origin inside oneself, or they are *false* and, in this case, demonstrate the falsity of the very person. In other words, as all good students of the Enlightenment know, one is only as good as his or her word.

It may not be as clear, however, why I might choose to lead this discussion with a quote from Thomas Jefferson, who in this example excuses himself from any imperative to produce original work. Implicitly, it seems, Jefferson is taking a stand on the legitimacy of intellectual property, a "dangerous" tendency he argued against in a variety of venues. Jefferson, like Lincoln after him, was deeply suspicious of the potential degradation of civic life by private interests. For this reason, Jefferson was adamant that the characteristics of property must not be applied to expression. In 1813 he wrote, "If nature has made any one thing less susceptible than all others of exclusive property, it is the action of the thinking power called an idea, which an individual may exclusively possess as long as he keeps it to himself; but the moment it is divulged, it forces itself into the possession of everyone, and the receiver cannot dispose himself of it."[30]

As the comment that opens this section illustrates, Jefferson viewed the invention process as a communal one in which an individual author does not bear the obligation of originality. Intellectual innovation was a *public endeavor*. However, Jefferson's conviction did not exempt him from much criticism on this point. For instance, his political adversaries, most notably John Adams, often sought to undermine Jefferson and his historical legacy by accusing him of plagiarizing the Declaration of Independence.[31] American studies scholar Jay Fliegelman points out that "the attacks on Jefferson all explicitly, in a new mode, identified authorship with originality and the novelty of thought rather than with the act of harmonizing—identified it, that is, with the articulation of one's individual personality rather than one's social nature."[32] As Fliegelman's observation illustrates, Jefferson stood at a crossroads at which Hobbes's notion of the "natural" versus "artificial" person expressed over a century earlier was blossoming in both the civic and artistic values of the New World. Ironically, the Enlightenment, bourgeois virtues that Jefferson so cherished were equally complicit in girding an absolutist category of the author that he adamantly rejected.[33]

For over two millennia, a central concern for rhetorical and political theorists has been to account for language's role in *constructing the human.* At least since the time of Isocrates, rhetoric has been afforded an ontological purpose—that is, it is our ability to cultivate civilizations through the strategic use of language, which supposedly separates humans from "the beasts." The Greek classical tradition did not distinguish between one's public ethos and one's private self; for example, the Athenian ideal of *arête*—excellence, or virtue—was fundamentally civic in nature. Later, the great Roman statesman Cicero argued that a speaker and his or her words were inseparable. During the Renaissance, authorship as we know it began to take root, but it had not yet been codified as it would come to be during the Enlightenment. As Lessig describes it: "The spirit of the times was storytelling, as a society defined itself by the stories it told, and the law had no role in deciding who got to tell what stories."[34] Storytelling was a communal event and, by its very nature, necessitated a vast and free body of archetypes, characters, and narrative threads from which to draw.

What shifted during the Enlightenment is that Westerners began to assume that rhetorical invention emerged from *within* the individual speaker or author. As Fliegelman puts it, during the Enlightenment, "No longer was the ideal of expression rooted in the authority of representativeness, the general will, and historical precedent; it appeared, rather, in the articulation of a sincere *particular will,* in a self-assertion that stigmatized the dissemination of traditional thought as but mechanical duplication."[35] Hence, Jefferson's position that it was not a thinker's responsibility to produce original work "seemed part of an old aesthetic."[36] The new aesthetic, in which creative expression was an articulation of a specific individual's inner workings, became increasingly codified in law over the next two centuries.

Legal scholar Rosemary Coombe, in her book *The Cultural Life of Intellectual Properties,* offers a sophisticated explanation of the most common critique of contemporary copyright and authorship. She writes:

> The law freezes the play of signification by legitimating authorship, deeming meaning to be valued properly redounding to those who "own" the signature or proper name, without regard to the contributions or interests of those others in whose lives it figures. This enables and legitimates practices of cultural authority that attempt to freeze the play of difference (or *différance*) in the public sphere.[37]

Here, Coombe voices a common concern about intellectual property and authorship: it operates ideologically to stop, or freeze, the polysemy inherent to signification itself. As we know, corporations spend more money and talent than ever before crafting their public images. Conventional marketing wisdom tells them it is in their best interest to control, as much as possible, how those images are understood by the public. Yet, as I argue later in this chapter, activists and artists too often assume that corporations are wholesale successful in this project and so, like *Adbusters,* spend much of their time and energy bemoaning the loss of rhetorical freedom.

Coombe herself complicates this assumption that corporations always succeed at "freezing" the playfulness of language, and her book offers a helpful analysis of the relationship between law and appropriation that acknowledges that the "blockages" invoked by the law can be productive as well. In her book, Coombe raises a point I explore further in chapter 5: blockages and obstacles are an intrinsic and valuable part of the invention process. She writes, "Such differentiations in interpretive practices may, however paradoxically, be inadvertently encouraged even as they are explicitly deterred by regimes of intellectual property."[38] As I discussed in chapter 2, it is the very expensive loglo that makes corporate imagery effective as rhetorical content in the first place. And it is copyright, trademark, and patent protections that, at least in part, enable this imagery to be so widely disseminated.

As Coombe suggests, "Law's constitutive or productive power, then, as well as its sanctions and prohibitions must be kept continually in mind."[39] Marketers can never freeze *différance* because *différance* produces the law. And, in turn, the law produces subjects as much as it prohibits them. So ultimately, an author-pirate dichotomy does not seem to hold when we think about artistic appropriation, because the same forces that produce and enable "authors" produce and enable "pirates." With this in mind, like Coombe, I remain equally skeptical of, on the one hand, romantic stories of rebellious pirate artists and, on the other, of omnipotent corporate image-makers wielding the legal system like a weapon against freedom. Both perpetuate an Enlightenment view of authorship that aids the goals of current regimes of intellectual property law. Corporations wield the powerful weapons of copyright and trademark in an attempt to *protect* an Enlightenment notion of discrete authorship, so it may not be helpful to replace one romantic version of author with another. Another powerful and longstanding category of the Enlightenment that, like authorship, mutually supports owners and outlaws is property.

Rhetoric as Property

Typically, an inherent characteristic of ownable property is that it is economically or politically *scarce.* Scarcity does not refer to an abundance or lack of a resource. Rather, as Marx and Rousseau have most famously shown, scarcity means that, absent explicit demarcation, conflicts are bound to arise.[40] This applies to tangible goods such as land, cars, or computers. The material things we own are discrete objects with defined boundaries. They are characterized by economists as "rivalrous" in that two people cannot simultaneously type at one computer or drive one car. Typically, others can share in the exploitation of rivalrous resources only upon agreement with the owner. In the rhetoric concerning the state of intellectual property law, the ill fit between property and ideas is often at the nub of the debate. Consider this oft-cited description from composer and sound-collage artist John Oswald: "If creativity is a field, copyright is the fence."[41] Oswald's comment represents a dominant sentiment of many activists and artists fighting increasingly restrictive intellectual property restrictions — that the laws configuring owned material stifle, limit, and degrade the free flow of rhetorical and artistic invention. Without the "fence" of copyright, Oswald suggests, aspiring rhetors would be at play in a vast and fertile field of creative fodder.

Again, Jefferson is often invoked on this point. Jefferson's dissent from many of his peers on the question of copyright—as his comments cited earlier about the inability to demarcate ideas illustrate—was based on his concern that thought could be turned into property, and that property, unlike thought, could be hoarded. Jefferson was careful to point out that thought and expression do not earn their value through material scarcity: "He who receives an idea from me, receives instruction himself without lessening mine; as he who lights his taper at mine, receives light without darkening me."[42] As Vaidhyanathan tells us, copyright legislation became another "Madisonian compromise, a necessary evil, a limited, artificial monopoly, not to be granted or expanded lightly."[43] Vaidhyanathan notes, however, that even Jefferson's political adversaries did not argue for copyright as property; it was a matter of civic policy. Copyright was a practice that was negotiated between the artist, the public, and the state. The assumption that intellectual works were property and could be passed down from one copyright holder to the next (an ability made possible through several commercially motivated extensions of copyright duration) is a contemporary phenomenon.

Ideas, thoughts, or rhetoric, as Jefferson nicely explains and as appropriation artists remind us, do not operate through scarcity; they act more like fire that grows and intensifies as it spreads. However, corporate brand managers want to have it both ways. On the one hand, they must protect, through legal demarcation, their investment in their symbolic *property*—be it Windows XP, the Nike swoosh, or *Gone with the Wind*. On the other hand, a brand's success depends on its ability to circulate, or catch fire, with the public. Advertisers speak explicitly about the need to dominate the public's "mindshare" as much as possible; that is, to succeed, their brand must insinuate itself into consuming publics' everyday consciousness, in order to make the stuff of our thoughts their property, and vice versa. So, corporations increasingly make it their business to encroach on our public and intellectual space as they extend their brands, media, and products, but they also want to control the ways in which we consume those texts. Colombia law professor Jeremy Waldron explains the tension well, so I will cite him at some length:

If one were to pursue an analogy with real property, one might get the idea . . . that Mickey Mouse was supposed to be the private domain of his creator, analogous to Walt Disney's home or a piece of land that he owned, and that all he was asking was that the courts should compel others to respect the "Keep Out" signs that defined the boundaries of his property. But of course any such analogy would be ludicrous. The whole point of the Mickey Mouse image is that it is thrust out into the cultural world to impinge on the consciousness of all of us.

We see this happening in an attempt of every advertiser to make the brand name of his product "a household word," to so inscribe his intellectual property in the mind of every consumer as to make it a part of their everyday vocabulary . . . it becomes ludicrous to continue insisting on the original proprietor's right to control their use.[44]

As corporate marketers endlessly repeat the images and catchphrases of their brands in the battle to conquer ever more mindshare, they find that this repetition, while perpetuating their brand's recognition, also fosters a breakdown in the structural consistency of the brand's "image." The majority of arguments against copyright do not put faith in that disintegration of brands as they spread; they see them only as a cancer that increasingly contaminates our formerly pristine public spaces. This expanding encroachment of and control by corporations has inspired a variety of activist publics to call for a return to the democratic notion of our shared commonwealth.

Conclusion: The Limitations of an "Art of Theft"

For more than twenty years, Rick Prelinger, a self-described "media archaeologist," has been archiving tens of thousands of cans of film stock—from educational films, to advertisements, to industrial and government footage. The Library of Congress recently acquired his "Prelinger Archives" and they are now available to the public through the library's Motion Picture, Broadcasting, and Recorded Sound Division. Although Prelinger is something of a patron saint for appropriation artists (his "Internet Archive" hosts over one thousand titles available for public use), he has his doubts about the ultimate viability of the practice as effective political strategy: "When we are obliged to defend ourselves against assaults motivated by someone else's agenda, we are fighting for freedom of expression on unfriendly turf, and are unlikely to win what we deserve. It also constrains us into thinking in limited terms, terms that might not necessarily be our own." Hence, he notes, appropriation art is "much more marginalized than it ought to be."[45]

Although appropriation is clearly part of any creative endeavor, Prelinger points out that it is too often framed as radical in the art world. Surely Zora Neale Hurston was right when she said, "Mimicry is an art in itself. If it is not, then all art must fall by the same blow that strikes it down."[46] That is, art *is* the appropriation of that which came before—not a necessarily radical premise. But radicalness has always been a double-edged sword for artistic communities. The appeal of one's art is often directly related to it being perceived as "outside" the mainstream, but its success usually depends on it being embraced by more than a few like-minded fans. Although appropriation art that attempts to call attention to the corporate hoarding of inventional resources has done much to bring public attention to increasing threats to freedom of expression, it may not be up to the task of offering alternatives to the fundamental assumptions that gird intellectual property regimes in the first place. As I have suggested, this may be because too much of the rhetoric meant to oppose intellectual property perpetuates authorship as the domain of an individual auteur, and property as something defined by scarcity. Furthermore, celebrating the role of the rebel-artist continues to assume that publics are things separate from markets, sacred spaces of invention which must stand in opposition to the practices of consumption. Unfortunately, this leaves activists and artists with little more than the subaltern identity of the pirate—who, although free in some senses, most often survives by stealing bits and pieces of property from the kingdom while leaving the monarchy intact.

If we perpetuate romantic notions of rebel auteurs stealing from established corporate authors ideas as *property* that can be hoarded or denied and a nostalgia for an open creative utopia, then a response to juridical restrictions as repressive, ideological, and prohibitive necessarily follows. This leaves publics in a perpetual game of cat and mouse with corporations, who will always have far more lawyers and resources with which to play. This is clearly not a fair game. And while crying "foul" and defiantly breaking the rules of the game without experimenting on one's own may make one feel like a momentary hero, it ultimately makes for frustrating play. The question here is whether a *hero* is needed at all.

I have suggested that the Robin Hood model of stealing from rich corporations and giving to poor publics reinforces the system it seeks to challenge. Perhaps funk legend George Clinton's model is a more viable one? Clinton generously makes his property available to newcomers to use in their projects. He is something of a creative philanthropist who understands that art always experiments with what came before. In effect, he takes stealing out of the equation for those who want to sample his work. As unselfish as Clinton is, however, relying on the occasional individual property owner who is friendly to trespassers is insufficient as well. This kind of hero can only become so *after* he has made his money. Up-and-comers, those who are trying desperately to piece together a livelihood from their creative endeavors, can hardly be expected to be as generous. Indeed, a reliance on generosity ultimately leaves the notion of scarcity unquestioned. We need alternative ways of thinking about intellectual property that do not reinforce notions of individuals fighting over scarce bits of property, even if the occasional individual, like George Clinton, graciously rises above the fray.

Prelinger asks, "What might a different kind of copyright law look like? It's time for us to sit down and work this out, so that we have solutions of our own, something more than simply reactive responses to existing law."[47] The next chapter will foreground another response to the injustices of intellectual property law that has emerged in recent years; one which promotes a communal rather than an individual ethic as it experiments with new ways to distribute and access cultural texts. Rather than simply react against the corporate hoarding of cultural property, Creative Commons augments copyright law in an attempt to intensify the circulation of resources. This response is an important step toward envisioning publics as characterized not by the qualities of property or ownership, but as something far more diffuse and dynamic.

Inventing Publics

Kairos and Intellectual Property Law

It is not a question any longer of appropriating their
instruments, their concepts, their places, or to begrudge
them their position of mastery. . . . Not to take
possession in order to internalize or manipulate,
but rather to dart through and to *"steal/fly."*

— Hélène Cixous, "The Laugh of the Medusa"

To speak is to lie — To live is to collaborate. . . . There are
degrees of lying collaboration and cowardice —
it is precisely a question of regulation.

— William S. Burroughs, *Nova Express*

f the pirate-as-hero model tends to perpetuate (however unwittingly)
the very notion of property and individual authorship it seeks to challenge, then it is worth considering approaches to the consumption-
invention dilemma for which "the public" does not depend on discrete
pieces of cultural turf. One area within humanities scholarship where this
approach is being explored is through a rethinking of the public as less a
Habermasian "sphere" that must be protected from the invasive tentacles
of the marketplace, than as "publics" as multiple and fluctuating bodies
made possible through the circulation of texts. One prominent theorist
of this approach is Michael Warner.

Warner's *Publics and Counterpublics* has been circulating widely through communication and cultural studies scholarship, creating a multiplicity of publics as it does so. Warner's preliminary essay on the subject appeared in *Public Culture* in 2000,[1] and a shorter version appeared in a 2002 issue of the *Quarterly Journal of Speech* as part of a forum of scholars commenting on his work.[2] Before the book even went to press, *Publics and Counterpublics*[3] had begun its process of creating publics. To wit: Warner argues that a public "comes into being only in relation to texts and their circulation."[4] That is, in a kind of reverse engineering of our traditional model of audience, Warner's publics only "exist by virtue of being addressed."[5] In Warner's model, publics do not exist a priori their textual interpolation, before they are called into being by the rhetoric that speaks to them. As such, publics are kinds of "fictions" — albeit fictions with identifiable properties and very real material effects. Publics, as Warner notes, "are queer creatures. You cannot point to them, count them, or look in the eye. You also cannot easily avoid them. They have become an almost natural feature of the social landscape, like pavement."[6] However, as even a cursory read of his argument illustrates, Warner's "publics" are really nothing like pavement. They are, he argues, shaped by the temporality of circulation, an ebb and flow of discourses demanding our attention and building on one another. Indeed, our public rhythms are shaped and punctuated by an endless systolic and diastolic *pulsing* of newspapers, Hollywood films, twenty-four-hour news channels, sitcoms, movies of the week, banner ads, billboards, reality television, presidential debates, novels, fashion magazines, hip-hop videos, porn, blogs, talk radio, bumper stickers, anime, political smear campaigns — the texts of everyday life that constitute the teeming and multicitational field in which publics are made.

What may make Warner's conception of the public so attractive to many contemporary scholars in the humanities is that he augments and nuances the traditional conception of the public sphere we have inherited (sometimes ambivalently) from Jürgen Habermas. As Dilip Parameshwar Gaonkar notes, "Warner draws out a series of conceptual implications with such rigor and insight that they significantly extend and modify our modernist Habermasian understanding of the public sphere."[7] Unlike Habermas's public, a pure, uncontaminated public free from the undue influence of both governmental bureaucracy and commercial enterprise, Warner's public has no clear telos. As Warner suggests, "I don't just speak to you; I speak to the public in a way that enters a cross-citational field of many other people speaking to the public"; hence, one can never predict where a particular public is going. We can only know that it moves in different directions, continually recalibrating in unexpected ways. This messier, dare I say "post-humanist" approach to publics, in Ronald Greene's words, "challenges the assumptions of communication models to explore the idea of a public through its relational understanding of self and other (speaker/audience; sender/receiver) and the norms envisioned for this communicative encounter."[8] If the Habermasian public sphere is a future and idealized space where interlocutors honor universal norms of discourse in the name of a common good, then Warner's is a fluctuating network, a self-reflexive and potentially infinite pattern of texts interpellating subjects in a variety of spaces and times.

At the risk of oversimplification, Habermas, heavily influenced by a Hegelian dialectic, offers a model of the public that is *centrally oriented*. Its goal is the reconciliation, or communion, of self and other. It longs for a space-time in which we can eradicate, or at least suspend, our differences in collective pursuit of a common goal. It is a telos organized around sameness. The appropriate inventional resources in this idealized public sphere are rational and universal norms of communication, including, paradoxically, the mandate that the matters discussed and the form itself be unregulated. He argues, for example, that in this ideal sphere, "citizens behave as a public body when they confer in an unrestricted fashion — that is, with the guarantee of freedom of assembly and association and the freedom to express and publish their opinions — about matters of general interest."[9] Many scholars have challenged Habermas's ideal public as one that superficially foregrounds freedom and communion but has the sublimation of difference written into its very code. Nancy Fraser's well-known critique that his model's failure to attend to the limitations of "actually existing" democracies is inherently masculinist is but one of many such challenges.[10] Although many scholars such as Fraser share Habermas's dream of a deregulated space for open democratic exchange, many reject the universalized and centralized identities such a sphere demands of its participants. The tensions that continue to surround Habermas's model illustrate the difficult challenge of imagining a commons that does not insist on commonality.

Many find Warner's conception of publics and counterpublics to be a productive alternative to Habermas's idealized public sphere. As I have suggested, Warner offers a more complex notion of publics as organic entities called forth and forced to respond to a "concatenation of texts through time."[11] This is a compelling model for scholars interested in public discourses. "Concatenation" gets at the interdependency of the texts that make publics and, hence, complicates models that, like Habermas's, insist upon the separation of certain textual worlds; for example, by keeping at bay the interfering interests of the market or the state.

Despite its fruitfulness, an important gap, or ambiguity, remains in Warner's discussion of publics, which may accommodate readings that ultimately domesticate the novelty of his insights — folding them back into the humanistic framework they seek to problematize. Specifically, if we are going to concede that publics are constituted by the circulation of texts, we need to consider seriously the political economies in which those texts are produced. *How* do they circulate? How does a text come to "be" in a manner that allows circulation? Without examining the conditions from which the texts that supposedly make publics emerge, there may be a temptation to read Warner in such a way that his model is taken as simply a hip analogue to Habermas. Might a reader, for example, see Warner's public as very different and revolutionary, but nevertheless weave a Habermasian call for deregulation into their reading? For example, Warner's metaphors such as "circulation" and "dissemination" might lend themselves to the position that the circulation of texts that constitute publics must be protected from obstructions of any kind. Put simply, one might find in Warner, as in Habermas, support for the position that regulation is the antithesis to healthy and diverse publics.

Through continuing the discussion started in chapter 4 of the debate over the regulatory effects intellectual property law has on the production of texts, I hope to discourage the temptation to conceive publics in this way. One of the most crucial issues facing the circulation of information today is the increased hoarding of intellectual material by the corporate sector. As many scholars and activists have recognized, the centralization of creative resources in the hands of the few is a potentially dangerous and antidemocratic tendency.[12] One might ask, as Kembrew McLeod does, what is the value of citizens' constitutional right to freedom of speech if corporate-sponsored legal restrictions increasingly prohibit public access to the venues and even the content through which to speak? In an age when technologies allow us to disseminate information as never before, corporate owners of intellectual properties — such as literature, film, music, and software code — are radically intensifying their attempts to control the flow and usage of their products and services. In response, a vast movement of activists, lawyers, writers, musicians, academics, and authors has mobilized to fight the extensions and aggressive deployment of copyrights and trademarks. For many, at the heart of the debate is freedom of speech and the capacity to create new and innovative works. At stake for many of those involved are *the possibilities for freedom of expression itself.*

Some who agree with Warner's notion that publics depend on the circulation of texts might see the regime of intellectual property as increasingly threatening the dynamism in which publics thrive. Such persons might be concerned that corporations are taking over the very stuff from which publics are made; that copyright *centralizes* our cultural texts in private hands and cuts off their circulation, enabling them to be hoarded. In this view, intellectual property law in its current state limits the potential of invention and, hence, acts as a tourniquet, stopping the pulses and flows that give publics vitality. Recall, for example, the chilling effect observed by many appropriation artists that the free flow of discourse is becoming frozen and stagnant, that the dynamism on which artistic publics thrive is withering in the current legal climate. From this perspective, our capacity to invent and be invented is in grave danger.

My goal is to help resolve a potentially unproductive impasse in both a Warner-like conception of publics and in the monopolization of intellectual property. I suggest that, as we saw from looking at the rhetorical strategies of activists fighting to maintain a rich public domain of ideas, many activists are fighting for a *deregulation* of the discursive field, for a "lightening" of the burden of intellectual property. Their approach correlates to a reading of Warner that would assume that because circulation is what thriving publics require, the appropriate strategy of resistance ought to be to *lift* regulations that bind them, to decentralize power, and to return to the notion of ideas as *common property.* Toward this end, many anticopyright activists, such as the "appropriation artists" in chapter 4, act as modern-day Robin Hoods, artistically pirating (or hacking) copyrighted and trademarked (that is, *owned*) material in an effort to call attention to corporate monopolies over information and to reinvigorate a sense of "the commons."

As I suggested, the copyright *pirate* model of resistance, despite its good intentions and often productive effects, perpetuates and solidifies the most harmful assumption girding current intellectual property law — that is, that intellectual materials can and should be treated as property. I suggest that the most compelling approach to this problem emerges from a public who may best understand current mechanisms of information circulation and innovation, from a public responsible for the speed and efficiency with which our digital and Internet culture has exploded — software programmers. As I will discuss, the open source software movement — which celebrates a mode of invention based on openness and collaboration, has become a model for some copyright activists. Now activists concerned with the private takeover of *cultural* material are adopting the shareware, peer-to-peer, hacker[13] ethic of open source, deploying it toward cultural production at large. In short, they are hoping to do for content what open source has done for code. The open content advocates I discuss in this chapter, particularly those at the Creative Commons project at Stanford Law School's Center for Internet and Society, demonstrate that successful publics need not function as centralized *or* decentralized networks. Unlike models advocated by other intellectual property activists — those who ostentatiously pirate corporate intellectual property in an effort to make a case for *deregulation* — the Creative Commons sharing model embraces a thoughtful and detailed *increase* in regulations; agreements that emerge in specific and ever-changing encounters between texts, the law, and publics.

I argue, perhaps controversially, that a conception of rhetorical and political innovation based on the classical Greek ideal of *kairos* (rather than property) offers a way of reimagining the public as being made *more* robust, *not less,* by regulations — albeit regulation of a different kind. Kairos, in the sense I propose here, is a rhetorical art for which, in Carolyn R. Miller's words, "the challenge is to invent, within a set of unfolding and unprecedented circumstances, an action (rhetorical or otherwise) that will be understood as uniquely meaningful within those circumstances."[14] My goal is to contribute to the conversation about publics by suggesting that kairos is an inescapable component of text making and, indeed, of public making. In the case of contemporary intellectual property law, this conception encourages responses that improvise on *what is,* rather than mourn a fantasy of *what was.* Ultimately, this chapter argues that strategies seeking to augment or even *intensify* aspects of the current discursive field may yield more innovative rhetorical and political opportunities than opportunities yielded by those whose goal is simply to sabotage (through parody) or appropriate (through pirating).

The Commons

If the controversies surrounding intellectual property discussed in chapter 4 tell us anything, it is that appropriation artists and other copyright activists are concerned about the possibilities for innovation and free expression under our current legal structure. In addition to appropriating, hijacking, and pirating cultural material in an effort to free up inventional resources, many activists are responding by promoting the notion of "the commons" as a space to be protected and nurtured if creative publics are to thrive. The most familiar model of the commons is detailed in David Bollier's *Silent Theft,* a book that outlines the trend toward the privatization of public resources that, for Bollier, includes the infringement of copyright law on the public domains of knowledge and art. Bollier worries we have "lost sight of our heritage as a commonwealth and lost control of our assets, and perhaps our democratic traditions, as private interests have quietly seized the American commons."[15] Duke law professor James Boyle describes this takeover as the "second enclosure movement," referring to the nineteenth-century English enclosure movement, in which common lands were fenced off and turned into private property.[16] What is at stake for Bollier, Boyle, and others who share their concerns is the vitality of the public sphere and its resources, what many in the movement call "the commons." Echoing Habermas's legitimate fears about the monopolizing tendencies of private enterprise, scholars and activists such as Bollier mourn the loss of a free space in which public discourse can thrive.

Keeping in mind the appropriation artists discussed in chapter 4, I return to a question I implied at the start of that chapter: Does the current state of intellectual property law restrict the possibility for rhetorical invention? Are corporations, as McLeod worries, saturating us with their imagery while forbidding us to respond? For the moment, I provisionally concede that yes, intellectual property law is increasingly prohibiting freedoms we have traditionally taken for granted. As Lütticken's comments on the art of theft suggest, appropriation has *always* been an integral component to artistic innovation. Many of our most notable and creative rhetorical texts, from Cicero's *De Oratore* to Jefferson's Declaration of Independence, are novel interpretations of works that came before. Their "authors," to appropriate the words of Sir Isaac Newton, unabashedly stood "on the shoulders of giants" during the invention process. As legendary literary critic Northrop Frye put it, "Poetry can only be made out of other poems; novels out of other novels."[17] Appropriation art is certainly not new, but it is making more politically explicit its suspicions of corporate ownership and monopolization of cultural content in a digital age.

The problems that copyright pirates and appropriation artists identify are quite real and are intensifying through the control mechanisms enabled by digital technology. As Lawrence Lessig reminds us, for example, it used to be that if I bought a book, the majority of things I could do with my book were unregulated. I could read it, sit on it, loan it to a friend, tear it to shreds, or wallpaper my bathroom with its pages. If I quoted from it, of course, I would have to cite it as a source, but that falls under the fair use provisions that protect certain kinds of speech, and I could do so without charge if I were publishing in a nonprofit venue.[18] The only thing that copyright could legally stop me from doing freely was copying and selling for profit the book or parts of it. However, in the digital age, things have radically changed. Our ability to copy and share digital information has exploded. So, however, has the ability of corporations to regulate every use of the material they own. Corporations can, in fact, write virtual stop signs and toll booths into the very code of digital texts. Lessig puts it thus: "Every act [on the Internet] is a copy, which means all of these unregulated uses disappear. Presumptively, everything you do on your machine on the network is a regulated use."[19] Texts can still circulate, but scholars such as Lessig worry that the nature of their circulation (and more importantly, the *publics* this circulation produces) is increasingly and more minutely controlled.

Although these fears are certainly valid, I suggest that the restrictions posed by intellectual property (for my purpose here, primarily copyright and trademark law) are more prohibitive if we accept the notion that intellectual material can *only* be imagined as property. Hence, I argue that the appropriation artists' strategy of "stealing" copyrighted material as an act of subversion is rhetorically productive, but is ultimately too limited. That is, perpetuating romantic notions of anticopyright artists as "pirates" or "Robin Hoods" stealing from monolithic corporate landlords leaves unquestioned the founding premise that ideas are *property* that can be hoarded. The most crucial argumentative terrain is ceded from the start.

The grounding premise of *this* version of the commons is an ironic concession to the concept of scarcity. In this version, the commons are described as a Habermasian ideal public sphere that is being blatantly stolen by private interests. Vaidhyanathan argues, for example, that "the corruptions of copyright have enforced, and been enforced by, the erosions of the public sphere."[20] Similarly, legal scholar Richard Posner, invoking the "marketplace of ideas" metaphor, argues "it is this marketplace, rather than some ultimate reality, that determines the 'truth' of ideas. . . . Such truths as we possess are forged in a competitive process that is distorted if potential competitors — unpopular or repulsive ideas — are forcibly excluded."[21] In other words, he argues that our *nomos*, the communal truths by which we live, are being subjected to the fickle whims of the market. This is an understandable and legitimate fear. The grounds for this fear, however, are exacerbated if we conceive the commons as only a discrete space that can be greedily appropriated by "the powerful" at the expense of "the people."

If we adopt this logic and preserve a nostalgia for an open public, free from government and corporate interference, a response to juridical restrictions as repressive, ideological, and prohibitive necessarily follows. Bollier's position serves as a clear example. He argues: "Any sort of creative endeavor—which is to say, progress—requires an open 'white space' in which experimentation and new construction can take place. There must be the *freedom* to try new things."[22] In *Silent Theft* he describes a private takeover of our commonly shared resources that diminishes our very ability to progress as a culture. Bollier idealizes an open, unregulated terrain for civic invention, unsullied by the interests of Private Enterprise. As he says, "an argument for the commons, then, is an argument for more 'white space.'"[23]

Open Content: A Creative Revolution?

Lessig uses a similar rhetoric to Bollier's to describe the creativity crisis, arguing, for example, that "always and everywhere, free resources have been crucial to innovation and creativity; . . . without them, creativity is crippled."[24] However, Lessig and his colleagues at Stanford Law School's Center for Internet and Society are responding quite differently than the "copyright pirates" I described earlier — specifically by capitalizing on the distributive logic of the Internet.

The commons are, Lessig argues, characterized by the public's access to certain free resources. In his oft-cited lectures on free culture, he offers a four-part refrain that clearly articulates the case against our current copyright culture:

1. Creativity and innovation always build on the past.
2. The past always tries to control the creativity that builds upon it.
2. Free societies enable the future by limiting this power of the past.
4. Ours is less and less a free society.[25]

Like the rhetoric of others concerned with the state of the commons, Lessig's rhetoric mourns a past when publics and the texts that constitute them were freer. However, rather than responding with a call for *less regulation,* Creative Commons, the project he founded, actually *augments* copyright law, offering more specific and nuanced options intended to proliferate cultural texts and people's access to them.

Creative Commons began as a pet project of Lessig's. He and a group of students and colleagues began the project through the Berkman Center for Internet and Society at Harvard University, and it is now housed at the Stanford University Law School and partially funded by the Center for Public Domain. Creative Commons is part of a larger attempt to do for cultural content what open source has done for software. Initially, open source was the norm in software development: code was readily distributed and shared among members of the international programmer community. Most in the industry agree that it is precisely this practical ethic of sharing that has enabled the so-called information revolution thus far. The logic of open source can best be described through Linus's Law, Linux founder Linus Torvalds's famous claim that "given enough eyeballs, all bugs are shallow." That is, making code open and available to users enables software to evolve more rapidly. In programmer Eric Raymond's seminal explication *The Cathedral and the Bazaar,* he compares the two competing models for the debugging of software, and offers perhaps the most influential case for open source. Whereas the "cathedral" describes the proprietary, protectionist model, in which corporations prefer to keep the inner workings of their products a secret from users, the open source model better takes advantage of Linus's Law, as it "resemble[s] a great babbling *bazaar* of differing agendas and approaches."[26]

Open source advocates assert that the *communal* mind of the bazaar, invested in finding and creatively addressing glitches, benefits everyone. Innovation, even if motivated by self-interest, can serve the whole community. Software designers and hackers have long recognized that what made the software industry so efficient and creative in its early years was a pragmatic ethic of information sharing. Even Bill Gates, who made his fortune on proprietary software, has said: "If people had understood how patents would be granted when most of today's ideas were invented and had taken out patents, the industry would be at a complete standstill today."[27] Indeed, the Microsoft empire, like the Disney empire, was built largely on the open appropriation of the creative visions of others. Mickey Mouse, the character formerly known as "Steamboat Willie," was based on Buster Keaton's "Steamboat Bill"; and Microsoft's Windows operating system was based on Apple's user-friendly Macintosh interface. A basic, governing assumption of open source is that sharing is not just more democratic, it is more pragmatic. It is simply more *efficient,* because it takes advantage of communal problem solving. If a programmer puts a program out into the world and allows the source code to be open to its users, they will collectively work out the bugs.[28]

It is easy to see why sharing information through an open distributed network might speed the evolution of software. But can what has worked for software source code work for cultural *content* as well? A variety of activists, lawyers, programmers, artists, and musicians who make up the experimental "open content," or "free culture" movement are asking this question, and others. After all, films, novels, and images do not involve problems to be solved in the same way software does. They are valued in different ways; they "catch fire" as much through pleasure as practicality. As one writer explains:

> What started as a technical debate over the best way to debug computer programs is developing into a political battle over the ownership of knowledge and how it is used, between those who put their faith in the free circulation of ideas and those who prefer to designate them "intellectual property." No one knows what the outcome will be. But in a world of growing opposition to corporate power, restrictive intellectual property rights and globalization, open source is emerging as a possible alternative, a potentially potent means of fighting back.[29]

Borrowing from the open source liberal "copyleft" licensing agreement, open content attempts to free up cultural material — music, images, prose, etc. — so people can share and access it through clearly articulated agreements. For example, Creative Commons, the most prevalent venue, helps artists disseminate their work through a collection of Creative Commons licenses, which allow for easier use for others.

Creative Commons is an attempt to designate a multiplicity of ways to share art, information, images, and music. It makes more complex and detailed the current zero-sum model of intellectual property. The all-or-nothing conventional model is based on rivalry: If it's *mine,* it cannot simultaneously be *yours.* In contrast, the Creative Commons model adds options not predicated on a proprietary binary. As explained at their Web site: "Creative Commons defines the spectrum of possibilities between full copyright — *all rights reserved* — and the public domain — *no rights reserved.* Our licenses help you keep your copyright while inviting certain uses of your work — *a 'some rights reserved' copyright.*"[30] Within this spectrum, one can tailor text-specific licenses by combining four different licensing conditions: "attribution" — a copyright holder can require they be given credit for the portion of their work used; "noncommercial" — a copyright holder can require their work not be used in commercial works without permission; "no derivative works" — allows others to copy and distribute copyrighted material if they agree not to alter it in any way; and "share alike" — one can use copyrighted material only if they agree to make the resulting work available under the same conditions determined by the original Creative Commons license. Copyright holders can combine these conditions in any way they wish, for any project they choose. Creative Commons, or open content, is an attempt to augment the available materials for rhetorical invention — by advocating a public sphere shaped by textually specific permission, rather than by uniform prohibition. Importantly, Creative Commons does not seek to repudiate copyright altogether. Rather, it seeks to make it more nuanced and attentive to specific moments of textual production. As I argue, it promotes a mode of rhetorical invention characterized more by kairos than by property.

The open content movement is an attempt to develop a robust pool of creative resources "donated" by artists, musicians, and filmmakers — a creative commons — from which others can draw for their own work. Both the resources and the process of rhetorical invention are opened up in a way that promotes greater experimentation and, potentially, greater diversity of inventing agents than the current corporate model of cultural production. Following Lessig's assertion that "Creativity and Innovation always build on the past,"[31] these artists, scholars, and activists are trying to make the past a bit more accessible. They do this through localized exchanges in textually specific moments, framed by licenses designed to *open up* the possibilities for rhetorical play, not preclude them.

It is important to distinguish projects like Creative Commons from Bollier's insistence on a pristine "white space" or Oswald's dream of a creative field free from any restrictive legal fencing. Whereas Bollier, Oswald, and the many others who decry the corporate takeover of our public cultural trust fantasize about a chaotic, borderless place unfettered by the regulations of the market, Creative Commons takes markets and regulation quite seriously. The Creative Commons experiment seems to capitalize on those characteristics that make markets so attractive in the first place. For example, markets of a particular character can be good at inspiring production and innovation and at making the most of *opportunities*.

Kairotic Invention: "Propriety" versus "Proprietary"

If we read Warner's publics and counterpublics thesis in a way that recognizes that circulation is not necessarily the dialectical opposite of regulation, then we remain open to the ways in which the intensification of regulatory categories (as exemplified by Creative Commons) can actually *increase* the circulation and vitality of our creative publics. In this section I propose that, for those interested in promoting a robust and democratic commons, the ancient rhetorical concept of kairos serves as a more appropriate rhetorical resource than property. During the golden age of Greece, Phillip Sipiora tells us, kairos was "typically thought of as 'timing,' or the 'right time,' although its use went far beyond temporal reference."[32] Unlike *chronos*, which was associated with linear, quantitative time, kairos was better understood as a moment of a particular *quality*. The word *kairos*, writes Sipiora, "carried a number of meanings . . . including 'symmetry,' 'propriety,' 'occasion,' 'due measure,' 'fitness,' 'tact,' 'decorum,' 'convenience,' 'proportion,' 'fruit,' 'profit,' and 'wise moderation.'"[33] To cite a prevalent example, it is kairos, not chronos, at the heart of this famous passage in Ecclesiastes: "For everything there is a season, and a time for every purpose under heaven: a time to be born and a time to die . . . a time to kill and a time to heal . . . a time to weep and a time to laugh" (Eccles. 3:1–8). The passage was appropriated and reworked into Pete Seeger's and the Byrds' call for "due measure" and restraint during that kairotic moment known as the Vietnam War.

In her essay "Kairotic Encounters," Debra Hawhee notes that rhetorical scholars have traditionally conceived the invention process in two ways.[34] The first imagines invention as "a process of discovery" in which the discerning rhetor simply apprehends existing rhetorical fodder. The second imagines it as "a creative process, emphasizing 'a generative *subjectivity*' in which discursive production depends on the rhetor's ability to produce arguments."[35] As an alternative to these conventional models — which both assume a discrete rhetorical subject who precedes the rhetorical moment — Hawhee, through the concept of kairos, promotes a notion of "invention-in-the-middle." In her analysis of Gorgias's *Encomium of Helen*, Hawhee demonstrates how "in the middle" reconceives the invention process as "'I invent and am invented by myself and others' (in each encounter)." She continues: "The middle, then, at once combines and exceeds the forces of active and passive. In the middle, one invents and is invented, one writes and is written, constitutes and is constituted."[36] A fuller consideration of kairos as a crucial component of rhetorical invention affords a better understanding of the disadvantages of perpetuating universal property metaphors in the debates over intellectual property and freedom of speech. Texts, publics, and rhetors are always in motion, distributing and redistributing across communicative networks. As such, they require legal restraints that enable their movement, rather than restraints that try to stagnate them behind the locked doors of intellectual property holders (to be seen and heard, but not touched).

These kairotic qualities of balance, in-betweenness, and proper proportion are essential to the spirit of Creative Commons and the open content movement in general. It is an ethic concerned more with "propriety" than with the "proprietary." Models ascribing the traits of property to ideas rely more on a sense of chronos, while those inspired by an open source ethic embrace the temporality of kairos. Kairos does not codify time and space through measures of quantity, but through their specific character; their quality. Kairos demands the capacity to strike a balance between this moment and that, to *respond* to a particular occasion in a way that maximizes its possibilities. Similarly, the kind of nuance the open content movement is calling for is not a call for the abolition of intellectual property, but a challenge to its universality. As software programmers have long understood about source code, rhetorical content must be open and accessible enough to be adapted to specific *situations.*

The famed Roman rhetorician Quintilian had it right millennia ago: "If the whole of rhetoric could be thus embodied in *one compact code*, it would be an easy task of little compass: but most rules are liable to be altered by the nature of the case, circumstances of time and place, and by hard necessity itself."[37] Indeed, the space-time promoted by "one size fits all" and "copyright should be forever minus a day" premises of contemporary copyright culture severely misunderstand the nature of rhetorical invention. The collaborative strategies of open source and open content activists enact Quintilian's assertion that rules often require case-by-case calibration. As rhetorical scholars well know, innovation cannot thrive under cookie-cutter conditions. Again, it is important to note that Creative Commons, my example here, does not promote the dismissal of "property" altogether. Rather, they promote a more exacting and nuanced approach to the rules that govern its specific uses.

Malcom Gladwell, writing on copyright and plagiarism for the *New Yorker*, discusses Lessig's charge that "a certain property fundamentalism" has destroyed the sense of balance between the past and the future that has traditionally defined American innovation. Gladwell notes that "the arguments that Lessig has with the hard-core proponents of intellectual property are almost all arguments about *where* and *when* the line should be drawn between the right to copy and the right to protection from copying, not *whether* a line should be drawn."[38] Both property and kairos are characterized by measures of time and space. But whereas property traditionally serves to make discrete a particular product or object for a set amount of time (chronos) and hence freezes both time and space, kairos suggests when and where to draw a line, when to seize and be seized by an opportune moment; and, in the case of collaborative invention, when and where to make the appropriate and prudent connection or contract with another artist.

Under an open content logic, users of cultural materials are encouraged to ask What can *I* do with this? This is not consumption of pre-packaged products waiting docile on supermarket shelves, or passive eyes mesmerized by Spectacular images on a film screen. Rather, open content creates the conditions for invention to become an ongoing and public process. Its direction is somewhat unpredictable, because the lines that feed it and are produced by it are multifarious. Opening up cultural content to collaborative augmentation embraces rather than rejects the viral and distributive character of publics. Publics do not thrive in a white space, or uncodified vacuum. Collaborative projects such as open source and open content offer publics more opportunities to circulate their work — not by lifting obligations, but by providing more ways and opportunities *to oblige one another*. Because Creative Commons propagates regulations that create the conditions for future appropriation, it promotes voluntary obligation and responsibility to one's community, not fear of punitive legal action.

The movement I describe here — whether we call it "open source," "free culture," or "open content" — promotes an alternative to a notion of property defined fundamentally through scarcity and chronos. Through customized agreements that explicitly announce the conditions under which specific texts can be used, Creative Commons offers tools that allow both protection and freedom for artists. Again, this model does not abolish property per se, but it does reconfigure it in ways that allow for more "balance, compromise, and moderation,"[39] values that promote innovation and, indeed, kairos. As the group's mission statement notes: "A single goal unites Creative Commons' current and future projects: to build a layer of reasonable, flexible copyright in the face of increasingly restrictive default rules."[40] Creative Commons rejects the bipolar dialectic that forces us to choose between a culture of total copyright control in which all rights are reserved, and utter anarchy in which artists are exploited and denied their livelihoods. Of course, should a dispute arise, traditional copyright is still in place to protect the artist. A Creative Commons license augments copyright by detailing the conditions under which use is permitted, rather than relying on the simple default of denial.

In essence, Creative Commons offers a model of property based more on *amplification* than scarcity. Opening cultural content through a "flexible layer" of regulatory options augments the possibilities for rhetorical invention. This more kairotic approach to property is achieved not through the wholesale repudiation of property, but through its intensification, its amplification, making it available to others. Erasmus, writing on the subject of amplification, suggested that it was "just like displaying some object for sale first of all through a grill or inside a wrapping, and then unwrapping it and opening it out and displaying it fully to the gaze."[41] Along a similar vein, Creative Commons provides free and easy tools that allow artists to open up their property to the public gaze. Doing so, as Lessig and others argue, lessens the past's grip on the future by "exploding" texts, by amping up their circulation. In other words, whereas traditional copyright offers prefabricated products for the public to consume under a priori conditions and restrictions, an open content approach opens cultural products to a public *process*, by "wrapping" content in a flexible, accessible layer of regulation.

The capacity for public texts to continuously mutate and differentiate enables them to thrive over time. Their "life" depends on the ever-shifting publics they infect, and which in turn infect them. That is, the vitality of texts and publics can best be measured by the degree to which they allow new meanings, codes, and interpretations to adhere to them, rather than by measures of integrity or coherence. The works of Shakespeare, for example, would have certainly withered on the vine many years ago had every instantiation been rendered as faithfully as possible. Although Shakespeare's work is often heralded for its ability to capture certain enduring truths about human nature, its malleability is at least as responsible for its lasting relevance for new generations. Rather than expecting texts to progress through time uncontaminated by new interpretations, circulation depends on textual interruptions and augmentations. Dilip Parameshwar Gaonkar and Elizabeth A. Povinelli state it well:

> If it is no longer viable to look at circulation as a singular or empty space in which things move, it is also no longer viable to reduce a form-sensitive analysis of culture to the captivating dialectics of meaning and its innervation. Translation — the (im)possibility of meaningful commensuration — has long been circulation's double, its enabling twin. And translation and circulation have long been seen as *both the value and the price* of a truly democratic public sphere.[42]

So, in this sense, Warner's use of "circulation" as a diagnostic metaphor is extremely helpful toward conceiving publics as distributed networks. Unlike "progress," which implies a teleological advance toward reconciliation, or "sphere," which demarcates a finite and timeless space, circulation connotes a process predicated on differentiation, a process sensitive to a qualitative and kairotic space-time. However, as Gaonkar and Povinelli suggest, we should be wary of assuming, as some commons advocates do, that circulation depends on "a singular or empty space in which things move." Rather, as I discuss in my concluding comments, circulation is invigorated by a kairotic "response-ability" to a busy and complicated rhetorical field.

Creative Commons licenses deploy a model of rhetorical invention based on kairotic relationships, not on exclusivity. Creative Commons and the open content movement in general are a burgeoning attempt to make the conditions for these kairotic relationships more robust and diverse. In response to the question with which I began — Does the current state of intellectual property law restrict the possibility for rhetorical invention? — most students of rhetoric would likely agree that we can only conclude that, no, rhetorical invention is never denied, because kairos, a key component of invention, can always respond in a specific encounter. It is a skill, a practice, not a discrete object that, like property, works on scarcity. Kairos can neither be owned, nor stolen. As thinkers such as Bollier and Oswald argue, the juridical landscape of copyright and trademark law *is* increasingly difficult to navigate. However, bemoaning the loss of some mythical free past does not do enough to cultivate a rhetorical *responsiveness* to *this* kairotic moment.

A better understanding of rhetoric and public discourse can enrich the debates over the laws fostering and undermining the circulation of texts. The metaphors, or "terministic screens," that govern our daily life *matter*.[43] In this case, it is by attending more specifically to the ways in which textual properties circulate, or can potentially circulate, that I hope to add a level of specificity to Warner's argument. A model in which the circulation of texts that transform subjects into publics is characterized exclusively by "circulation," and "punctuality" may not go far enough toward imagining the potential advantages of, say, *speeding up* the invention process by clearly designating rules for appropriation. Indeed, under our current model, intellectual property holders spend a staggering amount of time and money trying to ensure that every loophole is closed, that the proverbial wall around their property is impenetrable to would-be pirates. Likewise, artists wanting to incorporate fragments from existing culture into their own work must increasingly become amateur legal scholars in order to avoid the often costly penalties for ignorance.

Regarding the temporality of circulation, Warner argues that "the more punctual and abbreviated the circulation, and the more discourse indexes the punctuality of its own circulation, the closer a public stands to politics. At longer rhythms or more continuous flows, action becomes harder to imagine."[44] This dynamic, he suggests, attenuates the political efficacy of academic publishing, which relies on an archival model. Academic conversations, traditionally subject to the tortoise-like circulation of library stacks, are thus distanced from the pace of day-to-day politics. He writes, "In modernity, politics takes much of its character from the temporality of the headline, not the archive."[45] In other words, Warner juxtaposes the day-after-day-after-day temporality of newspapers (and, to a lesser degree, of magazines) to the dusty archival model of academe. Although I take Warner's point, I think an ambiguity remains that may too easily allow a reading in which the corporate control over the pace of this circulation is left uninterrogated.

Even Warner acknowledges that his concept of punctuality may be insufficient in the age of the Internet and digital media: "Highly mediated and highly capitalized forms of circulation are increasingly organized as continuous ('24/7 Instant Access') rather than punctual. At the time of this writing, Web discourse has very little of the citational field that would allow us to speak of discourse unfolding through time."[46] Indeed, given that our public texts are increasingly digitized (i.e., films, images, information, and sound are increasingly rendered in *one medium*), the opportunities for collaboration abound. Sharing is easier and speedier than ever before. Of course, so is the property holder's ability to police the use of digital texts. Although Warner speculates that, under the new digital infrastructure, "it may even be necessary to abandon 'circulation' as an analytic category,"[47] I disagree. Instead, I believe we need to theorize circulation outside of chronological notions of time (e.g., punctuality) and discrete notions space (e.g., conventional property). Chronos and space are framed through the language of scarcity. Because the temporality of the headline serves to *chronicle* events deemed significant by corporate media owners, and the temporality of the archive too easily stagnates ideas, it is worth theorizing the possibilities for the invention of publics that relies neither on the chronicle nor on the archive.

I argue that *distributed* publics, such as those emerging from the open source and open content movements, promote localized interventions and lateral access to texts, rather than centralized control or decentralized chaos. Their model is punctuated, yes, but this punctuation is not necessarily in the service of corporate attempts to control the rhythms of the market. Indeed, as rhetoricians have long known, and as Warner and Hawhee remind us, in "making do," in availing herself of the kairotic moment in which she finds herself, the rhetorical subject is also *produced.* The rhetorical subject is less the *origin* than a coproduct of a rhetorical situation, of a kairotic encounter—caught somewhere between texts and publics. On this point, I want to augment Warner's analysis. While he sees publics as the outcome of the punctuated concatenation of texts, I suggest the process of publics is much less linear. Texts circulate, yes, and call forth subjects and publics as they do. But we must keep in mind that these circulations occur on a much more dispersed terrain than Warner's argument might suggest. Kairotic moments are singular, albeit connected, events; they are not progressive. And we make texts at least as much as they make us.

Conclusion, or What If Rhetorical Invention Worked like a Pinball Machine?

Although appropriation art is a compelling and necessary part of a multilateral attack on the corporate hoarding of cultural resources, it may not go far enough in terms of experimenting with alternative responses. This may in part be because the art of theft, arguing on the ground of "rights," preserves the outdated and inefficient model of property it strives to undermine. Hence, it may unwittingly position publics as fighting for small scraps of property, rather than hastening a reconfiguration of the cultural field itself. Unlike many activists fighting the invasiveness of intellectual property law, I must conclude by arguing that rhetorical innovation is not precluded by intellectual property law, because intellectual property law, at least in part, structures the very cultural terrain over which artists and activists must navigate. So, while it is true that copyright and trademark constitute blockages to which artists and activists must respond, it is unproductive to approach these blockages as *antithetical* to the invention process — as restrictive tourniquets that, if removed, would reinvigorate the free flow of vital resources to atrophied publics. Instead, in this conclusion I argue that blockages and constraints have always been inextricably linked to invention.

I have suggested here that the pirating strategy of "theft," however unwittingly, perpetuates the very notion of property that it rejects. Perhaps more importantly, it celebrates as resistant a quality of discourse — its tendency to quote, appropriate, and steal — that is *inherent* to language's very function. In other words, appropriation is not antithetical to the law; it is mutually constitutive of it. The capacity to quote and play with language has all kinds of political effects, and not all of them are effects Lütticken and other proponents of the "art of theft" would so readily celebrate.

Although I believe that, as students of public discourse, we must support efforts to protect and even expand fair use, as well as a liberal approach to our cultural commons, I am left with many questions in the face of some critiques of copyright. As I have intimated throughout this discussion, I encourage us to be wary of models of rhetorical resistance in which democratic publics are perpetually on the losing side of an endless cat-and-mouse game with the corporate establishment. That is, I am not willing, after this brief exploration of the debate surrounding intellectual property, to merely conclude, "Yes, it stifles creativity." Certainly, corporations invoke and even lobby for laws so they can thwart certain kinds of critique; and it is true that copyright laws were never intended to be used ideologically — to silence political dissent. However, as may always be the case, when some kairotic moments are undermined, others are forgrounded. As Rosemary Coombe aptly notes in *The Cultural Life of Intellectual Properties,* "The imagery of commerce is a rich source for expressive activity."[48] This rich source is available, not despite intellectual property, but at least in part *because of it.*

I began this conclusion with the strange supposition that the field of rhetorical invention may be something akin to a pinball machine. I invoke that image because, in response to Bollier's position that creative progress "requires an open 'white space,'" I want to propose quite the opposite. Just as a pinball would gather no momentum, no speed, no direction without bumpers and pins to respond to, neither is rhetorical invention possible without the constraints and obstacles that define its "kairotic encounters."[49]

With this perhaps juvenile analogy in mind, I would like to return to Oswald's assertion that "if creativity is a field, copyright is the fence." Oswald's description is quite useful, though maybe not in the way he intended (language is funny that way). Intellectual property is not merely a fence that confines and makes discrete a piece of stagnant property — an impermeable boundary along which powerful corporations successfully post their "No trespassing" signs. Rather, it is a fence that gives shape and substance to specific fields of discourse. Importantly, fences can be straddled. They can be climbed under, over, and through. They can be extended, and reconfigured into playful mazes. They can be walked on like a tightrope. Taking advantage of the capacity publics have to move *rhetorically* — deftly negotiating amongst and between available and emerging texts — is a more appropriate way for a democratic society to approach the invention process. As Deleuze and Guattari explain: "*Between* things does not designate the localizable relation going from one thing to the other and back again, but a perpendicular direction, a transversal movement that sweeps one *and* the other away, a stream without beginning or end that undermines its banks and picks up speed in the middle."[50] That ability to walk delicately and precisely, in a state of in between, is precisely what defines kairos, perhaps the most crucial condition for rhetorical invention. As Hawhee reminds us: "The mythical figure Kairos . . . was depicted as a well-muscled wing-footed figure perched on a stick or ball, balancing a set of scales on a razor blade"[51] — almost as if walking along a fence. He is often depicted with winged feet — presumably for those moments when, like a pinball hitting a bumper, he is propelled off in some new and unknown direction, possibly picking up speed in the middle, as Deleuze might have it. Perhaps those of us interested in the possibilities for rhetorical and political invention in this age of increased corporate control of culture might take a cue from the ancient mythical figure of Kairos, who, like the contemporary mythical figure of the Who's Tommy, "plays a mean pinball" because he "plays by intuition"; and perhaps Kairos, like Tommy, knows that invention is about "becom[ing] part of the machine" and learning how to play it.

Conclusion

▌█▌ ▐ ▐▐ ▓▓▓▓▓ ▓▐▓▓▓▓▓ ▐▓ ▐ ▐▐ ▓▓ ▓▐▐

From Private Rights to Common Goods: OurSpace as a
Creative Commons

> Use political practice as an intensifier of thought, and
> analysis as a multiplier of the forms and domains
> for the intervention of political action.
>
> ▌█▌ ▐ ▐▐ ▓▓▓▓▓ ▓▐▓▓▓▓▓ ▐▓ ▐ ▐▐ ▓▓ ▓▐▐
>
> — Michel Foucault, preface to Deleuze and
> Guattari's *Anti-Oedipus*

> To be well wrought, a maxim does not need to
> be corrected. It needs to be developed.
>
> ▌█▌ ▐ ▐▐ ▓▓▓▓▓ ▓▐▓▓▓▓▓ ▐▓ ▐ ▐▐ ▓▓ ▓▐▐
>
> — Isidore Ducasse, aka the Comte du Lautréamont

ow then, should we envision today's "consuming publics"? Has
public life been reduced to little more than a scintillating barrage of lifestyle choices? Are our connections to one another nothing but thin and
fickle demographic categories we might share? Are we just publics who
consume? Or, worse, have the dictates of markets so successfully turned
us into mere consumers that anything like citizenship has been obliterated—rendering "our space" obsolete? That is, has postindustrial capitalism, with its tendency to turn products into brands and brands into the
vernacular of everyday life, *consumed publics*? I have argued that a vision
that casts publics as vulnerable and endangered, as stripped of their vitality by the processes of consumption, is untenable both as a descriptor of
what *is* or as a ground from which to launch meaningful political inter-

vention. This vision, one Foucault would likely describe as "sad and militant," dismisses the many provocative experiments being conducted with and within consumer culture, instead demanding that thoughtful citizens collectively repudiate the abject, dissembling Spectacle. Although I do not want to ignore the often dangerous superficiality and wastefulness that contemporary consumer culture promotes, I contend that any critical analysis that assumes we can neatly extricate ourselves from it is not only foolhardy, but ultimately unproductive as well.

I have tried to suggest that there is a third way we can understand consuming publics, one that is not predicated on a dialectical relationship between publics and markets (a relationship in which publics are perpetually on the losing side of the equation). We might also take our cue from the approach being explored by the open content movement, in which a consuming public is understood as an intensification of or an augmentation of the resources and logics markets can afford. From branding to copyright proliferation, publics that unabashedly lay claim to the agency and tools produced by brand logics may be better situated to intervene in the current economy in interesting and ultimately more democratic ways. By availing themselves of the creativity and innovation that markets can foster, Creative Commons, for example, promotes a vision of the public commons that rejects simple binaries and instead promotes "balance, compromise, and moderation." They do this not by finding some free space outside commercialism, but by "using private rights to create public goods."[1] In important ways, Creative Commons *intensifies* the logics of property and ownership—the sacred cows of the market—and in doing so, potentially transforms the zero-sum absolutist assumptions that have traditionally girded them. An open content perspective understands that publics are everywhere; they are all-consuming. They are not, despite the protectionist stance of many corporations, relegated to tiny and embattled spaces beyond the "No trespassing" signs of commerce, the market's version of the feeble "free-speech zones" allowed to protesters at political conventions.

What I hope to have demonstrated is that the stakes that attend this thinking of the public are extremely high. They involve not only the possibility of a political rejoinder to the logics of late capitalism (logics defined by brand culture), but also the scope of critical engagement with these logics, and, as such, the potential for invention and for intellectual and artistic responses to a society increasingly regulated by the legal dictates of corporate brand identity.

I have explored a variety of strategies through which artists and activists are engaging the commercialization of public life. By loosely categorizing these strategies in terms of "sabotage," "appropriation," and "intensification," I have attempted to highlight the differences between practices that position themselves outside commercial culture and those that more readily embrace the logics of commercialism. I have tried to be careful to acknowledge that I do not necessarily see these strategies as wholly different resistant practices, but rather as different rhetorical "postures." The advertising parodists of *Adbusters*, for example, following the situationists, position themselves as saboteurs *jamming* the corporate image factory through a kind of rhetorical monkey-wrenching. Like the industrial saboteurs of an earlier generation, their work is intended to clog the machinery of contemporary marketing; to pull back the curtain long enough for the public to see the mechanisms creating false consciousness. As I have argued, too often the project of the semiotic saboteur rejects a mode of power that in important ways has already changed into something else. The economic logic driving American (and, arguably, global) culture is no longer only a *disciplinary* one that functions through a rhetoric of denial and exclusion. Therefore, rhetorical saboteurs fail to address the ways in which the rhetoric of commerce itself claims to promote the same values as the saboteurs — difference, rebellion, and democracy.

Parodies, like those deployed on the pages and products of *Adbusters*, work by proposing they are outside the schema they oppose. They are, as such, a dialectic arrangement, but they are a dialectical response that fails to keep up with the times. When the situationists were first carving out a response to the commercialization of their cities and their everyday lives, capitalism offered a different set of surfaces against which to play. Consumption was increasingly the guiding principle of social organization, supplementing labor by transforming laborers into both the mistreated means of production and, simultaneously, the target audience for the goods being produced. The situationists had their share of problems, to be sure, but the successes they had, the successes that so captivate the contemporary subvertiser, were successes that made sense as an appropriate response to the time and economy from which they were generated. When the contours of consumption are formed by the products themselves, a play of meaning can at least be attempted that argues for different contours (psychogeography) or for new ways of traveling the spaces of consumption (détournement). But when those pathways give way to a play of surfaces on which brand identities flash and titillate, perpetuating themselves like viruses that infect context after context, the play of meaning changes substantively, and parody and other modernist models of dérive are no longer appropriate for the situation — in other words, they are no longer kairotic. There can be no outside to this play of branding and surfaces, at least no outside stable enough from which to mount something like a traditional opposition. As I have shown, if the history of brand culture teaches us anything, it is that this myth of the outside, this romanticizing of the cultural rebel, is precisely the trope that best spreads modern brand identity.

Sabotage is, of course, not the only response available to activists, artists, and those concerned with today's consuming publics. Appropriation artists — the pranksters and pirates of chapters 3 and 4 — position themselves more comfortably *within* the marketplace. They *jam with* rather than against the marketplace's instruments in an effort to take it in new directions. Engaging in something like rhetorical jujitsu, these activists study and deploy the logics of commercialism in an effort to use the power of the "beast" against itself. They understand that it is the form, not the content, of brand identity that must be engaged. As such, appropriation strikes me as a strategy that goes farther than sabotage toward the development of new lines of engagement with what Deleuze (and, in different ways, Hardt and Negri) has described as "control society." For example, Deleuze writes that in the information age, "computer piracy and viruses, for example, will replace strikes and what the nineteenth century called 'sabotage' ('clogging' the machinery)."[2] Hacking, as Deleuze anticipates, works from within information industries and is governed by an ethic that does not so much want to shut down those industries as to render them differently.

Unlike the danger of sabotage (the introduction of an external object intended to stop a disciplinary system) in a "control" society, for which the *computer network* is the model of the day, the "passive danger is noise and the active, piracy and viral contamination."[3] The appropriation response, as I have demonstrated, is different from that of sabotage, as it grounds itself in somewhat different ontologies. Appropriation is jamming, not through repudiation, but through *mutation.* To this extent, there seems to be real potential here. But is this promise fulfilled?

In this study, I have pointed to two different strategies of appropriation — appropriation art and pranking. These two strategies have promise, but I believe that in the end, it is a promise that these practices fail to keep. Pranking, for all its logic of diffusion, does little to respond to the proliferation of material conditions that govern brand cultures. A well-pulled prank is satisfying, no doubt, for pranksters and audiences alike, but can moments of "gotcha" pleasure, delighting in seeing at last that the emperor has no clothes, provide the grounds for substantive change? No matter how pronounced or noted the prank, it must remain primarily responsive to the flows of brand identities and corporate persona. Hence, pranking is not up to the task of providing new material, new ways of responding to or amplifying the legal substrates that make brands and markets work in the first place. It can, however, help call our attention to these substrates, an achievement that is not without political value.

It is the inability to forge new ground that prompts my critique of the other form of appropriation — that of the thief or pirate who steals back property for an increasingly frustrated and curtailed public. As I have argued, this model, which emerges from an antipathy to the big-brand, big-business, big-law model of late capitalism, seems promising. It foregrounds the complicated and dangerous trend in which corporations are effectively doing end-runs around publics and the democratic guarantee of freedom of expression. However, by ceding many of the more problematic aspects of this model, it sacrifices too much. Like the prankster, the pirate may unwittingly preserve the categories of property, author, and resistance in ways that continue to legitimate the commercial hoarding of cultural resources. This Robin Hood model of cultural advocacy is certainly more active than that of pranking, but its activism is defined first and foremost by recognizing the cultural hegemony of brand identity and consumption in late capitalism, and then by attempting to seek out new ways of rescuing the public from a dire fate.

As such, appropriation still operates via an oppositional stance, a dialectic between the structures of capitalism and a mythical outside. I believe this stance to be unsustainable, as it is still somewhat reactionary to the conditions in which it finds itself. That is, it is a stance that is insufficient on its own, as it gets stuck in its nay-saying role. Deleuze describes the political subject who is best able to respond to the new economy as one who is distinguished by the flexibility and dexterity to move among a variety of venues. I have argued that political strategies that rely on a dialectical *repudiation* of capitalism hinder from the start their own ability to *respond* to the speed and elasticity of the marketplace. If the market appropriates countercultural rebellion at the rate its critics suggest it does, then a "catch me if you can" avant-gardism seems a tiring and ill-fated game, to say the least. Deleuze likens to a surfer the subject who can better respond to control: "Control man undulates, moving among a continuous range of different orbits. *Surfing* has taken over from all the old *sports*."[4]

This analogy can be incredibly productive in understanding the limitations of appropriation. Sports are often defined by two forces in opposition to each other, a dialectic of sorts. In American football, to cite the most obvious example, two teams push each other out of the way in an effort to acquire more and more territory for their team. Football is a game based on the *scarcity of property*. One football team gains yardage at the expense of the other team. Surfing, on the other hand, is much more organic. The surfer does not *conquer* a wave as a football player conquers territory. For the surfer, the "ground" beneath her feet is not ground at all. It is unstable, it is fluctuating, it is permeable. The surfer succeeds neither by *overcoming* the ocean as if it were an obstacle, nor by appropriating it from another surfer. She succeeds by cultivating a way of being in the world that affords her the capacity to *respond* kairotically to what comes next. A good surfer must know something about wind, tides, ebbs, and flows and how they work together to create waves. She has to know something about her own body and how to position herself in a way that creates both balance and momentum. Surfing is not a dialectical operation; it is something far more fluid.

I play here with Deleuze's metaphor of the surfer because it offers a compelling alternative to both sabotage and appropriation; strategies that, to different degrees, perpetuate an oppositional relationship with their world. I should be clear that I do not mean "surf" in the point-and-click sense, as we might think of Web surfing, a metaphor that has, for many technology thinkers, outlived its usefulness as a descriptor of how we actually interact with Web technologies. I mean surfing — an experimentation with the creative play of shifting and multiple surfaces — as an alternative to dialectical processes that attempt to uncover hidden depths or to consume unknown territories.

In this study, concerned with the future possibilities of conceiving "consuming publics," surfing means reorienting our responses. It means no longer working *against*, but rather working *with*. It means taking the cultural logics of late capitalism so seriously that they begin to undo themselves. It means intensifying rather than negating. In chapter 5, I demonstrated that intensification finds one of its most profound expressions in the renewal of the public that operates under Creative Commons. By advocating for licensure law that makes cultural production easier to control and easier to copyright in a manner that improves the flexibility of artists and activists to share their work, Creative Commons offers a way of using regulations to explode the inventional resources available to the public. Unlike appropriation art, which begins by trying to rescue art from copyright, and in so doing, to rescue the public, Creative Commons offers a way of approaching publics viewed as replete with agency and creative potential, rather than viewed as an anemic body at the mercy of constrictive corporate forces. An open content model may not offer publics the tools with which to comment directly on Disney through, say, a parody of Mickey Mouse. Instead, it provides alternative artistic and political fodder — pooled from the community at large. As such, it displaces Disney's hold on the popular imagination, potentially making Disney, and brands like it, less relevant. Chapter 5 demonstrated the theoretical and critical potential of intensifications like Creative Commons. In support of this, I conclude by briefly noting similar efforts, and their political and critical potential.

Indeed, a number of interesting projects have emerged out of the new flexibility exemplified by Creative Commons licenses. For example, media scholar Douglas Rushkoff, author of *Media Virus!* and *Coercion,* in 2002 experimented with an open source novel, *Exit Strategy.* For one year, he allowed online readers to add their own notes to the text. Rushkoff then released the novel under a copyleft license, and is donating all proceeds to the Free Software Foundation and the Electronic Frontier Foundation. In another example, a number of musicians, including the Beastie Boys and David Byrne, contributed to an open content CD, distributed free with copies of *Wired* magazine and on the Internet and made available for use by the public through Creative Commons' new sampling licenses. As Creative Commons announced on its Web site: "These musicians are saying that true creativity needs to be open, fluid, and alive. When it comes to copyright, they are pro-choice. Here are 16 songs that encourage people to play with their tunes, not just play them."[5] Thanks to a burgeoning open content ethic, the resources and the process of rhetorical invention are opened up in a way that promotes greater experimentation and, potentially, greater diversity of inventing agents than the current corporate model of cultural production.

The Massachusetts Institute of Technology (MIT) has partnered with Creative Commons to create Science Commons, which seeks to "encourage stakeholders to create areas of free access and inquiry using standardized licenses and other means; a 'Science Commons' built out of voluntary private agreements."[6] Its board includes prominent scholars from the sciences, including two Nobel laureates. Following the open source, open content model of defining the "rules of the road" for information sharing, Science Commons works to "open up" scientific publishing, licensing, and databasing. "Uniprot," the world's largest protein database, is among recent databases made available through Science Commons licensure. Although the full effects have yet to be seen, Science Commons has the potential to reinvigorate an ethic of collaborative discovery that has long served scientific progress — an ethic that many would argue has been somewhat stifled by the litigious tendencies of the pharmaceutical behemoths.

Lessig and his colleagues have also experimented with an open source ethic in the production of legal arguments. When Lessig was constructing his case challenging the Sonny Bono Copyright Extension Act, he turned over the case to the Openlaw project at Harvard Law School. He invited law students from Harvard and other schools around the country to help craft arguments in an online forum. As journalist Graham Lawton explains, "Normal law firms write arguments the way commercial software companies write code. Lawyers discuss a case behind closed doors, and although their final product is released in court, the discussions or 'source code' that produced it remain secret."[7] Such a model is sometimes necessary, as many cases benefit from a "surprise" element when an argument is presented in court. However, with cases that provoke strong public interest, open sourcing can be advantageous. As Wendy Selzer, director of the Openlaw project, notes, "The gains are much the same as software. Hundreds of people scrutinize the 'code' for bugs, and make suggestions how to fix it. And people will take underdeveloped parts of the argument, work on them, then patch them in."[8] By turning his case over to the law community at large, Lessig helped to earn a hearing with the Supreme Court for a case that had earlier been deemed unwinnable.

Technological advances — funded in large part by corporate interests — have the potential to explode the possible arenas for open sourcing. For the first time in a long while, despite all the legal chicanery and the rollbacks on fair use, the means of production have evolved into low-cost mutations and are now increasingly in the hands of the public. Blogging, podcasting, and Flash animation, to name a few examples, are among a wide range of technologies that take advantage of the capacity of the Internet to disseminate content. Even the problems with new voting technologies — made painfully evident by the Florida debacle in 2000 — are now being addressed by open source. A handful of groups are now calling for the source code for electronic voting machines to be opened to the public, allowing anyone to critique and debug it. Doing so, advocates argue, would result in a more stable voting architecture, one of the essential components of a functioning democracy. The approach has been used in Australia for a state-level election and it apparently "ran like a well-oiled Chevy."[9] Clive Thompson, writing in the *New York Times Magazine,* argues that the United States needs to consider ending the secrecy surrounding voting machines if we are to avoid the rampant problems our elections have seen thus far. For example, the source code for Diebold, the primary manufacturer of electronic voting machines, has been described as buggy and hackable. The answer, for Thompson and advocates at groups like the Open Voting Consortium and Black Box Voting, is to get rid of for-profit software makers and instead hire a "crack team of programmers" who will take advantage of the "genius of the open source movement."[10]

Rushkoff, in his recent book *Open Source Democracy,* explores the potential of open source intensification on an even larger scale. He makes a case for the value of living interdependently in an increasingly competitive world. This interdependence is made possible in part by the new self-organized communities and dialogues being forged online, by interactive technologies that "could even help us understand autonomy as a collective phenomenon, a shared state that emerges spontaneously and quite naturally when people are allowed to participate actively in their mutual self interest."[11] Indeed, even MySpace, that commodified public owned by none other than Rupert Murdoch, recently served as a site for organizing collective action. In March 2006, tens of thousands of Los Angeles high-school students staged walkouts to protest a California house bill meant to crack down on illegal immigrants. The students reportedly organized the walkouts through text messaging and instant messaging as well as online through the hugely popular MySpace.[12] The *Los Angeles Times* reported that the high-tech community of MySpace allowed students to pull off "an event with surprising speed and dexterity. Planned in mere hours on little sleep, lacking any formal organization, the protests were chaotic and decentralized and organic."[13] This organicism, what Rushkoff calls "autonomy as a collective phenomenon,"[14] is at the heart of the best kind of consuming publics. This collective autonomy is made possible only by imagining publics not as embattled and atrophied, but as fluctuating, pervasive, and full of creative potential; not as bodies defined by opposition, but as interconnected and active agents who strategically navigate the vast resources of commercial culture and make them their own.

Notes

Introduction

1. Since then, MySpace has gone up and down in the overall traffic rankings for English-language Web sites, according to Alexa.com, an Internet-tracking site owned by Amazon.com. At the time of writing, MySpace remained one of the top twenty most-visited sites.

2. Alex Williams, "Do You MySpace?" *New York Times,* Style sec., August 28, 2005.

3. Nielsen//NetRatings, "MySpace Passes eBay, AOL and Google as the Third Most Page Viewed Site Online," *Business Wire,* November 18, 2005, http://www .findarticles.com/p/articles/mi_m0EIN/is_2005_Nov_19/ai_n15862059/pg_1.

4. Caleb Pate, cited in Aidin Vaziri, "There's Room for Everyone on MySpace, from Indie Rockers to Rupert Murdoch," *San Francisco Chronicle,* August 18, 2005.

5. Cited in Williams, "Do You MySpace?"

6. Steve Rosenbush, "Users Crowd into MySpace," *Business Week,* November 15, 2005, http://www.businessweek.com/technology/content/nov2005/tc20051115_908925.htm.

7. Cited in Williams, "Do You MySpace?"

8. Ibid.

9. Cited in Vaziri, "There's Room for Everyone on MySpace."

10. Julie Bosman, "Lesson for Murdoch: Keep the Bloggers Happy," Media Talk, *New York Times,* January 2, 2006, sec. C.

11. Cited in Nicholas Wapshott, "Get Out of MySpace, Bloggers Rage at Murdoch," Media_Internet, *Independent on Sunday,* January 8, 2006.

12. Cited in Bosman, "Lesson for Murdoch."

13. Bosman, "Lesson for Murdoch."

14. Jason Poland, "Murdoch Makes Myspace His Space," *Daily Cougar*, August 9, 2005.

15. Cited in Vaziri, "There's Room for Everyone on MySpace."

16. For a detailed discussion of this phenomenon, see Ruth Shalit, "The Inner Doughboy," *Salon*, March 23, 2000, http://archive.salon.com/media/col/shal/2000/03/23/doughboy/index.html.

17. Jim Walker, "Friending," *Nuvo*, January 25, 2006, http://www.nuvo.net/archive/2006/01/25/friending.html.

18. "MySpace Becomes Big Brand Space," *Adweek*, October 10, 2005, Adweek.com.

19. Saul Hansel, "High Anxiety," Convergence, *New York Times*, January 25, 2006.

20. Ibid.

21. Cited in Kris Oser and Abbey Klaassen, "Rupert Murdoch Wants His MySpace.com," *Advertising Age*, October 10, 2005, 3.

22. Ibid.

23. Kris Oser, "MySpace.com; Jamie Kantrowitz," *Advertising Age*, November 7, 2005, S16.

24. Naomi Klein, *No Logo: Taking Aim at the Brand Bullies* (New York: Picador, 2000), 3.

25. Ibid., 4.

26. Joseph Heath and Andrew Potter, *Nation of Rebels: Why Counterculture Became Consumer Culture* (New York: Harper Collins, 2004), 6.

27. Herbert Muschamp, "Seductive Objects," *New York Times*, July 2, 1999.

28. Abe Novick, "Time for the USA to Take Its Loftier Message to the World," Letter to the Editor, *Financial Times*, U.S. edition, October 31, 2001.

29. I want to acknowledge a limitation to this line of reasoning. Although I'm primarily focusing on controversies surrounding branding and advertising, I want to be careful not to afford branding more political import than it's due. That is, many corporations that are affecting, say, the environment, labor power, or national sovereignty, do not (perhaps purposely so) have high-profile brand identities. Although more and more corporations see the need for brand recognition, many powerful companies remain under the radar of the average consumer. See, for example, Monsanto, a biotech firm that has had a huge impact on global farming but is relatively unknown to the general public.

30. Thomas Petzinger Jr., "So Long, Supply and Demand," *Wall Street Journal*, January 3, 2000.

31. James MacKinnon, "Brand America," *San Francisco Chronicle*, January 27, 2003.

32. Cited in Tom Mashberg, "War on Terrorism; America Promises to Be a Hard Sell to Many Muslims," *Boston Herald*, November 11, 2001.

33. Cited in Martin Fletcher, "Publicity Queen Sells America to Muslims," *Times* (London), October 16, 2001.

34. Elisabeth Bumiller, "Bush Aides Set Strategy to Sell Policy on Iraq," *New York Times*, September 7, 2002.

35. Despite the fact that, as I write, Bush's dismal approval ratings remain stuck in the low thirties.

36. Mark Dery, "Culture Jamming: Hacking, Slashing, and Sniping in the Empire of Signs," Pyrotechnic Insanitarium, http://www.levity.com/markdery/culturjam.html.

37. Dery, "Culture Jamming."

38. Cited in Dery, "Culture Jamming."

39. Gareth Branwyn, *Jamming the Media: A Citizen's Guide* (San Francisco: Chronicle Books, 1997), 16.

40. Kalle Lasn, *Culture Jam: The Uncooling of America* (New York: Eagle Brook, 1999), xi.

41. Cited in Bob Paquin, "E-Guerrillas in the Midst," *Ottawa Citizen*, http://www.zmag.org/Bulletins/e_guerrilas.htm.

42. Gilles Deleuze, *Negotiations* (New York: Columbia University Press, 1990), 174.

43. Lasn, *Culture Jam*, 128.

44. Michael Hardt and Antonio Negri, *Empire* (Cambridge, Mass.: Harvard University Press, 2000).

45. As one of the more stark examples, see the launch of "State of Emergency," a Sony Playstation game in which gamers become antiglobalization activists battling the evil "American Trade Organization" in an unnamed U.S. city.

1. Detours and Drifts

Epigraph. The graffiti was documented in Bernard Edward Brown, *Protest in Paris: Anatomy of a Revolt* (Morristown, N.J.: General Learning Press, 1974), 89.

1. See Greil Marcus, *Lipstick Traces: A Secret History of the Twentieth Century* (Cambridge, Mass.: Harvard University Press, 1990), 340.

2. The complete leaflet is cited, among other places, in Marcus, *Lipstick Traces*, 340–41.

3. Serge Berna, Guy-Ernest Debord, Jean-L. Brau, and Gil J. Wolman.

4. Marcus, *Lipstick Traces*, 341.

5. Ibid., 343.

6. Branwyn, *Jamming the Media*, 23.

7. Lasn, *Culture Jam*, 101.

8. Steven Best and Douglas Kellner, "Debord, Cybersituationists, and the Interactive Spectacle," *Substance: A Review of Theory and Literary Criticism* 90 (1999): 131.

9. Guy Debord, *The Society of the Spectacle* (Detroit: Black and Red Press, 1983), aphorism 17. Emphases in original.

10. Mark Frauenfelder, Carla Sinclair, and Gareth Branwyn, eds., *The Happy Mutant Handbook* (New York: Riverhead Trade, 1995).

11. See, for example, Web sites such as Nothingness.org (http://www.nothingness.org/SI/); Bureau of Public Secrets (http://www.bopsecrets.org/); and Situationist International Online (http://members.optusnet.com.au/~rkeehan/).

Each site has extensive links to a variety of international situationist interest groups and Web sites. See also, recent anthologies of SI writings; for example, Thomas F. McDonough, ed., *Guy Debord and the Situationist International: Texts and Documents* (Boston: MIT Press, 2004); and Dark Star Collective, eds., *Beneath the Paving Stones: Situationists and the Beach, May 1968* (San Francisco: AK Press, 2001). And recent histories, including Roberto Ohrt, *Phantom Avant-Garde: A History of the Situationist International and Modern Art* (New York: Lukas and Sternberg, 2005); and Simon Ford, *The Situationist International: An Introduction* (London: Black Dog Press, 2005). See also, Debord biographies such as Anselm Jappe, *Guy Debord* (Berkeley: University of California Press, 1999); and Vincent Kaufmann, *Guy Debord: Revolution in the Service of Poetry,* translated by Robert Bononno (Minneapolis: University of Minnesota Press, 2006).

12. Cited in Brown, *Protest in Paris,* 4.

13. Ibid.

14. Andrew Feenberg and Jim Freedman, *When Poetry Ruled the Streets: The French May Events of 1968* (New York: State University of New York Press, 2001), 3.

15. Feenberg and Freedman, *When Poetry Ruled the Streets,* 3.

16. Brown, *Protest in Paris,* 89.

17. Marcus, *Lipstick Traces,* 49. Marcus traces the influence of the situationists on the punk movement—the Sex Pistols in particular—in this excellent book.

18. Brown, *Protest in Paris,* 89–90.

19. Ibid., 93.

20. Ibid., 99.

21. Ibid., 99.

22. From this point on, *IS* will refer to the journal *Internationale Situationniste* and a variety of other main situationist texts compiled in Ken Knabb, ed., *Situationist International Anthology* (Berkeley: Bureau of Public Secrets, 1981). SI refers to the group itself.

23. Lasn, *Culture Jam,* 108.

24. Simon Sadler, *The Situationist City* (Cambridge, Mass.: MIT Press, 1999).

25. Ibid., 17.

26. Knabb, ed., *Situationist International Anthology,* 55.

27. Best and Kellner, "Debord, Cybersituationists, and the Interactive Spectacle," 148.

28. Lasn, *Culture Jam,* 103.

29. However, the self-described "neo-situationists" at *Adbusters,* whom I will discuss in chapter 2, are much less ambiguous. The intended message of their ad parodies is always relatively clear.

30. Knabb, ed., *Situationist International Anthology,* 10.

31. Kenneth Burke, *Attitudes toward History* (Berkeley: University of California Press, 1984), 308–11.

32. Knabb, ed., *Situationist International Anthology,* 10.

33. Ibid.

34. Ibid.

35. Ibid., 11.

36. Ibid.

37. Ibid.

38. Ibid., 324.

39. For an excellent analysis of situationist architectural theory, see Sadler, *The Situationist City*.

40. Cited in Sadler, *The Situationist City*, 52.

41. Branwyn, *Jamming the Media*, 24.

42. Knabb, ed. *Situationist International Anthology*, 147. Emphasis in original.

43. Knabb, ed., *Situationist International Anthology*, 175. Godard himself said, "You know, I more or less agree with the situationists; they say that it's all finally integrated; it gets integrated in spectacle, it's all spectacle" (from a March 1969 newsreel interview documented at Ken Knabb's Bureau of Public Secrets Web site [http://listserv.cddc.vt.edu/Mirrors/SI/blindmen81.htm]). However, Godard took a different tactical response than SI. He acknowledged the inevitability of avant-garde work being appropriated by the Spectacle. Thus, rather than fighting for a place outside Spectacle, he sought to take the Spectacle in different directions. This tactic meant that avant-garde work must participate in rather than eschew (e.g., Godard's experiments with mise-en-scène).

44. Cited in Knabb, ed., *Situationist International Anthology*, 9.

45. Michel Foucault, *The Archeology of Knowledge*, translated by A. M. Sheridan Smith (New York: Pantheon Books, 1972), 235.

46. Anselm Jappe, *Guy Debord*, translated by Donald Nicholson-Smith (Berkeley: University of California Press, 1999), 118.

47. Knabb, ed., *Situationist International Anthology*, 45.

48. Ibid., 50.

49. Lasn, *Culture Jam*, 103.

50. André Breton, *Manifestoes of Surrealism*, translated by Richard Seaver and Helen R. Lane (Ann Arbor: University of Michigan Press, 1969).

51. Guy Debord, "Theory of *Dérive*," in Knabb, ed., *Situationist International Anthology*, 50.

52. I should pause here and note that SI did not discuss the notion of brands, per se. Although their political target was the false promises of the market as Spectacle, the group's heyday predated the level of branding that is so familiar to us today.

53. Cited in Knabb, ed., *Situationist International Anthology*, 50.

54. Debord, *The Society of the Spectacle*, 7.

55. Michel de Certeau, *The Practice of Everyday Life*, translated by Steven Rendall (Berkeley: University of California Press, 1988), 92–93.

56. De Certeau, *The Practice of Everyday Life*, 93.

57. Cited in Knabb, ed., *Situationist International Anthology*, 4.

58. Sadler, *The Situationist City*, 15.

59. Denis Cosgrove, "Maps, Mapping, Modernity: Art and Cartography in the Twentieth Century," *Imago Mundi* 57, no. 1 (February 2005): 35–54.

60. Cited in Sadler, *The Situationist City*, 83.

61. Ronnie Scott, "Pure Dead Magic: Glasgow's Enchanted Landscapes," *eSharp* 1 (Autumn 2003), http://www.sharp.arts.gla.ac.uk/issue1/scott.htm.

62. Sadler, *The Situationist City*, 77.

63. Stuart Ewen offers an excellent analysis of this phenomenon in *Captains of Consciousness* (New York: Basic Books, 2001).

64. The posters were produced by Paris art students who seized a university lithograph studio and distributed the posters anonymously and for free. They were posted on barricades and buildings throughout Paris in spring 1968. In a statement, the Atelier Populaire (Popular Workshop) insisted on the political role of the images: "The posters produced by the ATELIER POPULAIRE are weapons in the service of the struggle and are an inseparable part of it. Their rightful place is in the centers of conflict, that is to say, in the streets and on the walls of the factories. To use them for decorative purposes, to display them in bourgeois places of culture or to consider them as objects of aesthetic interest is to impair both their function and their effect. This is why the ATELIER POPULAIRE has always refused to put them on sale. Even to keep them as historical evidence of a certain stage in the struggle is a betrayal, for the struggle itself is of such primary importance that the position of an 'outside' observer is a fiction which inevitably plays into the hands of the ruling class. That is why these works should not be taken as the final outcome of an experience, but as an inducement for finding, through contact with the masses, new levels of action, both on the cultural and the political plane." For more information, see Mark Vallen's essay "Demand the Impossible" at http://www.art-for-a-change.com/Paris/paris.html.

65. Cited in Brown, *Protest in Paris*, 94.

66. Brown, *Protest in Paris*, 95.

67. Cited in Jappe, *Guy Debord*, 108.

2. Anti-Logos

1. *Adbusters*, "Blackspot," http://www.blackspotsneaker.html (accessed January 21, 2004).

2. Ibid.

3. Rob Walker, "Going after Nike," *Inc. Magazine*, October 2004, 124.

4. A popular slogan of Situationist International was "sous les paves, la plage!" (Under the paving stones, the beach!), indicating the natural terrain just beneath the surface of the city. See Dark Star Collective, eds., *Beneath the Paving Stones: Situationists and the Beach, May 1968*.

5. Lasn, *Culture Jam*, 24–25.

6. Ibid., 27.

7. Cited in Lasn, *Culture Jam*, 24.

8. Immediast Underground, *Seizing the Media*, Immediast Underground Pamphlet Series, http://deoxy.org/seize_it.htm. Emphasis added.

9. Ralph Nader, "Acceptance Speech for the Association of State Green Parties Nomination for President of the United States," http://www.c-span.org/campaign/2000/greenparty.asp (accessed September 27, 2000). For a more detailed

discussion of Nader's campaign and his rhetoric of purity and contamination, see my essay "The Green Virus: Purity and Contamination in Ralph Nader's 2000 Presidential Campaign," *Rhetoric and Public Affairs* 4 (Winter 2001): 581–603.

10. Lasn, *Culture Jam*, 11.

11. Ibid., xvii.

12. Cited in Lasn, *Culture Jam*, 32. Lasn also cites responses he received from other network executives: ABC New York's Art Moore: "There's no law that says we have to air anything—we'll decide what we want to air or not." CBS's Libby Hawkins: "I dare you to get any station manager in this town to air your message." CBS Boston's public affairs manager Donald Lowery: "We don't sell airtime for issue ads because that would allow people with the financial resources to control public policy." And, finally, NBC's Richard Gitter: "We don't want to take any advertising that's inimical to our legitimate business interests."

13. Carey Goldberg, "'Buy Nothings' Discover a Cure for Affluenza," *New York Times*, November 29, 1997.

14. Ibid.

15. Ibid.

16. Cited in *Adbusters*, "Buy Nothing Day," http://adbusters.org/campaigns/bnd/ (accessed November 20, 2002).

17. Klein, *No Logo*, 7.

18. Ibid., 8.

19. Ibid., 21.

20. Ewen, *Captains of Consciousness*, 1.

21. Cited in James B. Twitchell, *AdcultUSA: The Triumph of Advertising in American Culture* (New York: Columbia University Press, 1996), 193.

22. William Harmon, *A Handbook to Literature*, 10th ed. (New York: Prentice Hall, 2005).

23. Robert Phiddian, "Are Parody and Deconstruction Secretly the Same Thing?" *New Literary History* 28, no. 4 (1997): 681.

24. Ibid., 682.

25. Klein, *No Logo*, 348.

26. Ibid.

27. Ibid., 349.

28. Ibid., 282.

29. As legal scholar Rosemary Coombe explains, "Joe Camel came under scrutiny by the Clinton government in August 1996 when it ordered the Food and Drug Administration to introduce regulations that would curb underage smoking. As Clinton proclaimed, 'With this historic action that we are taking today, Joe Camel and the Marlboro Man will be out of our children's reach forever.'" Rosemary Coombe, *The Cultural Life of Intellectual Properties: Authorship, Appropriation, and the Law* (Durham: Duke University Press, 1998), 329, n. 152.

30. "Clinton Decries 'Heroin Chic' Fashion Look," CNN.com, December 1, 2000, http://www.cnn.com/ALLPOLITICS/1997/05/21/Clinton.Mayors/.

31. For more on heroin chic, see my essay "Tracking Heroin Chic: The Abject Body Reconfigures the Rational Argument," *Argumentation and Advocacy* 36 (Fall 1999): 65–76.

32. Robert Vida, "Fashion's Addiction," *Baltimore Sun,* May 29, 1997.

33. *Adbusters,* http://www.adbusters.com, October 19, 2002.

34. *Culture Jammers Video,* VHS (Vancouver, BC, Canada: Media Foundation).

35. Jean Kilbourne, *Killing Us Softly 3: Advertising's Image of Women,* VHS, directed by Sut Jhally (Northampton, Mass.: Media Education Foundation, 2000).

36. Examples include: A post by a subscriber to Chickknits.com read: "WAITWAITWAIT!!! What the f——!?! Is Harrison Ford dating Calista 'Feed Me!' Flockhart?? Please tell me it isn't true" (http://www.chicknits.com/ktalk/1019312209,95106,.html, accessed October 21, 2002). In the article "Us vs. Them" on the feminist e-zine *Genuine Article:* "On lonely Friday nights, my room-mate and I used to like to watch *Dateline,* every time Maria Shriver came on, we'd screech, 'Feed me!' Celine Dion was another favorite target of ours, 'Nour-rissez moi?'" (http://pages.ivillage.com/brookefinnigan2001/genuinearticleezine/id7.html, accessed October 21, 2002). Numerous blogs commenting on Nicole Richie and Lindsay Lohan feature the caption "Feed me!" See, for examples, http://popsugar.com/493 and http://conversationsfamouspeople.blogspot.com/2005/08/nicole-richie-feed-me.html.

37. Klein, *No Logo,* 286.

38. *Adbusters,* http://adbusters.org/uncommercials/obsession/ (accessed October 19, 2002).

39. Ibid.

40. Ibid.

41. Joe Friesen, "*Adbusters* Suing Networks for Not Airing Its TV Spots," *Globe and Mail,* September 15, 2004.

42. Jim Motavalli, "Cultural Jammin': The Media Foundation Uses Guerilla Tactics against Advertising Excess," *E-Magazine,* May–June 1996, http://www.emagazine.com/view/?604 (accessed October 21, 2002).

43. Cited in Jonathon Curiel, "Graphic Breast Cancer Ads Taken Down," *San Francisco Chronicle,* January 29, 2000.

44. Ibid.

45. Ibid.

46. Cited in Kim Curtis, "Breast-Cancer Ad Models in Lingerie — and Scars," *Sacramento Bee,* January 27, 2000.

47. Ibid.

48. Cited in Curiel, "A Sight to Shock."

49. Cited in Rachel Pinsky and Lisa Miya-Jervis, "Our Bodies, Our Bus Shelters," *Bitch: Feminist Response to Pop Culture* 12 (Summer 2000), 13.

50. Pinsky and Miya-Jervis, "Our Bodies, Our Bus Shelters," 13.

51. Curiel, "Graphic Breast Cancer Ads Taken Down."

52. Ruth Rosen, "Lack of Treatment, Not Ads, Is What's Obscene," *San Francisco Chronicle,* February 7, 2000.

53. Deleuze, *Negotiations,* 180.

54. *Merriam-Webster's Collegiate Dictionary,* 10th ed. (Springfield, Mass.: Merriam-Webster, 1993).

55. For more on this topic, see Kevin Michael Deluca, *Image Politics: The New Rhetoric of Environmental Activism* (New York: Guilford Press, 1999), 5.

56. Bryan Denson, "Biotech Sabotage Hits Oregon Company," *Oregonian*, June 6, 2000, http://www.oregonlive.com:80/news/oregonian/index.ssf?/news/oregonian/00/06/nw_31grass06.frame.

57. Kevin DeLuca and Jennifer Peeples, "From Public Sphere to Public Screen: Democracy, Activism, and the 'Violence' of Seattle," *Critical Studies in Media Communication* 19, n. 2 (June 2002): 125–51.

58. William Gibson, *Pattern Recognition* (New York: Putnam, 2003), 69. Emphasis added.

59. James MacKinnon, "First We Take Seattle," *Adbusters*, http://www.adbusters.org/campaigns/question/toolbox/seattleupdate/battle1.html.

60. Deleuze, *Negotiations*, 181.

61. Stuart Ewen, *All Consuming Images: The Politics of Style in Contemporary Culture* (New York: Basic Books, 1999), xvi.

62. I want to acknowledge that I borrow this insight from the wise Jeff Nealon.

63. Deleuze, *Negotiations*, 181.

64. Lasn, *Culture Jam*, 128.

65. From the "Culture Jammer's Manifesto." Available in Lasn, *Culture Jam*.

66. *Adbusters* 33, Letters sec., January–February 2001, 10.

67. Ibid.

68. Carrie McClaren, "Culture Jamming™: Brought to You by Adbusters," *Stay Free!* http://www.stayfreemagazine.org/9/adbusters.htm.

69. Ibid.

70. Ibid.

71. Negativland, *Over the Edge, Vol. 1: Jamcon '84* (ElCerrito, Calif.: SST/Seeland, 1985).

72. Mark Hosler, in discussion with the author, November 2002, New York University.

73. Klein, *No Logo*, 293.

74. Cited in Klein, *No Logo*, 295.

75. Sven Lütticken, "The Art of Theft," *New Left Review* 13 (January–February 2002): 97.

76. Lasn, *Culture Jam*, xi.

77. Lütticken, "The Art of Theft," 97.

78. Ibid., 97.

79. Ibid., 98–99.

80. Jeffrey T. Nealon, *Double Reading: Postmodernism after Deconstruction* (New York: Cornell University Press, 1993), 29. Emphases in original.

81. Ibid., 30

82. Ibid.

83. Michel Foucault, "Nietzsche, Genealogy, History," in *Language, Counter-Memory, Practice: Selected Essays and Interviews*, edited by Donald F. Bouchard (Ithaca, N.Y.: Cornell University Press, 1977), 142.

84. Herbert Muschamp, "Seductive Objects with a Sly Sting," *New York Times*, July 2, 1999.

85. Michael Hardt and Antonio Negri, *Empire* (Cambridge, Mass.: Harvard University Press, 2000), xv.

86. Randy Rucker, "Logomancer: William Gibson Forgets Virtual Reality and Takes a Wild Ride through the Hyperreal," *Wired*, February 2003, 64.

87. Thomas Frank, "Why Johnny Can't Dissent," in *Commodify Your Dissent: Salvos from the Baffler*, edited by Thomas Frank and Matt Weiland (New York: Norton, 1997), 34.

88. Gary Groth, "A Dream of Perfect Reception: The Movies of Quentin Tarantino," in Frank and Weiland, eds., *Commodify Your Dissent*, 183.

89. Frank, "Why Johnny Can't Dissent," 36–37.

90. Thomas Frank, *The Conquest of Cool: Business Culture, Counterculture, and the Rise of Hip Consumerism* (Chicago: University of Chicago Press, 1997), x.

91. Dick Hebdige, *Subculture: The Meaning of Style* (London: Methuen, 1979).

92. See, for example, three books by John Fiske: *Understanding Popular Culture* (New York: Routledge, 1989); *Media Matters: Race and Gender in U.S. Politics* (Minneapolis: University of Minnesota Press, 1996); and *Reading the Popular* (New York: Routledge, 1989).

93. Camille Paglia, "Madonna—Finally, A Real Feminist," *New York Times*, December 14, 1990.

94. Frank, "Why Johnny Can't Dissent," 38.

95. Ibid., 153.

96. Ibid., 37.

97. Peter Stallybrass and Allon White, *The Politics and Poetics of Transgression* (Ithaca: Cornell University Press, 1986).

98. Tom Peters, *Thriving on Chaos: Handbook for a Management Revolution* (New York: Knopf, 1987).

99. Carrie McLaren, "Radio Free Clear Channel," *Stay Free!* http://blog.stayfreemagazine.org/2005/05/radio_free_clea.html.

100. Robert Levine, "That Rebellious Voice Is No Pirate After All," business sec., *New York Times*, May 30, 2005.

101. Westhill Partners, http://www.westhillmarketingsciences.com/ (accessed January 2001). Emphasis added.

102. Frank and Weiland, eds., *Commodify Your Dissent*, 161.

103. Frank, *The Conquest of Cool*, x.

104. Hakim Bey, *The Temporary Autonomous Zone: Ontological Anarchy, Poetic Terrorism (1991)*, http://www.t0.or.at/hakimbey/taz/taz.htm.

105. Fredric Jameson, *Postmodernism, or, the Cultural Logic of Late Capitalism* (Durham: Duke University Press, 1991), 16.

106. Ibid., 17. Emphasis added.

107. Ibid., 18.

108. Gibson, *Pattern Recognition*.

109. Joseph Heath and Andrew Potter, *Nation of Rebels: Why Counterculture Became Consumer Culture.* New York: Harper Collins, 2004, 4.

110. Ibid.

Intermezzo

1. Frank, "Why Johnny Can't Dissent," 44.

3. Pranks, Rumors, Hoaxes

1. Friedrich Nietzsche, *On the Genealogy of Morals and Ecce Homo,* translated by Walter Kaufmann (New York: Vintage, 1989), 160. Emphasis in the original.

2. Michel Foucault, preface to *Anti-Oedipus: Capitalism and Schizophrenia,* by Gilles Deleuze and Félix Guattari (Minneapolis: University of Minnesota Press, 2000), xiv. Emphasis added. Foucault is here interpreting the themes of Delueze and Guattari's book.

3. Cited in V. Vale and Andrea Juno, eds., *Pranks!* (San Francisco: RE-Search, 1987), 36.

4. Kevin Michael Deluca, *Image Politics: The New Rhetoric of Environmental Activism* (New York: Guilford Press, 1999).

5. Vale and Juno, *Pranks!* 39.

6. Ibid., 40.

7. Ibid., 40–41.

8. Ibid.

9. Vale and Juno, "Quotations," in *Pranks!* no page number.

10. Vale and Juno, *Pranks!*

11. *Merriam-Webster's Collegiate Dictionary,* 10th ed.

12. Cited in Frauenfelder, et al., eds., *The Happy Mutant Handbook,* 40–41.

13. Ibid., 41.

14. Sniggle.net, "The Culture Jammer's Encyclopedia," http://www.sniggle.net/barbie.php (accessed February 18, 2003).

15. Ibid.

16. Brigitte Greenberg, "The BLO — Barbie Liberation Organization — Strikes," *Unit Circle,* http://www.etext.org/Zines/UnitCircle/uc3/page10.html (accessed October 12, 2006).

17. Ibid.

18. Cited in Mark Dery, "Hacking Barbie's Voice Box: 'Vengeance Is Mine!'" *New Media,* May 1994.

19. Ibid.

20. Cited in Virginia Eubanks, *Brillomag,* "Hacking Barbie with the Barbie Liberation Organization," http://www.brillomag.net/No1/blo.htm (accessed October 12, 2006).

21. Sniggle.net, "The Culture Jammer's Encyclopedia": http://www.sniggle.net/barbie.php, retrieved February 18, 2003.

22. Greenberg, "The BLO — Barbie Liberation Organization — Strikes."

23. Ibid.

24. Ibid.

25. Wayne Slater, "Bush Criticizes Web Site as Malicious," *Dallas Morning News,* May 22, 1999.

26. Rtmark, http://www.rtmark.com/ (accessed April 1, 2003).

27. Ibid. (accessed February 5, 2005).

28. Cited in Ian Walker, "B Is for . . . ," in *How to Make Trouble and Influence People,* http://www.abc.net.au/arts/headspace/rn/bbing/trouble/b.htm (accessed October 15, 2006).

29. Ibid.

30. Barbie Disinformation Organization, http://www-2.cs.cmu.edu/afs/cs/user/jthomas/SurReview/reviews-html/bdo.html (accessed February 18, 2003).

31. Peggy Marguiles, "The Barbie Disinformation Organization," *SurReview,* http://www-2.cs.cmu.edu/afs/cs/user/jthomas/SurReview/reviews-html/bdo.html (accessed February 18, 2003).

32. *The Pie's the Limit!* VHS, directed by A. Mark Liiv and Jeff Taylor (San Francisco: Whispered Media, 1999).

33. Ibid.

34. Ibid.

35. Ibid.

36. I borrow this phrase from DeLuca and Peeples, "From Public Sphere to Public Screen."

37. Mark Pauline, in an interview with Andrea Juno in Vale and Juno, *Pranks!*

38. *The Pie's the Limit!* Emphasis added to capture verbal emphasis in video.

39. *The Pie's the Limit!*

40. This phrase is reminiscent of Black Panther leader Huey Newton's famous phrase: "Violence is as American as cherry pie."

41. The Yes Men, "Hijinks," http://www.theyesmen.org/hijinks/wto.shtml (accessed October 15, 2006).

42. Ibid.

43. Ibid.

44. All quotes from Unruh's speech are drawn from *Harper's,* "Readings," November 2001, 15.

45. Michel Foucault, *Discipline and Punish: The Birth of the Prison* (New York: Vintage, 1995), 201.

46. Deleuze, *Negotiations,* 178.

47. For a detailed examination of the role of control in postindustrial capitalism, see Hardt and Negri, *Empire*; and Michael Hardt and Antonio Negri, *Multitude: War and Democracy in the Age of Empire* (New York: Penguin, 2004).

48. Deleuze, *Negotiations*, 175.

49. The Yes Men, "Hijinks," http://www.theyesmen.org/hijinks/wto.shtml (accessed October 15, 2006).

50. *Harper's*, "Readings," November 2001.

51. "Arnold Faces Anti-Smoking Challenges," *Adweek*, January 28, 2002.

52. G. Harris, "Just Say No to the Preaching and Scaremongering," *Scotsman*, January 16, 1996.

53. Essential Action, "Exposing the Truth: Tobacco Industry 'Anti-Tobacco' Youth Programs," http://www.essentialaction.org/tobacco/aofm/0103/ (accessed February 4, 2006).

54. "RJR Targeted Kids — Read Excerpts from the Documents [01/14–5]," ASH: Action on Smoking and Health, http://no-smoking.org/jan98/01-14-98-5 .html (accessed October 15, 2006).

55. Cited in "The Situationists and the New Forms of Action against Politics and Art," in *The Situationist International Anthology*, edited by Ken Knabb (Berkeley: Bureau of Public Secrets, 1981), 214.

56. "The Situationists and the New Forms of Action," 214.

57. Ibid.

58. Arthur Asa Berger, *Ads, Fads, and Consumer Culture: Advertising's Impact on American Character and Society* (Lanham, Md.: Rowman and Littlefield, 2000), 25.

59. American Legacy Foundation, "Truth Fact Sheet," http://www .americanlegacy.org/ (accessed May 28, 2005).

60. Marc Kaufman, "Survey Says Teen Smoking Is in Decline," *Washington Post*, September 19, 2002.

61. Fred Felder, *Media Hoaxes* (Ames: Iowa State University Press, 1989), 5.

62. Ibid., 9.

63. Ibid., 7.

64. Cited in Dery, "Culture Jamming."

65. Felder, *Media Hoaxes*, 20.

66. William S. Burroughs, "Electronic Revolution," in *Word Virus: The William S. Burroughs Reader*, edited by James Grauerholz and Ira Silverberg (New York: Grove Press, 1998), 295.

67. Ibid.

68. Ibid.

69. Cited in Brian Boling, "Corporate Myths," *Stay Free!* no. 19 (Spring 2002): 34, http://www.stayfreemagazine.org/.

70. Klein, *No Logo*, 75.

71. Ibid., 76.

72. Ibid.

73. About.com, "Tommy Hilfiger 'Racist' Rumor Is Fashionable Again," http://urbanlegends.about.com/library/weekly/aa121698.htm (accessed January 21, 2002).

74. Tommy Hilfiger, http://www.tommy.com/help/rumor/rumorTommy .jhtml (accessed January 21, 2002).

75. Cited in Alex Gramling, "Spread of Internet Lies Spooks Large Organizations," *New York Times*, "Technology" sec., May 15, 1997, http://www.nytimes.com/library/cyber/week/051597/lies.html (accessed February 13, 2003).

76. Fashion United, http://www.fashionunited.co.uk/news/tommy.htm (accessed January 21, 2002).

77. Tracie Rozhon, "Reinventing Tommy: More Surf, Less Logo," *New York Times*, March 16, 2003, sec. 3.

78. Ibid.

79. Cited in Rozhon, "Reinventing Tommy."

80. Jean-Nöel Kapferer, *Rumors*, translated by Bruce Fink (New Brunswick, N.J.: Transaction Publishers, 1990), 12.

81. Boling, "Corporate Myths."

82. Gary Fine, interviewed by Carrie McClaren, *Stay Free!* no. 19 (Spring 2002): 41.

83. Ibid.

84. See, for the most prominent examples, Douglas Rushkoff, *Media Virus!* (New York: Ballantine, 1996); and Malcolm Gladwell, *The Tipping Point* (New York: Little, Brown, 2000).

85. Vale and Juno, preface to *Pranks!*

86. For more information, see Malcom Gladwell, "The Cool Hunt," *New Yorker*, March 17, 1997, 82.

87. Vale and Juno, preface to *Pranks!*

4. Pirates and Hijackers

1. William Landes, "Copyright, Borrowed Images, and Appropriation Art: An Economic Approach," in *Copyright in the Cultural Industries*, edited by Ruth Towse (Cheltenham: Edward Elgar, 2002), 9.

2. See, for example, the U.S. 11th Circuit Court of Appeals case *Suntrust v. Houghton Mifflin* over the *Gone with the Wind* parody *Wind Done Gone*; and the 1994 Supreme Court case *Campbell v. Acuff-Rose Music, Inc.* over the rap act 2 Live Crew's sampling of Roy Orbison's "Oh Pretty Woman."

3. Lütticken, "The Art of Theft," 90.

4. Kembrew McLeod, *Owning Culture: Authorship, Ownership, and Intellectual Property* (New York: Peter Lang, 2001), 10.

5. According to communication scholar Ron Bettig, Clinton has estimated that "some 500 raps had been borrowed from his work, of which perhaps 25 percent generated royalties." Ron Bettig, *Copyrighting Culture: The Political Economy of Intellectual Property* (New York: Westview, 1996), 237.

6. John Perry Barlow, "A Declaration of the Independence of Cyberspace," February 8, 1998, http://homes.eff.org/~barlow/Declaration-Final.html (accessed October 15, 2006).

7. *Wired* magazine writer Steven Levy writes of Lessig: "In the realm of Internet politics and the law, no one even approaches Lessig's stature. He is the chief theorist, the most respected mind, the most passionate speechifier. He *is* cyberlaw." Steven Levy, "The Great Liberator," *Wired*, October 2002, 140. *New*

Yorker writer James Surowiecki writes: Lessig "earned a reputation as the most important thinker on intellectual property in the Internet era." James Surowiecki, "Righting Copywrongs," *New Yorker,* January 21 2002, 27.

8. Cited in Levy, "The Great Liberator," 144.

9. Lawrence Lessig, *Free Culture: The Nature and Future of Creativity* (New York: Penguin, 2005); Lawrence Lessig, *Code and Other Laws of Cyberspace* (New York: Basic Books, 1999); Lawrence Lessig, *The Future of Ideas: The Fate of the Commons in a Connected World* (New York: Random House, 2001).

10. See, especially, the Flash presentation of his 2002 OSCON lecture, "Free Culture," available, among other places, at http://lessig.org/freeculture/free .html.

11. Lawrence Lessig, *The Future of Ideas: The Fate of the Commons in a Connected World* (New York, Random House, 2001), 6.

12. Levy, "The Great Liberator." 11.

13. As of early 2006, the exhibit is touring the country. Readers can view a handful of the pieces at http://www.illegal-art.org/.

14. McLeod, preface to *Owning Culture*, ix–xv.

15. Ibid., xi.

16. Ibid, xv.

17. *Mattel, Inc. v. Walking Mountain Productions et al,* U.S. Court of Appeals for the Ninth Circuit.

18. Cited in Paul Brandu, "Hot Water: Starbucks Sues a Citizen: How a San Francisco Cartoonist Ticked Off the Seattle Java Giant" *Salon,* June 1, 2000, http://dir.salon.com/business/feature/2000/06/01/starbuckssuit/index.html.

19. Federal Trademark Dilution Act of 1996.

20. Sarah Mayhew Schlosser, "The High Price of (Criticizing) Coffee: The Chilling Effect of the Federal Trademark Dilution Act on Corporate Parody," *Arizona Law Review* (Winter 2001): 935.

21. Ibid., 939.

22. The risk may soon be even greater. As I write, the United States Senate is considering legislation that would ease the standard of proof necessary to claim trademark dilution. Under the Trademark Dilution Revision Act of 2005 (H.R. 683), companies will only be obliged to show the "likelihood of dilution." The Electronic Frontier Foundation, a vocal opponent of the act, calls it "a big company's dream," and warns Americans that "if it passes, the lawyers policing a trademark could sue businesses and individuals for using words, images, or even colors that look vaguely like a famous brand — without even having to prove that the company is being harmed." See Electronic Frontier Foundation, "Action Center, Stop the Trademark Act from Diluting Free Speech!" https://secure.eff .org/site/Advocacy?cmd=display&page=UserAction&id=113 (accessed February 6, 2006).

23. U.S. Constitution, art. I, § 8, cl. 8.

24. Levy, "The Great Liberator," 155.

25. Siva Vaidhyanathan, *Copyrights and Copywrongs: The Rise of Intellectual Property and How It Threatens Creativity* (New York: New York University Press, 2001), 186.

26. United States Copyright Act, "Section 107: Limitations on Exclusive Rights," 17 § U.S.C. 107, 1988, supp. 4. For an early, but still relevant, discussion of these issues, see John Shelton Lawrence and Bernard Timberg, *Fair Use and Free Inquiry: Copyright Law and the New Media* (Norwood, N.J.: Ablex Publishing Corporation, 1989).

27. 2 Live Crew could easily have found themselves the targets of another lawsuit when the group documented their experience in "Banned in the USA," which borrowed heavily from Bruce Springsteen's hit "Born in the USA." However, Springsteen, forever the champion of the little guy, readily consented to the usage.

28. Vaidhyanathan, *Copyrights and Copywrongs*, 146.

29. Edward Samuels, "*Campbell v. Acuff-Rose Music, Inc.* Bringing Fair Use into Focus?" *Media Law & Policy* (Spring 1994): 4.

30. Cited in Vaidhyanathan, *Copyrights and Copywrongs*, 23.

31. For examples of the charges, see Jay Fliegelman, *Declaring Independence: Jefferson, Natural Language, and the Culture of Performance* (Stanford: Stanford University Press, 1993), esp. 164–67.

32. Fliegelman, *Declaring Independence*, 165.

33. Because the work of Roland Barthes and Michel Foucault on the question of authorship has been well analyzed by a variety of scholars, I choose not to include a discussion of it here and instead stick close to the case of Jefferson. For more on the question of authorship, see Michel Foucault, "What Is an Author?" in *Language, Counter Memory, Practice*, edited and translated by Donald F. Bouchard (Ithaca: Cornell University Press, 1980); and Roland Barthes, "Death of the Author" in *Image, Music, Text*, translated by Stephen Heath (New York: Hill and Wang, 1978).

34. Lessig, *The Future of Ideas*, 8.

35. Fliegelman, *Declaring Independence*, 165.

36. Ibid.

37. Coombe, *The Cultural Life of Intellectual Properties*, 8.

38. Ibid.

39. Ibid., 11.

40. For a short, clear discussion of property and copyright from a conservative perspective, see Ilana Mercer and N. Stephan Kinsella, "Do Patents and Copyrights Undermine Private Property?" *American Partisan*, May 21, 2001.

41. John Oswald, "Plunderphonics, or Audio Piracy as a Compositional Prerogative," *Musicworks* 34 (Winter 1986), http://www.plunderphonics.com/xhtml/xplunder.html.

42. Cited in Vaidhyanathan, *Copyrights and Copywrongs*, 24.

43. Ibid.

44. Jeremy Waldron, "From Authors to Copiers: Individual Rights and Social Values in Intellectual Property," *Chicago-Kent Law Review* 68 (1993): 841–87.

45. Rick Prelinger, "Remarks on Appropriation Art" (remarks, Illegal Art panel, San Francisco Art Institute, July 7, 2003). The full text of Prelinger's remarks are available in *Other Zine* (Fall 2003), http://www.othercinema.com/otherzine/otherzine6/prelinger.html.

46. Zora Neale Hurston, "Characteristics of Negro Expression," in *Voices from the Harlem Renaissance,* 2nd ed., edited by Nathan Irvin Huggins (New York: Oxford University Press, 1995), 224–36.

47. Prelinger, "Remarks on Appropriation Art."

5. Inventing Publics

1. Michael Warner, "Publics and Counterpublics," *Public Culture* 14, no. 1 (Winter 2002): 49–89.

2. *Quarterly Journal of Speech* 88 (November 2002).

3. Michael Warner, *Publics and Counterpublics* (New York: Zone Books, 2002).

4. Warner, "Publics and Counterpublics," 50.

5. Ibid.

6. Warner, *Publics and Counterpublics,* 7.

7. Dilip Parameshwar Gaonkar, "The Forum: Publics and Counterpublics," *Quarterly Journal of Speech* 88 (November 2002): 412.

8. Ronald Greene, "Rhetorical Pedagogy as a Postal System: Circulating Subjects through Michael Warner's 'Publics and Counterpublics,'" *Quarterly Journal of Speech* 88 (November 2002): 435–36.

9. Jürgen Habermas, "The Public Sphere: An Encyclopedia Article (1964)," *New German Critique* (Fall 1974): 49–55.

10. Nancy Fraser, "Rethinking the Public Sphere: A Contribution to the Critique of Actually Existing Democracy," *Social Text* 25–26 (Spring 1991).

11. Warner, *Publics and Counterpublics,* 62.

12. See, for example, the work of Robert McChesney, *Rich Media Poor Democracy: Communication Politics in Dubious Times* (New York: New Press, 1999); and Vaidhyanathan, *Copyrights and Copywrongs.*

13. I mean "hacker" in its original, more generous sense, as a creative member of the open source community. Richard Kahn and Douglas Kellner make the distinction thus: "The term 'hacker' initially meant someone who made creative innovations in computer systems to facilitate the exchange of information and construction of new communities. However, largely through corporate, state and media co-optation of the term, 'hacking' eventually came to suggest a mode of 'terrorism.'" Richard Kahn and Douglas Kellner, "Oppositional Politics and the Internet: A Critical/Reconstructive Approach," *Cultural Politics* 1, no. 1 (March 2005): 77.

14. Carolyn R. Miller, foreword to *Rhetoric and Kairos: Essays in History, Theory, and Praxis,* edited by Phillip Sipiora and James S. Baumlin (New York: State University of New York Press, 2002), xiii.

15. David Bollier, *Silent Theft: The Private Plunder of Our Common Wealth* (New York: Routledge, 2003), 7.

16. James Boyle, "The Second Enclosure Movement and the Construction of the Public Domain," *Law & Contemporary Problems* 33 (Winter–Spring 2003).

17. Northrup Frye, *Anatomy of Criticism,*15th ed. (Princeton, N.J.: Princeton University Press, 2000), 4.

18. I take this illustration from Lawrence Lessig, "Free Culture" (lecture, O'Reilly Open Source Conference, San Diego, Calif., July 24, 2002). The content of this lecture is available, among other places, at Lessig.org, http://www.lessig.org/freeculture/free.html.

19. Ibid.

20. Vaidhyanathan, *Copyrights and Copywrongs*, 7.

21. Cited in Michael Rushton, "Copyright and Freedom of Expression: An Economic Analysis," *Copyright in the Culture Industries,* edited by Ruth Towse (Northampton, Mass.: Edward Elgar, 2002), 51–62.

22. Bollier, *Silent Theft,* 12.

23. Ibid., 13.

24. Lessig, *The Future of Ideas,* 14.

25. Lessig, "Free Culture."

26. Eric S. Raymond, "The Cathedral and the Bazaar," Catb.org, September 11, 2000, http://www.catb.org/~esr/writings/cathedral-bazaar/cathedral-bazaar/index.html#catbmain.

27. Bill Gates, "Challenges and Strategies" (memo, May 16, 1991), Bralyn Archives, http://www.bralyn.net/etext/literature/bill.gates/challenges-strategy.txt.

28. Although open source code has proven dramatically effective in producing stable operating systems and hack-resistant e-mail networks, its most profound contribution to American political life may be forthcoming. Open source advocates are pushing for Diebold, the manufacturer of the infamously untrustworthy electronic voting machines, to make its code available to the public. See Clive Thompson, "A Really Open Election," *New York Times Magazine,* May 30, 2004. One group, the Open Voting Consortium, has already written electronic voting software of its own, a system so "cheap, secure, accurate, and easy to use" that one reporter calls it the "holy grail of election officials." For more details, see the Open Voting Consortium Web site at http://www.openvotingconsortium.org/.

29. Graham Lawton, "The Great Giveaway," *New Scientist,* February 2, 2002, http://www.newscientist.com/hottopics/copyleft/copyleftart.jsp.

30. Creative Commons, http://creativecommons.org/learnmore (accessed October 15, 2006). Emphases in original.

31. Lessig, "Free Culture."

32. Phillip Sipiora, "Introduction: The Ancient Concept of *Kairos,*" in *Rhetoric and Kairos: Essays in History, Theory, and Praxis,* 1.

33. Ibid.

34. Debra Hawhee, "Kairotic Encounters," in *Perspectives on Rhetorical Invention,* edited by Janice Lauer and Janet Atwill (Knoxville: University of Tennessee Press, 2002), 16–35.

35. Ibid., 2.

36. Ibid., 3.

37. Cited in Sharon Crowley and Debra Hawhee, *Ancient Rhetoric for Contemporary Students* (New York: Pearson, 2004), 36.

38. Malcom Gladwell, "Something Borrowed," *New Yorker,* November 22, 2004, 44.

39. Creative Commons, "About Us," http://creativecommons.org/about/history (accessed October 15, 2006).

40. Ibid.

41. Cited in Crowley and Hawhee, *Ancient Rhetoric for Contemporary Students,* 393.

42. Dilip Parameshwar Gaonkar and Elizabeth A. Povinelli, "Technologies of Public Forms: Circulation, Transfiguration, Recognition," *Public Culture* 15, no. 3 (2002): 385–97. Emphasis added.

43. I take the phrase "terministic screens" from Kenneth Burke, *Language as Symbolic Action: Essays on Life, Literature, and Method* (Berkeley: University of California Press, 1968).

44. Warner, "Publics and Counterpublics," 68.

45. Ibid.

46. Ibid., 69.

47. Ibid.

48. Coombe, *The Cultural Life of Intellectual Properties,* 6.

49. Hawhee, "Kairotic Encounters," 5.

50. Gilles Deleuze and Félix Guattari, *A Thousand Plateaus,* translated by Brian Massumi (Minneapolis: University of Minnesota Press, 1987), 25.

51. Ibid.

Conclusion

1. Creative Commons, "About," http://www.creativecommons.org/ (accessed October 15, 2006).

2. Deleuze, *Negotiations,* 175.

3. Ibid., 180.

4. Ibid.

5. Creative Commons, "The Wired CD," http://creativecommons.org/wired/ (accessed October 11, 2006).

6. Science Commons, home page, http://www.sciencecommons.org (accessed March 2005).

7. Lawton, "The Great Giveaway."

8. Cited in Lawton, "The Great Giveaway."

9. Thompson, "A Really Open Election," 14.

10. Ibid.

11. Douglas Rushkoff, *Open Source Democracy: How Online Communication Is Changing Offline Politics* (London: Demos, 2003), 16.

12. Interestingly, the walkouts seem to have been inspired by the HBO film *Walkout,* which was being aired at the same time the walkouts took place. Directed by Edward James Olmos, *Walkout* is the true story of Chicano high-school students who staged a huge walkout in 1968 to protest their unfair treatment in East L.A. schools. So the 2006 walkouts were inspired, at least in part, by a story told on HBO (a commodified "space"), and were organized in MySpace (another commodified "space"). This small example suggests that we should at least remain

skeptical of arguments that insist that "real politics" require spaces outside of market forces.

13. Scott Gold, "Student Protests Echo the '60s, but with a High-Tech Buzz," *Los Angeles Times,* http://www.latimes.com/news/printedition/la-me-students31mar31,1,2174537.story?ctrack=1&cset=true (accessed March 31, 2006).

14. Rushkoff, *Open Source Democracy,* 16.

Index

Christine Harold is an assistant professor of speech communication at the University of Georgia.